DATE DUE

The Facts of
Reconstruction

The Facts of Reconstruction

❧ *Essays in Honor of John Hope Franklin*

Edited by

ERIC ANDERSON

&

ALFRED A. MOSS, JR.

LOUISIANA STATE UNIVERSITY PRESS
Baton Rouge and London

Designer: Rebecca Lloyd Lemna
Typeface: Sabon
Typesetter: Graphic Composition, Inc.
Printer and binder: Thomson-Shore, Inc.

Library of Congress Cataloging-in-Publication Data

The Facts of reconstruction : essays in honor of John Hope Franklin / edited by Eric Anderson and Alfred A. Moss, Jr.
    p. cm.
    Includes index.
    ISBN 0-8071-1666-1 (alk. paper)   ISBN 0-8071-1691-2 (pbk.: alk. paper)
    1. Reconstruction.   2. Southern States—History—1865–1877.   3. Afro-Americans—History—1863–1877.   I. Anderson, Eric, 1949–   .   II. Moss, Alfred A., 1943–   .   III. Franklin, John Hope, 1915–.
E668.F3'1991
973.8—dc20   90-47141
                                                                            CIP

Frontispiece photograph by Bill Weems

Contents

CONTENTS

ACKNOWLEDGMENTS

Throughout the long process of planning and editing *The Facts of Reconstruction*, we have had the help of many people who wished to join in honoring John Hope Franklin. If biological metaphors are appropriate to literary work, then Beverly Jarrett was the mother of this volume. During a coffee break at the Southern Historical Association convention, she first suggested the idea of a book such as this one. Bev helped us organize our ideas, politely prodded us to finish the project, and conspired with an ever-increasing group of people to keep the whole thing secret from John Hope.

At crucial points, Howard Rabinowitz and Louis Harlan were valuable counselors and critics. Experienced editors as well as scholars, they had a clear understanding of potential pitfalls. Thanks should also go to Marilyn Glaim, whose careful critique strengthened the Afterword.

We are also indebted to the editorial staff at Louisiana State University Press. Margaret Fisher Dalrymple, Catherine Landry, and John Easterly deserve special mention, both for their highly professional editing work and their enthusiastic support for the idea of paying tribute to the work of John Hope Franklin. We also owe warm thanks to our copy editor, Gerry Anders, who was efficient, thorough, and always considerate.

Last of all, we wish to thank Loretta Anderson, Matthew and Seth Anderson, and Daniel Moss, who were patient and long-suffering even when *The Facts of Reconstruction* intruded on family holidays.

INTRODUCTION

In 1913 an elderly black man named John R. Lynch wrote a book entitled *The Facts of Reconstruction*. As a participant in the reconstruction of Mississippi, former congressman Lynch believed that he was especially well qualified to challenge the scholars and journalists who had depicted Reconstruction as a "blunder-crime." Far from being a mistake, he declared, the congressional plan of reconstruction was the only possible one that "could have saved to the country the fruits of the victory that had been won on the battlefield." According to Lynch, "The adoption of any other plan would have resulted in the accomplishment of nothing but the mere physical abolition of slavery and a denial of the right of a state to withdraw from the Union." [1]

Although Lynch's revisionism "had little or no immediate impact on the historical profession," according to the later revisionist John Hope Franklin, it seems fitting to use Lynch's title, *The Facts of Reconstruction,* for this collection of essays honoring Franklin.[2] In the long run, Lynch's understanding of the period proved to be more accurate than the interpretations he attacked, including widely accepted works by James Ford Rhodes, James W. Garner, and William Archibald Dunning. Appropriately, the most important historian of Lynch's career—John Hope Franklin—was one of the leaders in the reappraisal of the nation's transition from slavery to freedom.

Franklin's contributions to Reconstruction historiography are so vast that, paradoxically, they risk being underrated. For when a scholar helps to discredit a previous understanding—if the job is done thoroughly enough—he often is rewarded in an odd way. Subsequent researchers may accept his insights as obvious, and consider the victory of the new view as easy and inevitable because it was so complete.

It is important to remember that Franklin's work on Reconstruc-

---

1. John R. Lynch, *The Facts of Reconstruction* (1913; rpr. New York, 1968), 110.
2. John Hope Franklin, "John Roy Lynch: Republican Stalwart from Mississippi," in *Southern Black Leaders of the Reconstruction Era,* ed. Howard Rabinowitz (Urbana, Ill., 1982), 54.

tion, especially his volume in the Chicago History of American Civilization series, *Reconstruction: After the Civil War* (1961), offered the first comprehensive response to William A. Dunning's *American Nation Series* volume *Reconstruction, Political and Economic* (1907), or at least the first one that scholars were willing to hear (Lynch's book could be dismissed as self-interested, while W. E. B. Du Bois's brilliant polemic *Black Reconstruction* was too sprawling, untidy, and tendentious to be fully understood or accepted).

The present volume is designed both to honor and engage John Hope Franklin. It is not a *festschrift*, at least in the conventional sense. Unlike the usual *festschrift*, this book is not limited to Franklin's students, nor is it made up of essays on a wide variety of topics. Readers should not look here for a formal tribute to Franklin's career as a teacher, a comprehensive list of his graduate students, or a complete record of his publications.

Instead, this work focuses on the Reconstruction era and Franklin's contributions to Reconstruction scholarship. The editors have asked each contributor to address an important aspect of Reconstruction, either in the form of a review essay or original research, always keeping in mind the impact of Franklin's *Reconstruction: After the Civil War*. Out of respect for Professor Franklin's lifelong aversion to "sweetheart sessions," we have requested critical analysis of his interpretation, not mere "appreciation." Part of the lasting significance of *Reconstruction: After the Civil War* is its persistent vitality, its ability to provoke discussion thirty years after it was published.

John R. Lynch was more cocksure about "the facts" than most professional historians. A reader may come away from this collection of essays with a better appreciation of the ironic interplay between fact and interpretation so evident in all historical writing—especially, perhaps, in work on Reconstruction. The primary difference between John Hope Franklin and William A. Dunning is not, after all, that one man got his dates and statistics and electoral returns correct and the other man did not. The difference is Franklin's ability to present a fully comprehensive interpretation, one that places both familiar facts and neglected evidence in a clearer context. Therein lies his claim to greatness as a historian.

The Facts of
Reconstruction

1

Rehearsal for Reconstruction
Antebellum Origins of the Fourteenth Amendment

~ PAUL FINKELMAN

The three constitutional amendments adopted between 1865 and 1870 were the capstones of Reconstruction. The formal abolition of slavery, the promise of "equal protection of the laws" for the freedmen, and the prohibition of racial discrimination in voting were designed to recognize the change in federalism brought about by the Civil War, to preserve permanently the Union victory, and to change forever the nature of race relations in America. Like the war itself, these amendments affected all subsequent American history.

Unlike the Thirteenth and Fifteenth amendments, the Fourteenth has been the subject of great debate among scholars, politicians, and jurists as to its meaning. Much of this discussion has centered on the intentions of the amendment's framers.

It is questionable whether Americans today, especially legislators and jurists, *ought* to be bound by the intentions of the generation of 1868—assuming we ever could agree on what those intentions were. A good deal of careful scholarship suggests that some of the framers intended the amendment to be open-ended, ambiguous, and subject to expansive interpretations. For example, John Bingham, one of the amendment's key framers, insisted on using the phrase "privileges and immunities" because "its euphony and indefiniteness of meaning were a charm to him."[1] It seems likely that other framers of the amendment

1. Michael Les Benedict, *A Compromise of Principle: Congressional Republicans and Reconstruction, 1863–1869* (New York, 1974), 170.

differed among themselves on specific policies and programs. Nevertheless, whatever the jurisprudential utility of "original intention," there is much historical value in trying to understand the broad goals of those who adopted the amendment.

To understand what the authors of the Fourteenth Amendment were trying to accomplish, it is necessary to examine the struggle for racial equality as carried on in the antebellum North by abolitionists, Free-Soilers, and ultimately Republicans. An examination of the prewar era reveals that contrary to what most scholars have argued, antebellum northern blacks had numerous legal rights, and their legal position was *improving* during the last antebellum decade. In terms of law and constitutional change, the "rehearsal for Reconstruction," to borrow Willie Lee Rose's phrase, actually began in the 1830s and continued through the 1850s.

Antebellum Race Relations and Modern Historians

Most scholars describe the conditions of antebellum northern blacks in the bleakest terms. The literature asserts that northern blacks were barely better off than southern slaves and that from 1800 to 1860, northern blacks continually lost rights. August Meier and Elliott Rudwick observe: "With the possible exception of certain New England states, the status of free blacks deteriorated in the course of the nineteenth century." Northern blacks were, in John Hope Franklin's words, "quasi-free." Vincent Harding asserts that they "had no secure rights which the masses of white people were bound by law to respect." Leon Litwack describes a fundamentally racist North, where in 1860 the "Negro remained largely disfranchised, segregated, and economically oppressed. Discrimination still barred him from most polls, juries, schools, and workshops, as well as from many libraries, theaters, lyceums, museums, public conveyances, and literary societies." On the eve of the Civil War, Litwack argues, "change did not seem imminent." One prominent legal scholar, Raoul Berger, has examined this history and concluded that the Fourteenth Amendment was not written to provide substantive equality for blacks; indeed, "the key to an understanding of the Fourteenth Amendment is that the North was shot through with Negrophobia." [2]

A careful reexamination of the antebellum North shows far greater complexity and ambiguity in northern race relations than the generally bleak picture these scholars paint. Such a reexamination demonstrates that progress toward racial justice in the North began long before the Civil War. By 1860, enormous legal changes, brought about by legislators, state executives, and jurists, had altered the status of northern blacks in dramatic ways. These changes, as well as unsuccessful attempts at greater change, are a critical part of the background to Reconstruction and the Fourteenth Amendment.

To rephrase Raoul Berger's assertions, the "key to an understanding of the Fourteenth Amendment" is *not* northern Negrophobia, but the fact that many antebellum northerners, especially Republican party leaders, fought for racial justice. Sometimes they failed, but their goals were always clear: they wanted to bring blacks within the full protection of the law. These same individuals worked to expand the Bill of Rights to apply to the states.[3] And later, from 1865 to 1870, many of these men used their new political power to implement their goals through the three Reconstruction amendments.

It is important to recognize at the outset that antebellum northern blacks never achieved complete social or economic equality; nor, with a few exceptions, did they achieve complete legal equality. In housing, employment, and education, northern blacks faced private and public discrimination that kept them, for the most part, on the bottom of the social and economic ladder. The majority of northern whites in this period never fully accepted the concept of black equality. When the radical congressman George W. Julian declared that "the real trouble is that *we hate the negro*," he was not speaking for himself, but he aptly described the view of many in the North.[4]

---

2. August Meier and Elliott Rudwick, *From Plantation to Ghetto* (3d ed.; New York, 1976), 90; John Hope Franklin and Alfred A. Moss, Jr., *From Slavery to Freedom: A History of Negro Americans* (6th ed.; New York, 1988), chap. 9; Vincent Harding, *There Is a River: The Black Struggle for Freedom in America* (New York, 1981), 118; Leon Litwack, *North of Slavery: The Negro in the Free States, 1790–1860* (Chicago, 1961), 279; Raoul Berger, *Government by Judiciary: The Transformation of the Fourteenth Amendment* (Cambridge, Mass., 1977), 10.

3. Any lingering doubts on this issue have been resolved by Michael Kent Curtis, *No State Shall Abridge: The Fourteenth Amendment and the Bill of Rights* (Durham, N.C., 1986).

4. Julian quoted in C. Vann Woodward, *American Counterpoint: Slavery and Racism in the North-South Dialogue* (Boston, 1971), 168.

PAUL FINKELMAN

What is remarkable is not that many antebellum northerners were antiblack, but that a substantial number, including most Republicans, worked to expand black rights. After the war these Republicans may have disagreed over tactics and particular programs, but the party was not nearly as "divided, hesitant, and unsure of its purpose" on black rights as C. Vann Woodward and other scholars have asserted. On the contrary, as Michael Les Benedict has demonstrated persuasively, their "common antislavery heritage, their shared desire to guarantee the security of southern loyalists, their determination to realize a Reconstruction that would firmly and permanently cement the Union, and their united wish to see justice done to the freedmen enabled Republicans to act in fundamental harmony" because they agreed on "fundamentals."[5]

The Complexity of Antebellum Race Relations

These Republican "fundamentals" were rooted in the legal and political history of the antebellum North. The North was, of course, profoundly racist. One should expect nothing less of an age when politicians and publicists were often unabashedly prejudiced, the scientific community supported white supremacy, and the Constitution protected slavery at every turn.[6] Even so, careful attention to localism and regionalism in the North reveals great variation in racial attitudes and practices. Throughout the period there was also a growing contradiction in the North between public manifestations of equality—in law and politics—and private racism. Antebellum Northern blacks gained legal and political rights, even though their economic and social condition did not markedly improve.

In this period there was also a critical connection between attitudes on slavery and those on race. To be sure, not all opponents of slavery were racial egalitarians. But even mildly antislavery attitudes

5. Woodward, *American Counterpoint*, 168; Benedict, *Compromise of Principle*, 48.
6. William Stanton, *The Leopard's Spots: Scientific Attitudes Toward Race in America, 1815–59* (Chicago, 1960); George Fredrickson, *The Black Image in the White Mind: The Debate on Afro-American Character and Destiny, 1817–1914* (New York, 1971); Paul Finkelman, "Slavery and the Constitutional Convention: Making a Covenant with Death," in *Beyond Confederation: Origins of the Constitution and American National Identity,* ed. Richard Beeman *et al.* (Chapel Hill, 1987), 188–225.

led to new protections and rights for free blacks. The vast majority of antebellum northerners never adopted notions of equality that Americans still strive for today. It would be anachronistic to expect them to have done so. But by the standards of the age, the antebellum North gradually was living up to its values in the treatment of blacks. The Civil War, Reconstruction, and the adoption of three constitutional amendments accelerated a process of expanding black rights that had begun well before the secession crisis.

Abraham Lincoln partially articulated the ideology of the North in his 1858 debates with Stephen A. Douglas. Although blacks could not vote in Illinois, and thus Lincoln could not expect any help from them in winning office, he nevertheless expressed a belief in fundamental equality and fairness (but not, it should be added, in complete political or social equality) that represented the ideology of most antebellum Republicans:

> I hold that . . . there is no reason in the world why the negro is not entitled to all the rights enumerated in the Declaration of Independence—the right of life, liberty and the pursuit of happiness. I hold that he is as much entitled to these as the white man. I agree with Judge Douglas that he is not my equal in many respects, certainly not in color—perhaps not in intellectual and moral endowments; but in the right to eat the bread without leave of anybody else which his own hand earns, he is my equal and the equal of Judge Douglas, and the equal of every other man.[7]

This appeal to life, liberty, and the pursuit of happiness was manifest in many areas of northern law and politics. Thus, despite its racism, the North failed effectively to discourage—and often indirectly encouraged—the growth of its black population. During this period most northern states not only protected their free black population from kidnapping, but also gradually expanded that population's civil and political rights.

The North did not actively seek black settlers. But unlike the states of the South, none in the North ever tried to expel its native-born black population; none even contemplated doing so.[8] Neither did the free states harass blacks with complicated laws and vicious enforcement,

7. Roy P. Basler, ed., *The Collected Works of Abraham Lincoln* (9 vols.; New Brunswick, N.J., 1953), III, 249.
8. Many southern states considered such laws and thus undermined the security of free blacks in the South, even though only Arkansas actually adopted such a law. *Arkansas Laws, 1860*, chap. 99; Ira Berlin, *Slaves Without Masters: The Free Negro in the Antebellum South* (New York, 1974), 372–80.

deny them access to courts of law, prohibit them from seeking an education, or bar them from various types of employment.[9] Most important of all, the North protected the fundamental rights and liberties of blacks.

Even at the height of antiblack sentiment in the mid-1830s, some states adopted new laws, or enforced old ones, that helped and protected blacks. For example, the disfranchisement of black men in Pennsylvania in 1837 must be balanced with the enfranchisement of black men in Rhode Island in 1842 and the majority vote in favor of black male suffrage in Wisconsin in 1849. Starting in the 1830s, northern courts often went out of their way to free slaves in transit from the South. Such decisions increased the number of free blacks in the North.[10] Similarly, from the 1830s on, northern "personal liberty laws" and rulings by northern judges not only served their ostensible purpose of helping to prevent the kidnapping and enslavement of free blacks, but also protected fugitive slaves living in the North. For example, by guaranteeing the writ of habeas corpus or the less common writ of homine replegiando to anyone arrested or seized as a slave, the new laws often functioned to impede the reenslavement of fugitives.[11] These statutes and court rulings, therefore, also resulted in more blacks living in the North. In 1860 and 1861, Republican-dominated northern legislatures were unwilling to repeal their laws protecting free blacks as part of a compromise to hold the Union together. This position reflected changes in northern law that, as noted earlier, had begun in the mid-1830s and increased throughout the 1840s and 1850s.[12] Contrary to the conclusion of Leon Litwack, on the eve of the

9. For examples of such harassment, see John Hope Franklin, *The Free Negro in North Carolina, 1790–1860* (Chapel Hill, 1943); Berlin, *Slaves Without Masters;* and Michael Johnson and James Roark, eds., *No Chariot Let Down: Charleston's Free People of Color on the Eve of the Civil War* (Chapel Hill, 1984). The Georgia Supreme Court discussed the legal disabilities of free blacks in *Bryan* v. *Walton,* 14 Ga. 185 (1853).

10. *Commonwealth* v. *Aves,* 18 Pick. (Mass.) 193 (1836). The case and its legal progeny are discussed in Paul Finkelman, *An Imperfect Union: Slavery, Federalism, and Comity* (Chapel Hill, 1981).

11. In some states the laws also established procedural requirements for the return of fugitive slaves. See, generally, Thomas D. Morris, *Free Men All: The Personal Liberty Laws of the North* (Baltimore, 1974). Such requirements were declared unconstitutional in *Prigg* v. *Pennsylvania,* 16 Peters (U.S.) 539 (1842). After this case some states limited the use of state facilities in the rendition process and/or prohibited state officials from participating in the rendition of fugitive slaves. Some state judges, acting on their own, refused to enforce the Fugitive Slave Law of 1793, citing *Prigg* as their reason for doing so. Paul Finkelman, "*Prigg* v. *Pennsylvania* and Northern State Courts: Antislavery Use of a Proslavery Decision," *Civil War History,* XXV (1979), 5–35.

12. On resistance to fugitive slave rendition in general, see William M. Wiecek, *The Sources of Antislavery Constitutionalism in America, 1760–1848* (Ithaca, N.Y., 1977) and Wiecek, "Lat-

Civil War change not only was "imminent," but in fact had been going on for some time.

Black Immigration to the North

Most historians believe that antebellum blacks faced restrictions if they moved North, because "nearly every northern state considered, and many adopted, measures to prohibit or restrict the further immigration of Negroes." [13] This assertion, if true, would be critical to the background of the Fourteenth Amendment, but it does not survive careful scrutiny.

There is no evidence that restrictive legislation was ever considered in New Hampshire, Vermont, Maine, New York, Michigan, Wisconsin, California, or Minnesota. Moreover, there is a great difference between states that "considered" such measures and those that adopted them. In Massachusetts, as Litwack's own evidence reveals, all proposals to prohibit or restrict black immigration died in legislative committees. [14] The history of Pennsylvania's consideration of restrictions on black immigration indicates the limits of northern racism.

From 1780 to the 1830s, Pennsylvania was one of the most egalitarian states in the North. Pennsylvania led the "first emancipation" with its Gradual Abolition Act of 1780 and became a haven for emancipated blacks and fugitive slaves. The Pennsylvania Supreme Court usually interpreted statutes in an antislavery, profreedom manner, while the legislature protected the freedom of Pennsylvania's blacks with various personal liberty laws. [15] In the mid-1830s attitudes changed, and the Pennsylvania 1837 constitutional convention disfranchised blacks. Attempts to prohibit black immigration into Pennsylvania, however, failed. The key figure in defeating this proposed clause was Thaddeus Stevens, a future Republican leader. [16]

imer: Lawyers, Abolitionists, and the Problems of Unjust Laws," in *Antislavery Reconsidered: New Perspectives on the Abolitionists*, ed. Lewis Perry and Michael Fellman (Baton Rouge, 1979).

13. Litwack, *North of Slavery,* 66.

14. *Ibid.,* 68.

15. "An Act for the Gradual Abolition of Slavery" (March 1, 1780), *Pennsylvania Acts, 1780.* Pennsylvania litigation is discussed in Finkelman, *Imperfect Union.*

16. Pennsylvania Constitution, 1838, Art. III, sec. 1, in *Journal of the Convention of the State of Pennsylvania to Propose Amendments to the Constitution . . . 1837* (2 vols.; Philadel-

Ten years after the 1837 constitutional convention, Pennsylvania adopted legislation freeing any slave entering the state who was not a fugitive.[17] The failure to adopt a constitutional prohibition on black immigrants in 1837 contrasts sharply with this antislavery success of 1847. Thus, Pennsylvania was a northern state that "considered" a prohibition on black migration but, significantly, rejected this prohibition and ten years later made itself into a haven for slaves-in-transit brought within its borders.

There is also an important difference between states that restricted black immigration and those that absolutely prohibited it. Equally important is the distinction between the adoption of laws and their enforcement. Sporadic enforcement of immigration restrictions and prohibitions may signify a change in attitude among prosecutors and judges that preceded a legislative change. Finally, it is imperative to investigate whether these restrictions changed over time. It is clearly misleading simply to tally up various immigration restrictions without regard to time or place, as in the following analysis from *North of Slavery:*

> The nature of restrictionist legislation varied from state to state. Several states required from incoming Negroes certificates proving their freedom and attesting to their citizenship in another state. Connecticut forbade, without the approval of civil authorities, the establishment of any educational institution for the instruction of non-resident Negroes. Most of the new states . . . either explicitly barred Negroes or permitted them to enter only after they had produced certified proof of their freedom and had posted bond, ranging from $500 to $1,000, guaranteeing their good behavior. If enforced, this requirement alone would have amounted to practical exclusion.[18]

A footnote to this paragraph reveals that the "several states" requiring certificates of freedom from incoming blacks were in fact only two states: Massachusetts (1788) and New Jersey (1798).

The Massachusetts law actually was concerned with vagabonds

---

phia, 1837–38), I, 148, 256, 779, 783, 516; John Agg, reporter, *Proceedings and Debates of the Convention of the Commonwealth of Pennsylvania, to Propose Amendments to the Constitution . . . 1837* (14 vols.; Harrisburg, 1837–39); Litwack, *North of Slavery,* 69; Ralph Korngold, *Thaddeus Stevens: A Being Darkly Wise and Rudely Great* (New York, 1955), 44–52.

17. "An Act to Prevent Kidnapping, Preserve the Public Peace, Prohibit the Exercise of Certain Powers Heretofore Exercised by Judges . . . and to Repeal Certain Slave Laws," *Laws of Pennsylvania,* 1847, No. 159, pp. 206–208.

18. Litwack, *North of Slavery,* 70.

and the support of indigents. This act indicates a stereotyped belief that free blacks and fugitive slaves were less capable than whites of supporting themselves, but does not prove that Massachusetts was opposed to black migration per se. Furthermore, there is no evidence that the law was ever enforced. It was repealed *sub silento* in the 1830s.[19] New Jersey's 1798 statute is even more problematic. The requirement that free black immigrants carry certificates of their freedom was part of an elaborate slave code. At the time, New Jersey was a slave state: not until 1804 did it pass a gradual emancipation statute. It is not surprising that the slave state of New Jersey regulated incoming free blacks. All slave states did this. Significantly, unlike other slave states, New Jersey did not prohibit the immigration of free blacks. In 1846, New Jersey finally ended slavery, and the few remaining slaves became indentured servants. The 1798 statute, which had been a dead letter since its passage, was repealed by the 1846 law.[20]

In 1833, Connecticut did (as Litwack states) allow localities to prohibit the establishment of schools for nonresident blacks. This law did not prohibit black immigration to the state, however. The law was a response to the opening of Prudence Crandall's school for black "young ladies" in Canterbury. Although Crandall was indicted under this law and eventually convicted, the Connecticut Supreme Court reversed the conviction. Five years after its passage the law was repealed.[21] Equally important, the same court ruled in 1837 that any slave brought into the state who was not a fugitive was immediately free. This decision was confirmed by the legislature in the state's revised statutes.[22] Thus, the Connecticut court and legislature took steps that both freed slaves and increased the state's black population.

The unenforced or short-lived restrictive laws in New Jersey, Mas-

---

19. "An Act for Suppression and Punishing Rogues, Vagabonds, Common Beggars, and Other Idle, Disorderly and Lewd Persons" (March 26, 1788), *General Law of Massachusetts, 1788*, pp. 680–82; repealed *sub silento* by "An Act for the Regulation of Gaols and Houses of Correction" (March 29, 1834), *Massachusetts Statutes, 1834*, chap. 151, pp. 189–207.

20. "An Act Respecting Slaves" (March 14, 1798), *Laws of New Jersey* (New Brunswick, 1800), 307–13; "An Act to Repeal Certain Acts and Parts of Acts" (April 17, 1846), *Statutes of the State of New Jersey, Revised and Published Under the Authority of the Legislature* (1847), 675–86.

21. "An Act in Addition to an Act for the Admission and Settlement of Inhabitants in Towns" (May 24, 1833), *Connecticut Public Acts, 1833*, chap. 9, p. 420; repealed by Act of May 31, 1838, *Connecticut Public Acts, 1838*, chap. 34, p. 30; *Crandall v. State*, 10 Day (Conn.) 339 (1834).

22. *Jackson v. Bulloch*, 12 Day (Conn.) 38 (1837); "An Act to Prevent Slavery," *Public Statute Laws of the State of Connecticut* (Hartford, 1839), Title XCVII, chap. 1, pp. 570–71, 571n.

sachusetts, and Connecticut hardly support the notion of a repressive northern legal code. Moreover, they must be balanced against the fact that no other northeastern or Middle Atlantic state passed such legislation.

The extent to which states actually required bonds from black immigrants or forbade them to immigrate is also questionable. At various times Ohio, Indiana, and Illinois enacted statutes requiring that immigrant blacks find sureties to promise bond in case the blacks were unable to support themselves. Despite the assertions of most historians, such laws did not in fact require that any money actually be posted.[23] Moreover, these statutes were rarely enforced. "The cumbersome legal machinery intended to impede black settlement could only be effective if county officials stalked the countryside and city streets in search of unregistered blacks; few officials appear to have taken the trouble."[24] What little enforcement there was could be found mostly in the southernmost counties—the "butternut" sections of the lower Midwest. Populated mostly by southerners hostile to blacks, these areas were usually Democratic party strongholds throughout the Civil War and Reconstruction, with little influence on national politics and policies from 1860 to 1870.

The Northwest's restrictive laws were based on an Ohio act of 1803. In 1849, Ohio repealed its "black laws," as these statutes were called. The repeal was secured by Free-Soilers who soon would form the backbone of the Republican party. The compromise that led to this repeal also sent the abolitionist Salmon P. Chase to the United States Senate.[25] For an understanding of Reconstruction, the 1849 repeal of the black laws is far more significant than the earlier existence of those laws. On the other hand, in the 1850s Indiana and Illinois became the

23. "An Act to Amend the Act, Entitled 'An Act Regulating Black and Mulatto Persons'" (January 25, 1807), *Ohio Laws, 1806–1807,* 53. One historian who does explain the distinction between cash and surety bonds is Richard Wade, "The Negro in Cincinnati, 1800–1830," *Journal of Negro History,* XXXIX (January, 1957), 43–57. "An Act Concerning Free Negroes and Mulattoes, Servants, and Slaves" (February 10, 1831), *Revised Statutes of Indiana, 1838,* chap. 83, pp. 418–19; "An Act Respecting Free Negroes and Mulattoes, Servants, and Slaves" (January 17, 1829), and the same act revised and amended by the Act of February 1, 1831, *Revised Laws of Illinois* (Vandalia, 1833), 462–65.

24. David Gerber, *Black Ohio and the Color Line, 1860–1915* (Urbana, Ill., 1976), 14. On the failure of enforcement in Indiana, see Emma Lou Thornbrough, *The Negro in Indiana: A Study of a Minority* (Indianapolis, 1957), 56–62.

25. "An Act to Authorize the Establishment of Separate Schools for the Education of Colored Children, and for Other Purposes" (February 10, 1849), *Ohio Laws, 1849,* 17–18; Stephen E. Maizlish, *The Triumph of Sectionalism: The Transformation of Ohio Politics, 1844–1856* (Kent, Ohio, 1983), 124–43; Frederick J. Blue, *Salmon P. Chase: A Life in Politics* (Kent, Ohio, 1987), 66–73.

only states east of the Mississippi absolutely to forbid all black immigration.[26] By this time, however, they were also the only eastern free states to place *any* restrictions on black immigration. Both states had strong Democratic parties and a large percentage of voters with southern backgrounds.

The states west of the Mississippi followed a similar pattern. California never adopted any restrictions on black immigration; Iowa and Oregon apparently did. The history of those restrictions illustrates the importance of the politics of the 1850s for understanding the 1860s.

In 1851 the Iowa legislature, dominated by Democrats, passed a law providing a two-dollar-a-day fine for blacks who remained in the state for more than three days. It is not entirely clear, however, whether this law was ever technically in force. Legislators sympathetic to blacks added a clause specifying that the law would "take effect, and be in force, by publication in the *Iowa True Democrat,*" published in Mount Pleasant. Despite its name, the *True Democrat* was a Free-Soil paper, and it refused to publish the law. Whatever its legal status, the law was never enforced, and between 1850 and 1860 the state's black population grew by more than 300 percent. A state judge declared the law unconstitutional in the only known attempt to enforce it.[27]

Republican electoral victories between 1856 and 1860 changed the entire nature of black rights in Iowa. The Republican-controlled 1857 constitutional convention wrote a bill of rights under which blacks "received legal rights in the state along with a measure of personal security," including the important right to testify in court against whites. The Republicans also provided for black suffrage, but to protect themselves from a feared white backlash they placed this constitutional provision before the electorate separate from the rest of the constitution. The constitution was ratified, but the black suffrage pro-

26. Indiana Constitution, 1851, Art. XIII; "An Act to Prevent the Immigration of Free Negroes into This State" (February 12, 1853), *Laws of Illinois, 1853,* 57–60.

27. "An Act to Prohibit the Immigration of Free Negroes into This State" (February 5, 1851), *Iowa Laws, 1851,* chap. 72. In 1864 the Republican-dominated legislature repealed the 1851 act. "An Act to Repeal . . . 'An Act to Prohibit the Immigration of Free Negroes into This State'" (February 5, 1864), *Iowa Laws, 1864,* chap. 6. According to its preamble, this act was passed to remove any "doubts" that the law was not in fact in force. For the other circumstances discussed in connection with this law, see Morton Rosenberg, *Iowa on the Eve of the Civil War: A Decade of Frontier Politics* (Norman, Okla., 1972), 15–16, and Jacques Voegeli, *Free but Not Equal: The Midwest and the Negro During the Civil War* (Chicago, 1967), 2. I am indebted to Professor Robert Dykstra of the State University of New York at Albany for information about the *Iowa True Democrat.*

vision failed. This outcome suggests that Republican leaders were well in advance of their constituents on racial issues. On the other hand, the Republicans successfully integrated Iowa's schools, and although the Democrats used this fact as a campaign issue, it had little effect.[28]

The case of Oregon also illustrates the importance of Republican opposition to racist restrictions. Oregon's 1859 constitution, written by a Democrat-controlled convention, prohibited all blacks, slave or free, from entering the state. Raoul Berger cites this instance of northern opposition to free blacks to bolster his interpretation of the Fourteenth Amendment. But Berger's analysis ignores the fact that Oregon came into the nation as a Democratic state, nurtured by the Negrophobic administration of James Buchanan. In 1859 the vast majority of Republicans in the Congress opposed Oregon statehood precisely because of the prohibition on black immigration. Put another way, the politicians and the party that would write the Fourteenth Amendment in 1866 opposed the racist provisions of the Oregon constitution in 1859. Equally important is the fact that the Oregon constitutional provision barring blacks was ignored in the state. Those few blacks who did come there were not expelled. The ideology of the Republicans was revealed in 1862 when they achieved control of the legislature. They could not repeal the prohibition on immigration without a cumbersome constitutional amendment. They were, however, able to give blacks the right to testify against whites.[29]

In 1860 only Indiana, Illinois, and Oregon—states with strong Democratic parties—restricted black immigration. Between 1820 and 1860, despite the restrictions in some states, the midwestern states in particular had continuous and impressive growth in their black populations.[30] Restrictionist legislation was of little significance for blacks

28. Rosenberg, *Iowa on the Eve of the Civil War*, 150–51. It also is worth noting that the 1851 restriction on black immigration did not appear in the Republican-sponsored 1860 revision of the Iowa code. *Revision of 1860 Containing All the Statutes of a General Nature of the State of Iowa* (Des Moines, 1860).

29. Oregon Constitution, 1859, Art. XVIII; Franz M. Schneider, "The Black Laws of Oregon" (M.A. thesis, University of Santa Clara, 1970), 4–35; Fred Lockley, "The Case of Robin Holmes vs. Nathaniel Ford," *Oregon Historical Quarterly*, XXIII (1922–23), 111–37; George H. Williams, "The Political History of Oregon from 1853 to 1865," *Oregon Historical Quarterly*, II (1901), 15–19; Berger, *Government by Judiciary*, 14. In 1863 the Republican-controlled legislature in California removed that state's prohibition on black testimony against whites. "Practice Act, Title XI, of Witnesses and Matter of Attaining Evidence," *General Laws of the State of California . . . 1850–1864* (San Francisco, 1865), 769.

30. U.S. Census Bureau, *Negro Population in the United States, 1790–1915* (Washington, D.C., 1915), 45. Between 1850 and 1860, for example, in Ohio and Illinois the black population grew by more than 40 percent. Between 1830 and 1850, despite restrictive legislation, Indiana's black population more than tripled.

seeking a better way of life north of slavery. Equally important, where Free-Soilers or Republicans gained power, such as in Ohio and Iowa, they repealed antiblack legislation.

Protecting Black Freedom

The free states did more than simply allow the settlement of free blacks. They also protected the freedom of blacks within their jurisdiction. In *Commonwealth* v. *Aves* (1836), Chief Justice Lemuel Shaw ruled that slaves brought into Massachusetts became free "because there is no law which will warrant, but there are laws . . . which prohibit" the "forcible detention or forcible removal" of a slave from the state.[31] Under *Aves,* any slave entering the Bay State (except a fugitive) was immediately free, and the full power of the state might be used to protect that freedom.

By 1860, every northern state except Indiana, Illinois, New Jersey, and California followed *Aves.* The Illinois Supreme Court had adopted the *Aves* precedent, but in 1853 the Democrat-controlled legislature passed a statute explicitly rejecting the *Aves* doctrine. This result illustrates that the legislature reflected the prejudices of the majority of the state. But it also reveals that a majority of the Illinois Supreme Court, including the influential chief justice John D. Caton and justice Lyman Trumbull, favored legal protection for blacks who were brought into the state.[32] Trumbull's role in this case is particularly significant: as a leading Republican senator during Reconstruction, Trumbull would write the Civil Rights Act of 1866—the forerunner of the Fourteenth Amendment.

In addition to freeing slaves-in-transit, most northern states protected the freedom of blacks within their jurisdiction. To repeat, the "personal liberty laws" of the North were designed ostensibly to protect free blacks from kidnapping. But they also were used to prevent the return of fugitive slaves, as thousands of northerners, including many legislators and governors, took a stand against returning blacks to slavery.

31. *Commonwealth* v. *Aves,* 18 Pick. (Mass.) 393 (1836) at 217. See also Finkelman, *Imperfect Union,* chap. 4.
32. Finkelman, *Imperfect Union,* 150–55.

A North thoroughly hostile to blacks would not have protected them from kidnappers. Indeed, kidnappers could have helped rid it of its unwanted blacks. Nor should such a North have been willing to protect fugitive slaves. The extent to which it did, in fact, protect free black citizens and fugitive slaves reveals the fundamental contradictions between the social racism of the North and the concepts of due process and fundamental rights inherent in northern culture.[33] When forced to choose between racism and due process, northerners often chose the latter, even though it was at odds with social practice, the dictates of the Constitution, and harmony within the Union. Thus, although most Republicans acknowledged the obligation to allow the return of fugitive slaves as part of the bargain over the Constitution, most also supported laws and court actions that, in practice, frustrated such returns.[34]

From 1780 to 1860, free blacks could count on fundamental due process rights to protect their liberty and freedom in the North. In 1860 the important due process right to testify in court without racial restrictions was available to blacks in all but four northern states. By 1863, this total had been reduced to just two states. (In the South, free blacks could testify against whites only in Louisiana.)[35] During Reconstruction, the Republican Congress would require that blacks' testimony be allowed in the South as well as the North.[36]

The liberty of free blacks was intimately connected to the protection of fugitive slaves. The only way to prevent the kidnapping and enslavement of free blacks was to guarantee due process for any black seized as a fugitive slave. The North's record on protecting fugitive

---

33. Herman Belz, *Emancipation and Equal Rights: Politics and Constitutionalism in the Civil War Era* (New York, 1978), xi–xiii, 108–113, discusses some of these issues.

34. Eric Foner asserts that "almost every Republican believed that it had been the intention of the founding fathers to restrict slavery and divorce it from the federal government." Foner, *Free Soil, Free Labor, Free Men: The Ideology of the Republican Party Before the Civil War* (New York, 1970), 84. Republicans interpreted the Constitution to fit their program. At this distance it seems clear that the founders did not in fact divorce the federal government from slavery. William M. Wiecek, "The Witch at the Christening," in *The Framing and Ratification of the Constitution*, ed. Leonard Levy and Dennis Mahoney (New York, 1987), 167–84; Finkelman, "Slavery and the Constitutional Convention."

35. The two northern states were Indiana and Illinois. Oregon and California removed their prohibitions in 1862 and 1863 (see n. 29 above). On black testimony at this time, see Paul Finkelman, "Prelude to the Fourteenth Amendment: Black Legal Rights in the Antebellum North," *Rutgers Law Journal*, XVII (1986), 415–82.

36. Robert Kaczorowski, *The Politics of Judicial Interpretation: The Federal Courts, Department of Justice, and Civil Rights, 1866–1876* (New York, 1985), 4–7.

slaves shows that its commitment to fundamental due process exceeded its racism. Some judges refused to aid in the rendition process or actively opposed it by issuing writs of habeas corpus for alleged fugitives. Other northerners protected their black neighbors by arresting or indicting federal marshals, slave owners, and slave catchers who seized blacks.

By 1860, every free state except Minnesota and Oregon had enacted some sort of personal liberty law that not only helped prevent the kidnapping of free blacks but also impeded the return of fugitive slaves by guaranteeing all persons, free or fugitive, the rights to counsel, jury trial, and habeas corpus. Some free states closed their jails to slave catchers or threatened them with criminal prosecution. Popular opposition and resistance to slave catching was also widespread. Even in notoriously Negrophobic Indiana, hunting down slaves could be a dangerous enterprise.[37] In sum, by guaranteeing basic legal protection to everyone, including fugitive slaves, the North tolerated a growing black population.

The personal liberty laws and the willingness of whites to cooperate with blacks in fighting the rendition of fugitive slaves made the 1793 Fugitive Slave Law unworkable and led to the 1850 law. Passage of the 1850 law produced a brief exodus of some fugitive slaves from the North to Canada because they feared enforcement of the new law by federal officials.[38] Frederick Douglass complained that "fugitive slaves who had lived for many years safely and securely in western New York and elsewhere, and bought little homes for themselves and their children, were suddenly alarmed and compelled to flee to Canada for safety as from an enemy's land—a doomed city—and take up a dismal march to a new abode, empty-handed, among strangers." But Douglass' fears were short-lived. By 1852, the Jerry rescue in Syracuse

---

37. Morris, *Free Men All*, 219–22, provides a useful list of personal liberty statutes. On state judges, see Finkelman, "*Prigg* v. *Pennsylvania* and Northern State Courts." For other examples of resistance to fugitive slave rendition, see Paul Finkelman, *Slavery in the Courtroom* (Washington, D.C., 1985), 103–97; Wiecek, "Latimer"; *Vaughn* v. *Williams*, 28 F. Cas. 1115 (1845); George K. Hesslink, *Black Neighbors: Negroes in a Northern Rural Community* (Indianapolis, 1968), 48n; *Norris* v. *Newton*, 18 F. Cas. 322 (1850); *Norris* v. *Crocker* 13 Howard (U.S.) 429 (1851).

38. Fred Landon, "The Negro Migration to Canada After the Passage of the Fugitive Slave Act," *Journal of Negro History*, V (1920), 22–36, suggests that 3,000 fugitive slaves went to Canada after the passage of the 1850 law. This figure suggests the extent to which fugitives were able to settle in the North before 1850.

and the Christiana slave "rebellion" in Pennsylvania had made the Fugitive Slave Law a dead letter in upstate New York and other parts of the North.[39]

Even where it was not a dead letter, the 1850 law was never very effective. Between 1850 and 1860, only 298 fugitives were returned, even though more than 1,000 slaves escaped in 1850 alone. Many northerners refused to stand aside quietly when their black neighbors were threatened with enslavement. Twenty-two slaves were rescued from slave catchers or federal authorities between 1850 and 1860.[40] Rescues in Boston, Syracuse, Oberlin-Wellington (Ohio), and Racine (Wisconsin) electrified the North. Some might argue that these were isolated events, carried out by atypical northerners. But the careers of many public leaders illustrate the popularity of protecting fugitives and fighting for black rights.

Gerrit Smith's election to Congress in 1852 was directly connected to his role in the Jerry rescue. Sherman Booth remained a key figure in the Wisconsin Republican party after his imprisonment for rescuing Joshua Glover; indeed, his role in the case "enhanced his political importance." His attorney, Byron Paine, won election to the Wisconsin Supreme Court "on the strength of his defense of Booth"; moreover, the Wisconsin court suffered no loss of prestige for its opposition to federal law in the Ableman-Booth controversy.[41] Salmon Chase's reputation as the "attorney general for fugitive slaves" and his strong civil rights positions did not prevent his election to the United States Senate in 1849 and 1860, with two terms in between as Ohio's governor. John Andrew's reputation as a defender of fugitive slaves and his open admiration for John Brown helped him become governor of Massachusetts. Lyman Trumbull's career as an antislavery lawyer and judge in Illinois helped set the stage for his election to the Senate. Ben Wade was elected to the Senate after his public declaration, while he was on the Ohio bench, that he would never enforce the Fugitive Slave Law. Governors Dennison of Ohio and Seward of New York scored politi-

39. Frederick Douglass, *The Life and Times of Frederick Douglass* (1892; rpr. New York, 1962), 279–82. On the Jerry rescue and the Christiana affair see Finkelman, *Slavery in the Courtroom*, 95–107.

40. Stanley Campbell, *The Slave Catchers* (Chapel Hill, 1970) 7, 199–207. Campbell's own evidence undermines his argument that the 1850 law was enforced.

41. Richard Current, *The History of Wisconsin: The Civil War Era, 1848–1873* (Madison, 1976), 271, 276, 568–70. "Booth, Sherman Miller," *Dictionary of Wisconsin Biography* (Madison, 1960); Ex parte *Booth*, 3 Wisc. 145 (1854).

cal points by refusing to extradite men accused of aiding fugitive slaves.[42]

The personal liberty laws passed in the last antebellum decade demonstrate the profound desire of Republicans to protect the rights and liberties of blacks. Similarly, the actions of local juries and judges indicate the availability of state legal institutions to defend fugitive slaves and their abolitionist friends, black or white. For example, a jury in Elkhart County, Indiana, found a group of southerners guilty of riot for attempting to capture a fugitive slave. In 1855 the Indiana Supreme Court upheld the right of a free black not only to sue for false arrest, but also to assault the federal marshal who seized him as a fugitive slave. After the abortive attempt to remove the fugitive slave Jerry from Syracuse, New York, a local grand jury indicted a federal marshal for kidnapping.[43]

The responses to the Oberlin-Wellington rescue illustrate the political context of opposition to fugitive slave renditions. This incident also illuminates later developments during Reconstruction, when Ohio was a vital Republican stronghold.

In 1858, free blacks and white abolitionists—including most of the students and faculty of Oberlin College—rescued a fugitive slave in nearby Wellington. A federal grand jury subsequently indicted thirty-seven rescuers, two of whom, Simeon Bushnell and Charles Langston, were convicted in federal court. Bushnell and Langston then sought writs of habeas corpus from the Ohio Supreme Court. This case forced the court to choose either to support the imprisoned abolitionists and confront the federal authority or to allow the abolitionists to remain in jail, thus avoiding a state-federal confrontation. In *Ex parte Bushnell, Ex parte Langston*, the Ohio court voted three to two to deny the writs.[44]

42. Henry G. Pearson, *The Life of John A. Andrew* (2 vols.; Boston, 1904); Maizlish, *Triumph of Sectionalism*, 121–239; Blue, *Salmon P. Chase;* Hans Trefousse, *Benjamin Franklin Wade: Radical Republican from Ohio* (New York, 1963), 62–63, 95; Hans Trefousse, *The Radical Republicans: Lincoln's Vanguard for Racial Justice* (New York, 1969) 7–9; Mark Krug, *Lyman Trumbull: Conservative Radical* (New York, 1965) 53–72; Paul Finkelman, "Antebellum States' Rights, North and South," in *Uncertain Tradition: Constitutionalism and the History of the South,* ed. Kermit Hall and James Ely, Jr. (Athens, Ga., 1988); *Kentucky v. Dennison,* 24 Howard (U.S.) 66 (1861); Paul Finkelman, "The Protection of Black Rights in Seward's New York," *Civil War History,* XXXIV (1988), 211–34.

43. Morris, *Free Men All; Graves and Others* v. *The State* 1 Ind. 258 (1848); *Freeman* v. *Robinson,* 7 Ind. 321 (1855). Freeman lost the case because of technical error in his original suit. Finkelman, *Slavery in the Courtroom,* 103–107.

44. Jacob R. Shipherd, *History of the Oberlin-Wellington Rescue* (Boston, 1859). These prosecutions are not reported, but records of them are found in the National Archives Records

Joseph Swan, Ohio's chief justice, destroyed his promising political career by refusing to support the habeas corpus petitions. Swan, an antislavery Republican, provided the tie-breaking vote and wrote the majority opinion. In voting this way, Swan avoided challenging the Supreme Court and the federal government as the Wisconsin court had done in the litigation surrounding Sherman Booth. Swan did not act out of hostility toward blacks, for he previously had supported black rights in Ohio. Rather, as Robert Cover argues, Swan felt constrained by legal formalism and his oath of office to uphold federal law. Whatever his motives, Swan's vote was unacceptable to Ohio Republicans, who refused to renominate him for the court. They obviously were not sympathetic to a legal formalist who failed to protect the liberty of black and white abolitionists. On the other hand, Jacob Brinkerhoff, who dissented in the case, received full Republican support in 1860 and won reelection in the "most brilliant" victory "ever achieved in the State by the Republican party." This, of course, was the same Ohio Republican party that sent John Bingham to Congress.[45]

Some Republicans may have supported personal liberty laws for political gain, but even that explanation implies that the rank and file supported such legislation. Eric Foner is probably correct that "the Republican stand on race relations went against the prevailing opinion of the 1850s." [46] This Republican stand on race, however, helped move the "prevailing opinion" in an egalitarian direction. The Republican position on race did not cripple the party's electoral appeal; throughout the North, men with known egalitarian and integrationist sentiments won local and state offices. Legislation, judicial opinions, the results of grand and petit jury deliberations, and electoral results demonstrate that on the issue of basic protection for free blacks and fugitive slaves, "prevailing opinion" often favored due process for all people. More important, these Republicans who were ahead of northern opinion in the 1850s would write the Fourteenth Amendment in the 1860s.

Center, Chicago, and in the actions of the defendants in the state cases of *Ex parte Bushnell, Ex parte Langston,* 9 Ohio 77 (1859).

45. Robert Cover, *Justice Accused: Antislavery and the Judicial Process* (New Haven, 1975); Eugene Roseboom, *The Civil War Era, 1850–1873* (Columbus, 1944), 370–71, Vol. IV of *A History of the State of Ohio,* 8 vols. The statewide support for Brinkerhoff undermines Berger's argument that Ohio was a "hotbed of Negrophobia" and that Bingham's intentions for the Fourteenth Amendment were limited and constricted.

46. Foner, *Free Soil,* 262.

Antebellum Education and the
Fourteenth Amendment

In *Brown* v. *Board of Education,* the Supreme Court held that the Fourteenth Amendment prohibits segregated education. During the evolution of this case, the Court sought to determine "the circumstances surrounding the adoption of the Fourteenth Amendment in 1868." The record of the congressional debates over the amendment revealed that many framers had conflicting intentions and that many of the politicians involved in the debates were far from candid. Wisely, the Court concluded that the historical question was "at best . . . inconclusive." The justices found that both the rudimentary system of public education in the South and "the effect of the Amendment on the Northern States" were "generally ignored in the congressional debates." In short, there was "little in the history of the Fourteenth Amendment relating to its intended effects on public education." [47]

This analysis is undoubtedly correct. As Robert Cottrol has argued, the Thirty-ninth Congress "probably did not plan to abolish school segregation," because education was not on its agenda. But as Cottrol also argues, Congress *did* "intend to establish equality of treatment before the law." [48] The history of abolitionist, Free-Soil, and Republican attempts to provide greater educational opportunity for antebellum northern blacks offers insight into the relationship between education and "equality of treatment before the law." This history shows that educational opportunity for blacks increased as these groups gained political power.

In the antebellum years, American public education was in its formative stages. Education was not yet a "right" or an "entitlement." Nevertheless, throughout the antebellum North, blacks found limited but growing educational opportunities. By 1860, almost all of the North provided some public education for blacks. In Massachusetts and Iowa, segregated schools were illegal. [49] In other places practice

47. *Brown* v. *Board of Education of Topeka, Kansas,* 347 U.S. 483 (1954) at 489, 490; Richard Kluger, *Simple Justice: The History of "Brown v. Board of Education" and Black America's Struggle for Equality* (New York, 1976), 617–56.
48. Robert J. Cottrol, "Static History and Brittle Jurisprudence: Raoul Berger and the Problem of Constitutional Methodology," *Boston College Law Review* XXVI (1985), 375.
49. "An Act in Amendment of 'An Act Concerning Public Schools,' Passed March 24, 1845," *Massachusetts Acts, 1855,* chap. 256; Iowa Constitution, 1857, Art. IX, sec. 12; Rosenberg, *Iowa on the Eve of the Civil War,* 204.

varied. Rural Rhode Island had integrated schools, while Providence remained segregated—some blacks in that city opposed integration because the segregated schools provided jobs for black teachers, whose salaries were paid mostly by white taxpayers. In New York some districts were segregated, others were totally integrated, and still others fell somewhere between these extremes. More than three hundred blacks, including such abolitionists as Austin Steward, Henry Highland Garnet, William C. Nell, and J. W. C. Pennington, taught in New York's schools in the antebellum era. In Ohio, Cleveland's schools were integrated, Cincinnati's segregated. Only Indiana refused to provide statewide public education for blacks.[50]

The test of Republican commitment to antebellum black education cannot be the twentieth-century one of integration. In his important study of the post-Reconstruction South, Howard Rabinowitz demonstrated that the development of segregated institutions—where previously there had been *no* institutions for blacks—was an improvement.[51] This was true of the antebellum North as well. Where no schools for blacks existed, the creation of separate schools was a step forward; where private schools were the only ones available for blacks, the appropriation of public funds for black education was a positive development.

The history of antebellum black education in Massachusetts illustrates a full cycle of development. In 1798 a private school educated blacks in Boston. In 1800 the city refused to fund a public school for blacks. In 1820 the city changed its mind and established a segregated school for blacks. By the 1840s, schools throughout Massachusetts were integrated, but Boston still maintained separate schools for blacks. In 1846 Boston's black community, led by William C. Nell, petitioned the Boston School Committee to integrate. This agitation led to the nation's first school desegregation case, *Roberts v. Boston*, in 1849. Roberts was represented by Charles Sumner, a leading white

50. Robert J. Cottrol, *The Afro-Yankees: Providence's Black Community in the Antebellum Era* (Westport, Conn., 1982), 99–100; Carleton Mabee, *Black Education in New York State* (Syracuse, 1979), chaps. 8, 9; Kenneth Kusmer, *A Ghetto Takes Shape: Black Cleveland, 1870–1930* (Urbana, Ill., 1979), 16–17; Finkelman, "Prelude to the Fourteenth Amendment"; Carter G. Woodson, *The Education of the Negro Prior to 1861* (Washington, D.C., 1919), 307–35.

51. Howard Rabinowitz, *Race Relations in the Urban South, 1865–1890* (New York, 1978). On Republicans and education during Reconstruction see [Henry Barnard], *Special Report of the Commissioner of Education on the Improvement of Public Schools in the District of Columbia* (Washington, D.C., 1871).

antislavery activist and future United States senator, and by Robert Morris, Jr., the first black attorney in the United States. In his brief, Sumner made constitutional, political, and psychological arguments similar to those used in *Brown,* but unlike the attorneys in *Brown,* he lost the case. In the first use of the "separate but equal doctrine," Chief Justice Lemuel Shaw upheld Boston's system of segregating black children.[52]

In *Government by Judiciary,* Raoul Berger cites Shaw's decision as evidence that the Fourteenth Amendment was inappropriately used to integrate schools.[53] He writes: "What matters it that 'antislavery idealists were backing judicial assault upon segregated schools' when not long before the Civil War they were rebuffed by the Supreme Courts of Massachusetts and Ohio?" Berger apparently believes that the intentions of the framers of the Fourteenth Amendment can somehow be divined by reading a decision written nineteen years before the amendment was adopted.[54] His analysis, however, fails to account for three key aspects of the *Roberts* case that shed light on the meaning of the Civil War amendments.

First, Berger does not acknowledge that *Roberts* was argued *before* the Fourteenth Amendment was adopted. Sumner's argument stressed the inherent equality of all people, but he did not have an equal protection clause to help his case.[55] Second, Berger looks at the wrong men for his precedents. Chief Justice Shaw never joined the Republican party. In 1860 he campaigned against Lincoln. His 1849 opinion can hardly be seen as a precursor of the Fourteenth Amendment. Sumner, on the other hand, was an important Republican before

---

52. Leonard W. Levy and Douglas Jones, *Jim Crow in Boston: The Origin of the Separate but Equal Doctrine* (New York, 1974); *Roberts v. Boston,* 5 Cush. (Mass.) 198 (1849); James Horton and Lois Horton, *Black Bostonians: Family Life and Community Struggle in the Antebellum North* (New York, 1979), 71.

53. This is part of a superficial and in many ways quite wrong analysis of abolitionist thought, in which Berger attempts to show that congressmen such as John Bingham did not intend to provide substantive rights for blacks through the due process clause of the Fourteenth Amendment. Berger, *Government by Judiciary,* chap. 13.

54. Berger, *Government by Judiciary,* 233. Earlier in the book, Berger attempts to undermine the significance of Charles Sumner's views on racial equality by pointing out that "Chief Justice Shaw held against him." *Ibid.,* 88. Oddly, Berger seems unaware that Sumner's election to four terms in the Senate was probably a greater measure of public views on race than Shaw's decision, which the legislature subsequently overturned.

55. Sumner's argument, as published in Charles Sumner, *Equality Before the Law: Unconstitutionality of Separate Colored Schools in Massachusetts* (Boston, 1849), is reprinted in Paul Finkelman, ed., *Abolitionists in Northern Courts* (New York, 1988), 493–524, Ser. 3 of Finkelman, ed., *Slavery, Race, and the American Legal System,* 16 vols.

and during Reconstruction. In the period from 1866 through 1868, Sumner and his Republican allies fought to constitutionalize, through the Fourteenth Amendment, their views on equality. Finally, Berger fails to tell the full story of school segregation in Boston.

Berger is correct that Chief Justice Shaw rejected Sumner's arguments and upheld segregated education, but he incorrectly ends his analysis of segregation in Massachusetts with *Roberts*. Neither Boston's black community nor Sumner gave up after *Roberts*. Blacks in Boston redoubled their efforts to eliminate segregated schools. A boycott "reduced black [school] attendance dramatically." Some blacks relocated, "taking advantage of integrated schools in several towns outside Boston." Meanwhile, blacks petitioned the legislature, which in 1855 prohibited segregated schools in Massachusetts.[56] Thus, if the antebellum history of segregated schools in Massachusetts is of value in understanding the meaning of the Fourteenth Amendment, then Berger's analysis, which truncates this history, is clearly erroneous. Indeed, the history in Massachusetts suggests gradual change over time, leading to integration in 1855.

The history of black education in antebellum Ohio is especially revealing because Ohio was the home of John Bingham, the author of the Fourteenth Amendment, as well as a key Republican stronghold during Reconstruction. Although Ohio initially excluded blacks from the public schools, in 1834 the Ohio Supreme Court ruled that mulattoes who were more than one-half white could not be excluded from those schools. By the early 1840s, in spite of prohibitory legislation, blacks attended some Ohio public schools.[57]

An 1848 law allowed integration if no whites openly opposed it. Some communities, such as Cleveland, immediately integrated. If whites protested integration, the statute provided for segregated black education paid for by taxes collected from blacks, with school trustees elected by black (male) taxpayers. If school districts refused to set up any schools for blacks, blacks were exempt from all school taxes.[58]

---

56. Horton and Horton, *Black Bostonians*, 74–75; [Barnard], *Special Report*, 357; Leonard W. Levy, *The Law of the Commonwealth and Chief Justice Shaw* (Cambridge, Mass., 1957), chap. 7.

57. [Barnard], *Special Report*, 370–74; Kusmer, *A Ghetto Takes Shape*, 16–17; *Williams v. Directors of School District*, Wright Ohio Chancery Reports 578 (1834); *Jeffries v. Ankney*, 11 Ohio 372 (1842); *Thacker v. Hawk*, 11 Ohio 376 (1842); *Lane v. Baker*, 12 Ohio 237 (1843).

58. "An Act to Provide for the Establishment of Common Schools for the Education of Children of Black and Mulatto Persons. . . ." (February 24, 1848), *Ohio Laws, 1848*, p. 81; Kusmer, *A Ghetto Takes Shape*, 16–17.

An 1849 law left the decision to integrate up to local school boards, thus eliminating the possibility that a few whites could block integration. Towns now were required to provide some form of public education for blacks, although segregated schools remained an option for school districts. An 1856 law required that school funds in Cincinnati be distributed on a per capita basis. Thus, the segregated schools in that city were partially funded by white taxpayers. Throughout Ohio, numerous black teachers taught in the state's segregated institutions.[59]

The failure of Ohio's antislavery Republicans to create a fully equal school system is not surprising. As with his analysis of Massachusetts, however, Raoul Berger misses the importance of the evolving changes in Ohio. Similarly, he fails to understand that those politicians who lost equality battles in the 1850s had gained political power by the 1860s. Thus, when Ohioans such as John Bingham adopted the Fourteenth Amendment, they were attempting, at least in part, to win at the national level what they had failed to achieve a decade earlier at the state level.

The North certainly did not offer blacks equal education. But developments in the 1840s and 1850s indicate that the trend in the North was toward greater educational opportunity. Meanwhile, educational opportunity for southern blacks declined. By 1860, many southern states absolutely prohibited the education of free blacks. In that year more black children attended school in Ohio than in all fifteen of the slave states combined; more blacks attended schools in Indiana than in all eleven states that would form the Confederacy.[60]

By 1860, most northern governments appropriated tax dollars for black education. This was a critical indication of the growth in black rights. Put simply, the North accepted its obligation to educate blacks with taxes collected from whites. This obligation eventually would lead to legal requirements for integration. These changes were brought about through the efforts of Whigs, Free-Soilers, and Republicans in the 1840s and 1850s. By 1866, many of those who had brought about

59. "An Act to Authorize the Establishment of Separate Schools for the Education of Colored Children, and for Other Purposes" (February 10, 1849), *Ohio Laws, 1849*, p. 17; "An Act to Amend an Act Entitled 'An Act to Amend the Act to Provide for the Maintenance and Better Regulation of Common Schools in the City of Cincinnati,' Passed January 27, 1853 and April 18, 1854," (April 6, 1856),*Ohio Laws, 1856*, p. 117; [Barnard], *Special Report*, 370–72.

60. [Barnard], *Special Report*, 394. See also Berlin, *Slaves Without Masters*, 303–304. Statistics on schooling of blacks and whites in this period are available in Finkelman, "Prelude to the Fourteenth Amendment," 472–75.

such changes—William Seward and Charles Sumner, for example—
were leaders in the Republican party.

Blacks, Republicans, and the Franchise

The greatest civil disability antebellum northern
blacks faced was at the ballot box, although by 1860 blacks could
legally vote in every New England state but Connecticut. If they met
property qualifications, they could vote in New York. Ohio courts had
held that mulattoes could vote. In addition, Ohio blacks could vote in
school board elections where segregated schools existed; this guaranteed blacks a certain level of autonomy in running their schools, which
distinguished these segregated schools from those of the post-
Reconstruction South. In Michigan blacks could vote in all school
board elections. In the upper Midwest some blacks voted in regular
elections and were not challenged. Even without black votes, John
Mercer Langston was elected to a number of offices in Ohio between
1855 and 1860.[61]

The struggles to further enfranchise blacks in the antebellum
North illustrate the nature of Republican thought before the adoption
of the Fourteenth and Fifteenth amendments. Even though they understood that such a position risked losing white votes, Republicans in a
number of states fought for black suffrage. During Reconstruction,
Republicans sought to enfranchise southern black males through section 2 of the Fourteenth Amendment. When this tactic failed, the Republicans quickly moved to guarantee blacks the vote through the Fifteenth Amendment. This amendment fulfilled Republican goals that
predated the Civil War.

That a number of attempts to extend the franchise to blacks failed
in the 1850s should surprise no one. That they were even attempted is
significant. At Ohio's 1851 constitutional convention a group of dele-

---

61. Frank R. Levstik, "John Mercer Langston," in *Dictionary of American Negro Biography* (New York, 1982), 382–84; *Anderson v. Milliken*, 9 Ohio 568 (1859); Kusmer, *A Ghetto
Takes Shape*, 7–9; David Katzman, *Before the Ghetto: Black Detroit in the Nineteenth Century*
(Urbana, Ill., 1973), 33–34. Cottrol, *Afro-Yankees*, 93, discusses the election of a black to an
office in Providence, Rhode Island. Although the election was a fluke, Cottrol notes that "what
is most significant is . . . the fact that he was able to get a grudging measure of acceptance as he
fulfilled his duties for one year."

gates who would soon form the Republican party in Ohio argued for black suffrage. In Iowa, Wisconsin, and New York, Republicans managed to place equal suffrage on the ballot. In 1857, New York's Republican legislators unanimously supported equal suffrage. In Connecticut a proposal to enfranchise blacks passed the Republican state senate but died in the house.[62]

Republican support for equal suffrage suggests the willingness of politicians to risk electoral defeat over issues of fundamental rights. This support also indicates a lessening of antiblack attitudes in the North. A majority of northerners were clearly not ready to grant political equality to their black neighbors, but a sizable minority, including the leaders of what was emerging as the section's dominant party, did favor such changes. The agitation of the 1850s helped pave the way for postwar success. After the Civil War, Republicans were able to nationalize concepts of due process and political equality that were politically impossible to attain in their own states. Because state legislatures, and not the voters themselves, approved amendments to the national Constitution, it proved easier to amend that document than some state constitutions.

Freedom North of Slavery

The antebellum North did not welcome free blacks with open arms. But in crucial ways free blacks were far better off in the North than the South. In the North there was a legal presumption of freedom; furthermore, as John Hope Franklin has noted, "the essential difference between the South and the North and West was that in the latter sections blacks had more of the law on their side and could therefore resist encroachments on their rights." The North guaranteed blacks basic legal rights and protections. Habeas corpus was theirs for the asking, except when a federal act interfered. Blacks could buy and

---

62. Richard Sewell, *Ballots for Freedom: Antislavery Politics in the United States, 1837–1860* (New York, 1976), 323, 333–35; Foner, *Free Soil*, 281–95; Phyllis Field, *The Politics of Race in New York: The Struggle for Black Suffrage in the Civil War Era* (Ithaca, N.Y., 1982); Current, *History of Wisconsin*, 265–71. See also *Gillespie v. Palmer* et al., 20 Wisc. 572 (1866), declaring that in an 1849 referendum Wisconsin had in fact adopted black suffrage. This case, argued by a leading Republican and decided by Republican jurists, indicates the continuity of thought between antebellum and postbellum Republicans on black rights.

sell property, educate themselves and their children, and establish churches. They could contract and sue. In most places they could be witnesses against whites. In some states they could vote. In all the free states they could agitate, petition, publish their views, hold public meetings, and in many other ways seek to persuade the white majority that they deserved better. "Northern Negroes could organize and fight for what they believed to be their rights," and in spite of the extreme racism of the North, "there was a substantial group of white citizens who gave them both moral and material support." [63]

On the eve of the Civil War, northern blacks had more rights than at any time in the previous thirty years, and they could reasonably expect change for the better.[64] The growing interest of northern politicians in an equal franchise boded well for blacks. Equally important, there existed by this time a political party dedicated to protecting and expanding black rights. Between 1865 and 1870, that party would rewrite the Constitution to achieve those ends.

The contrast with the South was striking. Long before 1860, most of the South discouraged emancipation. Recently freed slaves were required to leave most slave states. In Charleston, South Carolina, blacks who had lived as free persons for decades suddenly were threatened with enslavement as dormant laws were enforced with a vengeance. Free blacks in other southern states faced enormous pressure to migrate elsewhere. As John Hope Franklin has noted, even in "rather liberal" North Carolina free blacks were an "unwanted people," fearful of reenslavement or expulsion and "looked upon with growing suspicion" by whites. As the Civil War approached, Arkansas actually adopted legislation requiring all free blacks to leave the state.

63. John Hope Franklin, *From Slavery to Freedom: A History of Negro Americans* (5th ed., New York, 1974), 183.

64. Lincoln and other Republicans often argued that blacks had lost rights during the nineteenth century. For example, in 1857 Lincoln condemned Chief Justice Roger Taney for assuming "that the public estimate of the black man is more favorable *now* than it was in the days of the Revolution. This assumption is a mistake. In some trifling particulars, the condition of that race has been ameliorated; but, as a whole, in this country, the change between then and now is decidedly the other way; and their ultimate destiny has never appeared so hopeless as in the last three or four years." Basler, ed., *Collected Works of Lincoln*, II, 403. The position of Republicans on this issue has, I think, misled historians. It was in Lincoln's interest to argue that the standing of blacks had declined, because that allowed Lincoln to blame the decline on Taney, Stephen A. Douglas, and other Democrats. Lincoln also blamed this decline on federal actions such as the Fugitive Slave Law of 1850, the Kansas-Nebraska Act, and the *Dred Scott* decision. Lincoln, of course, offered an answer to this problem—the election of Republicans like himself. More significant than Lincoln's recital of the decline of black rights was the fact that even in Illinois, one of the most Negrophobic states in the North, Lincoln and other Republicans were willing to raise the issue of black rights as part of their campaign.

Only a governor's veto stopped a similar law in Missouri. Other southern states seriously considered such legislation.[65]

Throughout the antebellum period, free blacks and fugitives moved North despite the lack of full equality there. By voting with their feet, antebellum blacks showed that they understood where their rights and liberties were most protected.

The Civil War and Reconstruction would change forever the nature of American race relations. Raoul Berger has argued that the Fourteenth Amendment was not meant to provide full racial equality; indeed, "the key to an understanding of the Fourteenth Amendment is that the North was shot through with Negrophobia." [66] It is, of course, meaningless to talk about a single "key" to the Fourteenth Amendment. There were many keys, one of which may be the Negrophobia of many Americans of the Civil War era. But those Americans had been defeated politically in the North and militarily in the South.

The core of the Republican party—from conservatives such as Trumbull to moderates such as Bingham to radicals such as Stevens and Sumner—had been working for black equality for two decades or more. Throughout the North they had struggled, often with great success, to end inequality. They were ultimately victorious on the battlefield and in the struggle for the meaning of the Constitution. Of all the "keys" to the Fourteenth Amendment, perhaps the most important is the history of the struggle for equality in the period preceding the Civil War. The expansion of black rights in the antebellum North set the stage for providing at least formal constitutional equality for all Americans after the Civil War.

---

65. Berlin, *Slaves Without Masters,* 379–80; Johnson and Roark, eds., *No Chariot Let Down;* Michael Johnson and James Roark, *Black Masters: A Free Family of Color in the Old South* (Chapel Hill, 1984); Franklin, *The Free Negro in North Carolina,* 192, 220. The southern consideration of bills to force blacks out differed substantially from the consideration of immigration restrictions in the North. Northern "consideration" would have had little effect on blacks thinking about moving North. It is unlikely they even would have known of such debates. Southern free blacks, however, might very well have followed the debates over their fate. Their personal sense of security would have been diminished by such debates even when no laws actually were adopted.

66. Berger, *Government by Judiciary,* 10.

2

Presidential Reconstruction
Ideology and Change

❧ ROBERTA SUE ALEXANDER

In 1948, John Hope Franklin called for a new direc-
tion in Reconstruction historiography, one rejecting interpretations
that, like those of William Dunning, treated blacks with contempt, ignored Presidential Reconstruction, and saw southern whites uncriti-
cally as heroes.[1] From this time onward, Reconstruction would be a
major theme in Franklin's writings, and in 1961 he made one of his
most important contributions to the new direction he was advocating.
That contribution was *Reconstruction: After the Civil War,* the first
major synthesis of the revisionist interpretation of Reconstruction.

Nineteen years later, in his presidential address to the American
Historical Association, Franklin again reflected on the state of Reconstruction scholarship. Applauding the insights found in many recent
monographs, he cautioned the new scholars to be careful lest they repeat the errors made by the Dunning school: they must not, he
warned, use the events of the Reconstruction era either "to support
some current policy" or to seek "analogies that are at best strained and
provide little in the way of an understanding of that era or our own."
In order "to assure ourselves and others that we are serious about the

---

1. John Hope Franklin, "Whither Reconstruction Historiography?," *Journal of Negro
Education,* XVII (1948), 446–61. Works that exemplify the Dunningite interpretation include
William A. Dunning, *Reconstruction, Political and Economic, 1865–1877* (New York, 1907);
Walter Lynwood Fleming, *The Sequel to Appomattox: A Chronicle of the Reunion of the States*
(New Haven, 1919) and *Civil War and Reconstruction in Alabama* (New York, 1905); Claude J.
Bowers, *The Tragic Era* (Boston, 1929); James W. Garner, *Reconstruction in Mississippi* (New
York, 1901); and E. Merton Coulter, *The South During Reconstruction, 1865–1877* (Baton
Rouge, 1947).

postbellum South," Franklin added, "we would do well to cease using Reconstruction as a mirror of ourselves and begin studying it because it very much needs studying." In such a process, he predicted, "Reconstruction will doubtless have much to teach us all." [2]

Those who have studied the era of Presidential Reconstruction have not always been successful in judging this period within its own context. Historians of the Dunning school were influenced by the pervasive nationalism and racism of late nineteenth- and early twentieth-century America. Focusing on national politics, they contended that repentant former Confederates accepted defeat and eagerly followed the compassionate policies promulgated by President Andrew Johnson, policies based on the wise program Abraham Lincoln had formulated during the Civil War. Unfortunately, the Dunningites concluded, these policies were overthrown by vindictive radical Republicans who imposed a corrupt, incompetent rule on the South for their own selfish ends.

Early revisionists such as Franklin, Kenneth Stampp, LaWanda and John Cox, Eric McKitrick, W. R. Brock, and James M. McPherson effectively challenged this picture. Because of his inflexible states' rights ideology and his stubborn, rigid, hypersensitive personality, Andrew Johnson could not rise to the challenge of leading the nation through Reconstruction. As Franklin wrote, Johnson's Proclamation of Amnesty and Pardon and his Proclamation for North Carolina exhibited "leniency . . . [that] far outstripped his predecessor." Congress, motivated chiefly by a desire to protect the freedmen and to assure southern loyalty so that the fruits of victory would not be lost, concluded that additional requirements were necessary before the South could be readmitted to the Union. Initially, legislators moved cautiously in formulating a program, hoping to gain the president's support. That hope was shattered when Johnson vetoed the modest Freedmen's Bureau and Civil Rights bills and verbally assaulted several leading Republicans in his Washington's Birthday speech. Faced with an open split, congressional Republicans presented a platform based on the Fourteenth Amendment and representing compromises between the moderate and radical factions within the party. The northern electorate, horrified by the South's arrogance, pride, and racism

2. John Hope Franklin, "Mirror for Americans: A Century of Reconstruction History," *American Historical Review,* LXXXV (1980), 14.

and chagrined by Johnson's intemperate actions, overwhelmingly supported Congress' plan in the election of 1866. With increased strength, Congress launched its reconstruction program on March 3, 1867, and Presidential Reconstruction came to a deserved close.[3]

Franklin and other early revisionists also rejected the contentions of previous scholars that vindictiveness, political opportunism, or economics were the chief motivations of the Republicans. The revisionists believed that most policy makers of the era were driven largely by a desire to make the world a better, fairer place in which to live. Brock, for example, concluded that "Reconstruction was an ideological struggle, and the crisis must be understood in emotional terms and not merely as a record of personal rivalries, conflicting interests, and political maneuvers."[4]

Scholars writing during the last two decades have continued to focus on ideology as a principal means by which the course of Presidential Reconstruction can be explained. That is, they concentrate on examining the basic beliefs and value systems as well as the fears and prejudices of the participants. This is not to say that these scholars ignore contemporary political concerns; however, they argue that politics is best seen as a reflection of ideology. Custom, culture, race, class, and economic interests are paramount in shaping one's world view. This vision forms the basis for an ideology, which in turn is used by its adherents in making political decisions. Increasingly, therefore, historians today argue that Presidential Reconstruction can best be understood as a clash between competing ideologies—that is, as a conflict between different value systems based on conflicting sets of moral beliefs and racial assumptions. Despite this agreement that ideology was the prime force that shaped the policies and actions of the Reconstruction era, current scholars differ markedly on their assessment of the impact of these competing world views.

One of the clearest ideological struggles of the Reconstruction era took place between the president and Congress. Early revisionists such

---

3. John Hope Franklin, *Reconstruction: After the Civil War* (Chicago, 1961), 31. Early revisionist works besides Franklin's include Kenneth M. Stampp, *The Era of Reconstruction, 1865–1877* (New York, 1965); Rembert W. Patrick, *The Reconstruction of the Nation* (New York, 1967); Eric L. McKitrick, *Andrew Johnson and Reconstruction* (Chicago, 1960); John H. Cox and LaWanda Cox, *Politics, Principle, and Prejudice, 1865–1866: Dilemma of Reconstruction America* (New York, 1963); William R. Brock, *An American Crisis: Congress and Reconstruction, 1865–1867* (New York, 1963); and James M. McPherson, *The Struggle for Equality: Abolitionists and the Negro in the Civil War and Reconstruction* (Princeton, 1964).

4. Brock, *American Crisis*, 14.

as McKitrick, the Coxes, and Brock depicted Johnson as a stubborn leader inflexibly clinging to his ideology, which combined states' rights and a strict interpretation of the Constitution with strong racist assumptions shaped by a lifetime in Tennessee. The president was opposed by a Congress dominated not by radical but by moderate Republicans. Reflecting northern public opinion, these moderates differed from Johnson in their commitment to a Union based on equal political rights.

Some recent works have presented a more sympathetic interpretation of the seventeenth president. James E. Sefton agrees with the early revisionists that national politics can best be understood as a struggle over constitutional principles, with Johnson clinging to his lifelong belief in states' rights. But Sefton downplays the racism that the Coxes found central to understanding Johnson's actions. Instead, he argues that Johnson, although "clearly not a spokesman for political equality for blacks," nonetheless supported "a different sort of equality—equality of expectations." Therefore, "he judged blacks, whether unrealistically or not, by the same standards he had always applied to white yeoman farmers and mechanics."[5]

Albert Castel's *The Presidency of Andrew Johnson* is an even more sympathetic treatment. Castel claims that his purpose is to determine not whether Johnson's policies were right or wrong, but "whether he was good at using power." This, he believes, will lead to a more objective, historically sounder assessment of Johnson as president. Castel agrees with the revisionists that Johnson must be considered "a failure as president." Blaming this failure on Johnson's "ineptness in using . . . power," Castel finds little to criticize in Johnson's policies themselves. On the contrary, he believes that Johnson's policies and actions were realistic and certainly "far from being altogether wrong." He disagrees with McKitrick, Michael Perman, Hans L. Trefousse, and Michael Les Benedict, who attack Johnson for misusing power and preventing "the achievement of a true reconstruction of the South"; Castel accuses them of viewing the reconstruction process from their own radical perspective. Instead, he maintains, one has to understand Reconstruction within the context of its time. If one does that, one must conclude that Johnson was wiser than the Republican Congress, for he correctly saw

5. James E. Sefton, *Andrew Johnson and the Uses of Constitutional Power* (Boston, 1980), 127.

"that ultimately the blacks in the South would have to come to terms with the whites and that it would be the whites who would set the terms." In short, Castel sees Johnson as a courageous president who should be respected for his integrity and adherence to principle as well as for his attempts to promote a realistic approach to Reconstruction.[6]

Castel's observation that blacks and whites would have to reach their own accommodation in the South is quite perceptive. But it is not removing Johnson from his times to criticize him for failing to see what quickly became apparent to the vast majority of northerners— that if the federal government did nothing more than follow Johnson's lenient program, blacks would not have equal opportunities and racial accommodation would be solely in the white landowners' interests.

Although comparatively little new work has been done on Andrew Johnson in the last two decades, several important monographs have examined the motivations and policies of northern Republicans.[7] Franklin, the Coxes, Brock, and many other early revisionists, in detailing the evolving Republican policy, argued that Johnson's program only emboldened the recalcitrant white majority in the South. Therefore, as Patrick W. Riddleberger concluded, in the critical year of 1866 moderate Republicans took the lead in trying to save the reconstruction process. After breaking with Johnson, the Republicans showed a unity of purpose that culminated in the adoption of the Fourteenth Amendment, "which in the long run may be the most important of all constitutional amendments."[8] Rejecting Howard K. Beale's contention that the Republicans were motivated by economic concerns, the early revisionist scholars concluded that Republican policy was influenced by a sincere commitment to equal rights and equal justice.

Most of the recent analysis of the Republican program that emerged from the clash with Johnson supports Franklin and other early revisionists' belief in the sincerity of Republican motivations. The historians engaged in such analysis agree that "the principle of equal rights was a cardinal feature of the Republican ideology." The party was determined to restore the Union "on a firmer foundation

---

6. Albert Castel, *The Presidency of Andrew Johnson* (Lawrence, Kans., 1979) vii, 230, 224.

7. The continuing publication of the Andrew Johnson papers may stimulate new work on the Johnson presidency. Leroy P. Graf *et al.*, eds., *The Papers of Andrew Johnson* (7 vols. to date; Knoxville, 1967–86). The next volume will deal with Johnson's first years as president.

8. Patrick W. Riddleberger, *1866: The Critical Year Revisited* (Carbondale, Ill., 1979), 105.

than the one that had crumbled in 1861." The fruits of victory demanded equal rights and a new leadership for the South. After examining Republican beliefs in more detail, however, these scholars contend that northern policy makers evidenced a "constitutional conservatism" when they called for southern voluntarism and "state-centered federalism." This ideology "kept reconstruction policy from veering off into revolutionary radicalism" of land confiscation and redistribution or the total disfranchisement of white southerners.[9]

Despite this broad area of agreement, recent monographs differ sharply in their assessment of the Republican program. A handful of recent scholars even deny that there was an egalitarian strain in Republican thought. Examining federal labor policies toward blacks during the war, Louis S. Gerteis rejects the notion proposed by those he calls "liberal" historians that "the Civil War and Reconstruction wrought dramatic and fundamental changes in the society and economy of the South." Gerteis strongly condemns northern policy as being limited by a conservative constitutional ideology tinged with racism and committed to maintaining the economic and social status quo, for which reasons the government developed a contract labor system that merely perpetuated black subordination, dependence, and poverty. Gerteis grants that federal officials did protect blacks and tried to insure that they received humane treatment, but he argues the ultimate goal was stability and the maintenance of the traditional social order. Freedmen's Bureau agents and military commanders, "like Southern planters . . . saw the mass of blacks as field hands necessary for the cultivation of cotton. . . . [Therefore,] they encouraged and, when necessary, forced blacks to accept plantation labor. Their aim, as the nation's aim, was not revolutionary."[10]

---

9. Herman Belz, *Emancipation and Equal Rights: Politics and Constitutionalism in the Civil War Era* (New York, 1978), 106, xi; Michael Les Benedict, *The Fruits of Victory: Alternatives in Restoring the Union, 1865–1877* (Philadelphia, 1975), 7. Glenn M. Linden, *Politics or Principle: Congressional Voting on the Civil War Amendments and Pro-Negro Measures, 1838–69* (Seattle, 1976), Martin E. Mantell, *Johnson, Grant, and the Politics of Reconstruction* (New York, 1973), and Larry Kincaid, "Victims of Circumstance: An Interpretation of Changing Attitudes Toward Republican Policy Makers and Reconstruction," *Journal of American History,* LVII (1970), 48–66, also see remarkable unity among Republicans during Presidential Reconstruction. Republicans, they argue, were motivated by an idealism based on a northern ideology of racial equality. J. Michael Quill, in *Prelude to the Radicals: The North and Reconstruction During 1865* (Washington, D.C., 1980), agrees that northerners early insisted that the reconstruction process must accomplish the regeneration of southern society to conform to northern thought and northern principles so that the fruits of victory would be preserved.

10. Louis S. Gerteis, *From Contraband to Freedman: Federal Policy Toward Southern Blacks, 1861–1865* (Westport, Conn., 1973), 3, 181. See also Peter Camejo, *Racism, Revolution, Reaction, 1861–1877: The Rise and Fall of Radical Reconstruction* (New York, 1976).

Other historians have not been quite as critical as Gerteis. Phillip S. Paludan, Allen W. Trelease, and Donald G. Nieman, for example, grant that Republican ideology had an egalitarian strain. But because most Republicans also clung to a state-centered view of the Constitution and to an unbending belief in the sanctity of private property, they were unwilling "to make fundamental changes in the nature and configuration of American governmental-legal institutions." They failed, for example, to give the Freedmen's Bureau sufficient resources and authority, they refused to consider land confiscation, and they rejected the kind of legislation needed to protect blacks in any meaningful way from white southern political and economic domination. In sum, Republicans could not see that a powerful federal government was necessary to the achievement of meaningful equality.[11]

The problem with these arguments is that they remove analysis from its historical context. It is true that nineteenth-century Republican ideology was conservative by twentieth-century standards. Confiscation and land redistribution were never truly viable options in an America with such a strong ethic of laissez-faire capitalism.[12] To northerners of the nineteenth century, a free society guaranteed "freedom of speech and of the press, the right to travel, free public education, and equal citizenship irrespective of race."[13] It did not take from one group to protect others. Freedom had a self-help implication—one was free from government restraints, but government did not even up the competition. By viewing the world from a twentieth-century perspective, these historians tend to miss the significant differences in outlook among those struggling to formulate Reconstruction policies.

Michael Les Benedict, Richard H. Abbott, and David Donald, unlike the historians just discussed, emphasize that the Republicans' strong commitment to egalitarianism was central to their ideology. They agree that Republican policy was conservative, but pinpoint the cause of this conservatism as the moderate Republicans' fear that

11. Quotation from Donald G. Nieman, *To Set the Law in Motion: The Freedmen's Bureau and the Legal Rights of Blacks, 1865–1868* (Millwood, N.Y., 1979), xvii. See also Phillip S. Paludan, *A Covenant with Death: The Constitution, Law, and Equality in the Civil War Era* (Urbana, Ill., 1975); Allen W. Trelease, *Reconstruction: The Great Experiment* (New York, 1971); Michael Perman, *Reunion Without Compromise: The South and Reconstruction, 1865–1868* (New York, 1973).

12. See Herman Belz, "The New Orthodoxy in Reconstruction Historiography," *Reviews in American History,* I (1973), 106–13; Belz, *Emancipation and Equal Rights;* and Herman Belz, *A New Birth of Freedom: The Republican Party and Freedmen's Rights, 1861–1866* (Westport, Conn., 1976).

13. Belz, *Emancipation and Equal Rights,* 77.

"radical terms would alienate Northern white voters." Thus, the moderates' egalitarianism was tempered by practical and political considerations.[14] What these historians fail to emphasize is that these limited policies still could bring about significant changes.

Herman Belz insists that Republican policies, "viewed in historical perspective," were "undeniably radical." He and others agree that many Republicans tended to be constitutionally conservative. They grant that policies were modified for the sake of political expediency. They maintain, however, that even though "the extension of civil and political equality to Negroes may seem less radical than the confiscation and land allotment plans that Congress rejected, . . . they were exceedingly radical when measured against the antebellum conditions of blacks that most people considered the relevant basis for comparison in evaluating the postwar situation." Furthermore, "if slavery was primarily a matter of individual freedom . . . as contemporaries believed, then the conclusion is irresistible that blacks made significant gains during Reconstruction." Despite the persistence of discrimination, poverty, disfranchisement, and segregation, blacks had more opportunity and more control over their lives.[15]

Moreover, if Republican policy was conservative, what label would one put on Johnson and the northern Democrats? Edward L. Gambill's *Conservative Ordeal* convincingly demonstrates that northern Democrats provided a clear alternative to Republican policies. Gambill argues that the Democratic ideology, with its roots in the antebellum era, stressed conservative, states' rights constitutionalism and a laissez-faire approach to economic problems, social issues, and Reconstruction. Like the Republicans, Democrats faced party factional-

14. Quotation from Richard H. Abbott, *The Republican Party and the South, 1855–1877: The First Southern Strategy* (Chapel Hill, 1986). See also Michael Les Benedict, *A Compromise of Principle: Congressional Republicans and Reconstruction, 1863–1869* (New York, 1974) and David Donald, *The Politics of Reconstruction, 1863–1867* (Cambridge, Mass., 1965).

15. Belz, *Emancipation and Equal Rights,* 107, 146. See also Harold M. Hyman, *A More Perfect Union: The Impact of the Civil War and Reconstruction on the Constitution* (New York, 1973), and Michael Les Benedict, "Equality and Expediency in the Reconstruction Era: A Review Essay," *Civil War History,* XXIII (1977), 322–35. This same debate over the nature of northern Republicanism and the extent to which expediency overtook principle is seen in some significant new works on politics in northern states during the early postwar years. See, for example, Felice A. Bonadio, *North of Reconstruction: Ohio Politics, 1865–1870* (New York, 1970); Phyllis F. Field, *The Politics of Race in New York: The Struggle for Black Suffrage in the Civil War Era* (Ithaca, N.Y., 1982); James C. Mohr, *The Radical Republicans and Reform in New York During Reconstruction* (Ithaca, N.Y., 1973); and Eugene H. Berwanger, *The West and Reconstruction* (Urbana, Ill., 1981).

ism as the "apostles of principle" fought the "advocates of expediency." Democrats squabbled over whether the South should make concessions to the North, how to deal with Andrew Johnson and his attempt to form a National Union party, and other matters of policy and politics. Still, Democrats shared a common ideology that led them to advocate full restoration of political rights for all southerners as well as local control over race relations. This approach was certainly very different from the one supported by the Republicans.[16]

While some historians continue to examine the political scene in Washington, many more are focusing their attention on the South, recognizing that Presidential Reconstruction can best be understood by examining events in that region. It was in the South that the pattern of race relations for the next hundred years evolved. Historians of the Dunning school, as well as many early revisionists, basically ignored Presidential Reconstruction in the South. Franklin, in *Reconstruction: After the Civil War,* was a rare exception; he devoted an entire chapter to the white southern response to national policy. Franklin's writings, along with the works of Vernon Wharton and Joel Williamson, helped stimulate state-centered research. Yet as late as the mid-1970s, Otto Olsen and Michael Les Benedict found that much of this essential local research still needed to be done.[17]

Recently, many innovative and rewarding monographs have helped to fill this serious gap in Reconstruction historiography and enhanced understanding of the South during the early postwar years.[18]

16. Edward L. Gambill, *The Conservative Ordeal: Northern Democrats and Reconstruction, 1865–1868* (Ames, Iowa, 1981), 39.

17. For examples of early revisionist state studies, see Vernon Lane Wharton, *The Negro in Mississippi, 1865–1890* (Chapel Hill, 1947) and Joel Williamson, *After Slavery: The Negro in South Carolina During Reconstruction, 1861–1877* (Chapel Hill, 1965). For calls for additional research on the local level, see Otto H. Olsen, "Setting the Record Straight on the Reconstruction South," *Reviews in American History,* III (September, 1975), 333–34, and Benedict, "Equality and Expediency."

18. This essay focuses on works examining southern society during Presidential Reconstruction, but valuable studies have been done in other areas as well. Some of these relatively recent works focus on economic reconstruction, evaluating the success of the free labor system and the extent to which that system allowed blacks greater opportunities. See, for example, Stephen J. DeCanio, *Agriculture in the Postbellum South: The Economics of Production and Supply* (Cambridge, Mass., 1974); Robert Higgs, *Competition and Coercion: Blacks in the American Economy, 1865–1914* (Cambridge, Mass., 1977); Jay R. Mandle, *The Roots of Black Poverty: The Southern Plantation Economy After the Civil War* (Durham, N.C., 1978); Roger L. Ransom and Richard Sutch, *One Kind of Freedom: The Economic Consequences of Emancipation* (New York, 1977). See also Lawrence Powell, *New Masters: Northern Planters During the Civil War and Reconstruction* (New Haven, 1980), for the problems of the transition from slave to free labor as seen from the perspective of northerners who became planters. Powell examines

This work focuses on the connections between the motivations and actions of southern whites, the accomplishments and limitations of the northerners working in the South, and the emergence of the free black community. From these studies one begins to see much more clearly what Eric Foner has called the "complex triangular debate . . . played out among freedmen, northern whites, and southern planters, over the nature of the South's new free labor system" and southern society.[19]

John Hope Franklin labeled the years from 1865 to 1867 "reconstruction, Confederate style." Focusing his attention on southern whites, he stressed that under Johnson's policy, they were left almost entirely to their own devices as far as demonstrating to the nation their regret over the Civil War, their renewed loyalty, and their ability to treat the freedmen fairly. With this relatively free hand, white southerners failed to meet northern expectations. Instead, the North perceived a South controlled by "those who had fought against the Union" yet were still "pursuing most of their prewar policies as though there had never been a war. This was reconstruction, Confederate style!"[20]

Recent scholarship, accepting this revisionist thesis, has continued to explore in much more detail southern thinking and actions. Whether writing detailed monographs of a single community or state or undertaking broader surveys of white southern opinion, historians of the last twenty-five years show remarkable agreement. For these scholars "reconstruction, Confederate style," is the story of southern leaders doggedly struggling to maintain the South's antebellum culture based on its proslavery ideology. The "planters' basic ideas about slavery, blacks, agriculture, and Southern civilization revealed a remarkable resistance to change." Unable to picture "a decent and enduring Southern civilization without slavery," the planters' "primary political

---

the causes for the failure of these men, focusing (as many of the other economic studies do) on the interplay of nature, the market, and ideology on labor and economic recovery.

In another important area of research, the educational efforts of northern missionaries, scholars have analyzed the extent to which a conservative ideology limited the success of those efforts and stifled the black struggle for autonomy. See Ronald E. Butchart, *Northern Schools, Southern Blacks, and Reconstruction: Freedmen's Education, 1862–1875* (Westport, Conn., 1980); Jacqueline Jones, *Soldiers of Light and Love: Northern Teachers and Georgia Blacks, 1865–1873* (Chapel Hill, 1980); Robert C. Morris, *Reading, 'Riting, and Reconstruction: The Education of Freedmen in the South, 1861–1870* (Chicago, 1981); Joe M. Richardson, *Christian Reconstruction: The American Missionary Association and Southern Blacks, 1861–1890* (Athens, Ga., 1986).

19. Eric Foner, *Politics and Ideology in the Age of the Civil War* (New York, 1980), 100.
20. Franklin, *Reconstruction*, 53.

objective . . . after 1865 was to make the region a safe place for plantation agriculture." White southerners viewed any policy that challenged planter political control and the plantation labor system as suicidal. To them, northern arguments about free-black labor were the "foolish prattle of an alien and inferior Northern culture." James L. Roark put it well when he noted that "ideologies, once constructed, have lives of their own." Nothing could be truer of the white South immediately after the Civil War.[21]

There are, of course, areas of disagreement. For example, historians debate the question of how flexible the South was immediately after the war. Some agree with Eric McKitrick that the South was prepared to do whatever its conquerors demanded, and that if the federal government had been firmer, the South probably would have responded.[22] Others lean toward Michael Perman's judgment that even if Johnson had been firmer, "it could have made only a marginal difference." The South's rejection of Johnson's policies and northern expectations was not the result of a northern failure to communicate its requirements clearly to the South (as McKitrick has argued). Instead, this group maintains, southerners consciously pursued a policy of "masterly inactivity" based on their belief that once the northern white racial backlash limited Republican demands, they would be able to rejoin the Union on their own terms. But even if southerners had read northern opinion correctly, these historians continue, they would have resisted change. There is no evidence that the majority of white southerners would have accepted "any truly radical requirements in 1865." The South clung too fiercely to its antebellum ideology.[23]

Historians differ as to the reasons for the South's rejection of northern requirements, but nearly all would agree that the postbellum white South was a cohesive society whose actions were driven almost irresistibly by antebellum assumptions. Any alternative to a plantation economy based on landless black labor was rejected as unviable. "The

21. James L. Roark, *Masters Without Slaves: Southern Planters in the Civil War and Reconstruction* (New York, 1977), 95, 195, 107, 108. See also works cited in notes 23 through 28.

22. See, *e.g.*, C. Peter Ripley, *Slaves and Freedmen in Civil War Louisiana* (Baton Rouge, 1976); Jerrell H. Shofner, *Nor Is It Over Yet: Florida in the Era of Reconstruction, 1863–1877* (Gainesville, 1974); Joe Gray Taylor, *Louisiana Reconstructed, 1863–1877* (Baton Rouge, 1974); Ted Tunnell, *Crucible of Reconstruction: War, Radicalism, and Race in Louisiana, 1862–1872* (Baton Rouge, 1984).

23. Perman, *Reunion Without Compromise*, 143; Dan T. Carter, *When the War Was Over: The Failure of Self-Reconstruction in the South, 1865–1867* (Baton Rouge, 1985), 275. See also Roberta Sue Alexander, *North Carolina Faces the Freedmen: Race Relations During Presidential Reconstruction, 1865–67* (Durham, N.C., 1985).

proslavery argument—shaken but unbroken by emancipation—drew the overwhelming majority of whites into the same web of crippling assumptions."[24] Some dissenters and consistent Unionists offered a different vision, but southern leaders ignored their advice.[25] The southern majority also rejected the die-hard Confederates, although perhaps less so in 1866 than in 1865.[26]

Thus, the "reluctant secessionists" were in firm control. They may have bickered about certain specific strategies and policy choices, but they remained united because of their shared world view. Almost all of them firmly believed that blacks were innately inferior and would not work unless forced. Therefore, southerners united in support of policies to insure a stable labor force, to keep wages low, to impose restrictive contracts on laborers, and to resist any efforts by the freedmen to buy or rent land. Legislators, by large majorities, enacted Black Codes to insure black economic dependency. Law enforcement officials and the courts also aided in these efforts. More important, perhaps, southerners united to promote white supremacy. Nearly all shared the belief that the subordination of blacks was necessary to preserve a peaceful society. Therefore, in addition to economic restrictions, the Black Codes provided for the legal and social subordination of blacks. "Any black assertion of freedom met with resistance perpetrated by individual whites, organized terrorist groups, or outlaw gangs, who often received active or passive support from most members of the white community." Black efforts to achieve an education or religious independence often were opposed violently by whites. White crowds attacked blacks for being "too sassy and stubborn." Law enforcement officers often sided with these whites, regularly arresting blacks for breaches of the peace—which included attempts by the freed people merely to behave as free people. For example, in North Carolina a black man was jailed for "giving insolence" to a white woman. Justice

24. Carter, *When the War Was Over*, 175.
25. LaWanda Cox, in "Reconstruction Foredoomed? The Policy of Southern Consent," *Reviews in American History*, I (1973), 541–47, and Peter Kolchin, in Review of Perman, *Reunion Without Compromise*, in *Journal of American History*, LXI (1974), 494–95, criticize Michael Perman for giving "an exaggerated picture of southern unity." Carter, early in *When the War Was Over*, also criticizes Perman and others for seeing a united South. Carter argues that white southerners held "quite diverse" views; however, his own conclusions contradict this argument. Indeed, despite these occasional criticisms that white southerners were divided along class, regional, or other lines, most research suggests an overriding unity.
26. See esp. James Smallwood, *Time of Hope, Time of Despair: Black Texans During Reconstruction* (Port Washington, N.Y., 1981), and Alexander, *North Carolina Faces the Freedmen*, for detailed examples of increasing conservatism in 1866.

in the courts for blacks who faced such violence or discrimination was selective at best.[27] Historians have come to understand that the white South, given its basic beliefs and assumptions, could hardly have been expected to act in ways other than it did.[28]

While white southerners struggled to recapture their antebellum world, northerners working in the South had some influence on the policies that eventually emerged. Before revisionism, these northerners were seen as interlopers influencing and controlling blacks for Republican political purposes. Early revisionists like Franklin and Stampp, although recognizing that federal policy limited the impact that northern philanthropists and Freedmen's Bureau agents might have had, nevertheless emphasized the valuable, necessary work these people accomplished.[29] Seeking to understand the "failure of Reconstruction," many recent historians have tended to emphasize the limits of northern efforts. These scholars accept the arguments of those who emphasize the conservative nature of Republican ideology in formulating reconstruction policy. They see a similar lack of radicalism among army officers, Freedmen's Bureau agents, and northern missionaries. According to this interpretation, northerners working in the South did make a difference in the lives of southern blacks, but a limited federal government and the northerners' belief in black self-help restricted their effectiveness.

For example, Joe Gray Taylor, C. Peter Ripley, John Cimprich, Robert Engs, and others argue that during the war army officers, often racist, sometimes corrupt, and definitely committed to a free-labor ideology that insisted that blacks work, led the way in developing the contract labor system. In Tennessee the army forced blacks to sign labor contracts and encouraged employers to withhold half the freed people's wages until the end of the contract year. Elsewhere, the army

27. Smallwood, *Time of Hope*, 160; Alexander, *North Carolina Faces the Freedmen*, 133, 143.
28. George M. Fredrickson, "A Comparative Study of White Responses to the New Order of Race Relations in the American South, Jamaica, and the Cape Colony of South Africa," in *What Was Freedom's Price?* ed. David G. Sansing (Jackson, Miss., 1978), 71–92, emphasizing a similar unity of purpose among whites in the postemancipation societies of Jamaica and South Africa, asserts that all whites showed a stubborn "desire to keep as many of their old privileges as possible" (76). Eric Foner, in his comparative study of emancipation in the British Caribbean and the United States, *Nothing but Freedom: Emancipation and Its Legacy* (Baton Rouge, 1983), also describes a united white community, although he emphasizes class interest more than race as the primary ingredient "for continuing conflict" (72; see also esp. 10–38).
29. See Franklin, *Reconstruction*, 37–39, 57–58; Stampp, *Era of Reconstruction*, 131–35. See also Willie Lee Rose, *Rehearsal for Reconstruction: The Port Royal Experiment* (New York, 1964).

forced blacks to labor, often cruelly abused them, and in other ways cooperated with southern whites to enforce old slave patterns and control devices such as the pass system. Thus, army policies set "a precedent for the notorious Black Codes." [30]

After the war, the Freedmen's Bureau took over from the army, and in the view of these recent historians, O. O. Howard and his agents were paternalistic at best, racist at worst. These scholars contend that most agents agreed with southern whites that blacks had to stay on the land and that compulsion was necessary to accomplish this. Howard and his agents, limited by their ideology, were more concerned with stability and order than with black autonomy. Although they attempted to achieve some fairness in the labor system and often ameliorated white abuses, they also helped southern whites keep blacks on the land by enforcing the contract labor system and allowing contracts with demeaning and restrictive provisions. As Donald Nieman concludes, bureau agents chose stability "at the expense of blacks' independence and self-reliance." Black collective action such as strikes, unionization, and the formation of credit unions might have led to greater autonomy, but "bureau officials' attitudes—their fear of social disorder, faith in the operation of laws of the market, and concern for instructing blacks in their obligations of freedom—had prevented them from urging freedmen to follow such a course." Thus, in the words of Leon Litwack, "the Freedmen's Bureau ultimately facilitated the restoration of black labor to the control of those who had previously owned them." Some scholars even contend that southern whites were misled by bureau agents and other northern governmental officials. These historians argue that southerners, in enacting their Black Codes and discriminatory educational policies, merely adopted policies already in place in the North or established by the Freedmen's Bureau or the military in the South before southerners regained control. Even the bureau's efforts to assure equal justice in the courts, this group maintains, were limited by a misplaced faith in classic liberalism. The bureau's belief that "with the simple transformation of the statute law of the Southern states, with the mere elimination of dis-

30. Quotation from Taylor, *Louisiana Reconstructed*, 39. See also John Cimprich, *Slavery's End in Tennessee, 1861–1865* (University, Ala., 1985); Edmund L. Drago, *Black Politicians and Reconstruction in Georgia: A Splendid Failure* (Baton Rouge, 1982); Ripley, *Slaves and Freedmen;* Robert F. Engs, *Freedom's First Generation: Black Hampton, Virginia, 1861–1890* (Philadelphia, 1979); and Leon F. Litwack, *Been in the Storm So Long: The Aftermath of Slavery* (New York, 1979).

criminatory legislation, justice would . . . follow" was unsuited to postwar southern conditions. Only too late did some agents realize that "harshly unjust practices could go on even if state laws made no distinction of race or color." [31]

These historians, in judging northerners in the South during Reconstruction by twentieth-century standards, fail to see the real dynamics that occurred. Bureau agents were not New Dealers committed to a policy of strong federal intervention. If they were not completely colorblind, they were certainly more enlightened than were the southern whites in control of the state governments during Presidential Reconstruction.

Historians such as Martin Abbott, who is more appreciative of the accomplishments of the Freedmen's Bureau, recognize the important differences in the assumptions of northerners and southerners. These historians also tend to emphasize how the national authorities limited the bureau. For example, Andrew Johnson's insistence that land be returned to white southerners, as well as his other efforts to curtail the power of the bureau, prevented that agency from carrying out policies that might have promoted black freedom. Moreover, Congress never provided the necessary funding for staffing sufficient to protect blacks from white abuse. As Abbott concluded, the bureau "stumbled badly" because it was restricted "by its sponsors." Yet despite these limitations, the bureau was "a qualified success." It got better pay and better treatment for blacks from whites. Contracts supervised by the bureau were fairer than those that were not. The bureau forced whites to compromise and concede much to blacks. Many agents, once legislation was enacted, helped blacks get land, especially under the Southern Homestead Act. The bureau also tried, with notable success, to protect blacks from white violence. Agents pushed for equal treatment of blacks in the courts and helped moderate the legal restrictions against blacks in the Black Codes and in practice in state courts. Unlike the pessimists, then, such scholars as Martin Abbott, Herman Belz, Joe Richardson, and Roberta Alexander argue that despite the limits of the bureau's vision, despite the paternalistic attitudes of most agents, these northerners were "committed to the independence of the freedmen in a way that former masters and most white southerners were not." As

31. Nieman, *To Set the Law in Motion,* 158, 222; Litwack, *Been in the Storm,* 386; James Oakes, "A Failure of Vision: The Collapse of the Freedmen's Courts," *Civil War History,* XXV (1979), 75.

ROBERTA SUE ALEXANDER

Belz emphasizes, one must strive to understand the Reconstruction era on its own terms. "To give the freedmen legal recourse to protect themselves," he points out, was to nineteenth-century liberal northerners "to treat them as freemen with equal rights." [32] And this was certainly a vision of race relations different from that held by the southern planter leadership.

Until recently, most accounts of Presidential Reconstruction would have ended here, with northern and southern whites struggling for control of the South. New research, however, has emphasized the active role of southern blacks. This role was ignored by the Dunning school and only briefly examined by Franklin and other early revisionists, who tended to concentrate on national politics and southern whites' reactions to federal policies. Franklin, however, did start a new generation thinking about the role of the freed people. For example, he noted that southern black conventions provided northerners with much of the basis for the latter's critique of Presidential Reconstruction. The blacks "declared that they were being victimized by the merciless and inconsiderate policies of the former Confederates." Franklin also pointed out how the freedmen exhibited an "eagerness" for education. Finally, he showed that despite southern whites' fears, by the end of 1865 most former slaves had agreed to return to the plantations and work on white terms. But that is where the story ended. [33]

Much of the most provocative and important recent work on Presidential Reconstruction attempts to re-create the life of southern blacks, to trace the development of the free black community, and to detail the interaction of this newly emerging black community with whites who saw its members more as dependents than as autonomous human beings with their own goals and dreams. Reexamining Freedmen's Bureau records, reports of mass meetings, WPA narratives, county court marriage records, church documents, and the like, historians have formed a new picture of the freed people and their post-emancipation community. These studies clearly indicate the impor-

32. Martin Abbott, *The Freedmen's Bureau in South Carolina, 1865–1872* (Chapel Hill, 1967), 133–35; Belz, *Emancipation and Equal Rights*, 72, 73.
33. Franklin, *Reconstruction*, 56, 108, 6. See also Rose, *Rehearsal for Reconstruction*. For a discussion of the state of historical scholarship on the black community at the end of the 1960s, see John Hope Franklin, "Reconstruction and the Negro," and August Meier, "Comment on John Hope Franklin's Paper," in *New Frontiers of the American Reconstruction*, ed. Harold M. Hyman (Urbana, Ill., 1966), 59–86.

44

tance of Presidential Reconstruction. As Peter Kolchin has noted, it was during the "short transition period" of Presidential Reconstruction that "many old modes of thought and behavior among blacks gave way to new ones." Blacks had dreams, and their determination to achieve these dreams led to continual conflict with southern whites.[34]

On one level, it is hardly surprising that planters and freedmen clashed. As Eric Foner has pointed out in his comparative study of postemancipation societies, "Everywhere, emancipation was succeeded by struggle for control of the scarce resources of plantation economies, paramount among them, the labor of the former slaves themselves." Thus, "irreconcilable interests" led to "continuing conflict."[35]

No one would deny that the different attitudes held by whites and blacks stemmed in part from their different economic and class interests. But these differences do not explain why nonplanter whites supported the planter class. Planter and poor white alike subscribed to an ideology that clashed with the black community's aspirations and views of itself.

Recent scholarship has proved convincingly that blacks, from the start of the Civil War, asserted their independence. Historians such as Cimprich, Litwack, Ripley, and Kolchin have demonstrated how blacks during the war years continually exploited the tumultuous situation to seek new rights and privileges. Those who remained on the plantations often demanded new work conditions: to labor at a slower pace; to be paid, if not in cash, then with a share of the crop; to have more land to grow their own crops; and the like. Thousands of others escaped to Union lines to free themselves. Many served as spies and informants. At least 186,000 became soldiers, and in this way helped transform public sentiment in the North and increase racial pride among the freedmen. In Union-occupied Louisiana—especially in New Orleans, with its affluent, well-educated, free black population— blacks organized to demand equal political rights, including suffrage, as being essential to the preservation of freedom and economic security. They formed equal-rights leagues and other such groups to insure that their demands would be heard. Freed people in the countryside

34. Peter Kolchin, *First Freedom: The Responses of Alabama's Blacks to Emancipation and Reconstruction* (Westport, Conn., 1972), xix.
35. Foner, *Nothing but Freedom*, 37, 72.

fought General Nathaniel Banks's paternalistic labor system, with its dependency and its pass system.[36]

Such responses during the war should not be exaggerated. Historians have found it impossible to determine how widespread such assertiveness was, especially by blacks still on plantations far from Union lines. For most slaves, emancipation came with great suddenness in the spring of 1865. But if these slaves remained quietly on the plantation during the war, they soon changed their demeanor as they tested their freedom. Throughout the South—almost universally, if planters' complaints are to be believed—blacks walked off plantations to test their freedom or to search for loved ones so that their families could be reunited.[37]

When they returned to the land, blacks refused to return as slaves. In many ways, they asserted their independence and their freedom. Initially, many dropped their old slave demeanor, refusing to abide by antebellum race etiquette. In many other ways, despite their lack of political power or even necessary legal rights and protections, blacks struggled to become free. They had a clear vision of what they wanted and worked with purpose to fulfill their dreams. Most important, they sought autonomy—not mere freedom from the restraints of slavery, but freedom from all white supervision, authority, and control. One can see this vision of freedom in every facet of life: in agriculture, in family relations, in education, in religion, in other social relations, and in the political arena.

Individually and collectively, the freed blacks took control of their lives. They tried to buy land or negotiate contracts that would free them from white supervision. They saved in the Freedman's Bank and elsewhere, postponing immediate desires in order to achieve their goal of independent landownership. In their conventions and meetings they protested white oppression and demanded fair treatment and equal rights. They continually clashed verbally or physically with whites as

36. See, for example, Kolchin, *First Freedom*; Cimprich, *Slavery's End*; Litwack, *Been in the Storm*; Ripley, *Slaves and Freedmen*; Engs, *Freedom's First Generation*. Mary Berry, *Military Necessity and Civil Rights Policy: Black Citizenship and the Constitution, 1861–68* (Port Washington, N.Y., 1977), 79, 86, 96, points to the clear connection between blacks' becoming soldiers and northern recognition of their right to citizenship. See also Belz, *Emancipation and Equal Rights*, 67, and Benedict, *Fruits of Victory*, 17.

37. See, for example, Litwack, *Been in the Storm*; Smallwood, *Time of Hope*; Alexander, *North Carolina Faces the Freedmen*; Williamson, *After Slavery*; Shofner, *Nor Is It Over Yet*; Taylor, *Louisiana Reconstructed*; Kolchin, *First Freedom*; and Edward Magdol, *A Right to the Land: Essays on the Freedmen's Community* (Westport, Conn., 1977).

they sought to assert or protect their interests, rights, and community institutions. They struggled to protect their family life from white control; parents vigorously protested the forced apprenticeship of their children. Freed people sacrificed to educate themselves and their children, accepting northern aid but insisting on controlling their education and their schools. They formed their own churches, resisting southern white and northern missionary efforts to influence or control their religious institutions and practices.

From these struggles emerged a new black leadership that would help the black community thrive. Moreover, these experiences enhanced the freed people's image of their abilities, encouraging them to continue to meet and to organize to assert their rights and their interests. In labor relations, education, religion, family affairs, and politics, the former slaves "had an immediate and real awareness of their best interests." They wanted the opportunity to shape their own destinies free from white control and white interference.[38]

Although historians agree on this general picture, they disagree on certain specifics. Some, such as Herbert G. Gutman and Edward Magdol, argue that freed blacks created a unique Afro-American culture. They stress the distinctive characteristics of the black family, black religious practices, and black naming practices; Magdol points especially to black collective efforts—what he calls the ethos of "mutuality." These historians conclude that the black community was a unique blend of the African and slave heritage. Gutman and Magdol have made a valuable contribution by examining some of the unique features of the southern black community, but they base their conclusions on scanty evidence.[39]

Most historians, although admitting that postbellum black culture was influenced by some remnants of African heritage and a great deal by slave experiences, are struck more by the *similarities* between the freed people and white Americans. Examining the entire range of black culture and community, they conclude that to blacks, the white culture was a free culture. Thus, even while developing their own subculture and institutions, the freed people adopted the "value system of the predominantly white society because these values represented free-

---

38. Ripley, *Slaves and Freedmen,* 159.
39. Magdol, *Right to the Land;* Herbert G. Gutman, *The Black Family in Slavery and Freedom, 1750–1925* (New York, 1976); Jones, *Soldiers of Light and Love.* See Alexander, *North Carolina Faces the Freedmen,* 65–66, for a critique of some aspects of Gutman's work.

dom." Black institutions usually paralleled those of whites and served the same purposes. Freed blacks formed patriarchal families and strove to remove wives and mothers from the fields—southern whites continually complained that black women were staying home and "playing the lady." Most historians conclude that blacks made every effort to follow the white family model; this, to them, was what a free family was like and what had been prohibited to them in slavery.[40] Thus, as blacks sought autonomy, they accepted American middle-class, Victorian values and strove by the same means (industriousness, sobriety, hard work, thrift) to achieve the same ends (individual success and economic prosperity).[41]

A second major area of disagreement concerning the black community is the extent of its unity. Most who address this issue argue that the more affluent, better-educated free blacks, realizing that "they could rise only as a result of the strength of numbers," worked to aid the freed people. These historians grant that there were class divisions and that free mulattoes often saw themselves as superior to black freed people. They point out, however, that the elite refused to be tempted by offers of rights and privileges reserved to them alone. Free and freed cooperated "to achieve common goals."[42]

Thomas Holt, on the other hand, asserts that the free-born, affluent black leaders, with their "bourgeois" goals of life, liberty, and property, had different needs and ambitions than the "slave-born black peasantry." The black bourgeoisie was more concerned with its image. It stressed harmony and moderation in working with southern whites and called for black self-help and hard work. The bourgeois leadership sold out the black peasant, who wanted (and needed) land; the leaders pushed instead for suffrage. They were even willing to accept limited

40. Quotation on value system from Smallwood, *Time of Hope,* 109. See also John W. Blassingame, *Black New Orleans, 1860–1880* (Chicago, 1973); Williamson, *After Slavery;* Alexander, *North Carolina Faces the Freedmen;* Campbell, *A Southern Community;* Litwack, *Been in the Storm;* Shofner, *Nor Is It Over Yet;* Foner, *Nothing but Freedom;* Kolchin, *First Freedom.* Gutman, in *Black Family,* and Magdol, in *Right to the Land,* agree with many of the major conclusions of this group—for example, that the black family was stable, monogomous, and patriarchal—while emphasizing, on balance, the unique Afro-American characteristics of the family. Taylor, *Louisiana Reconstructed,* 426, disagrees. He argues that blacks exhibited lax morals, which he claims was a result of slavery and did not change with emancipation. He also argues that the free black family, like the slave family, was matriarchal in structure.

41. See Williamson, *After Slavery;* Kolchin, *First Freedom;* Blassingame, *Black New Orleans;* Alexander, *North Carolina Faces the Freedmen;* Smallwood, *Time of Hope;* Richardson, *Christian Reconstruction;* and Carl R. Osthaus, *Freedmen, Philanthropy, and Fraud: A History of the Freedman's Savings Bank* (Urbana, Ill., 1976) as well as the sources in note 40 above.

42. Quotation from Blassingame, *Black New Orleans,* 154. See also Cimprich, *Slavery's End,* and Ripley, *Slaves and Freedmen.*

suffrage based on education or wealth as long as it was applied equally to blacks and whites.[43]

The truth about the extent of the unity within the postbellum world of southern blacks probably lies somewhere between Holt's class-torn society and the harmonious community postulated by John W. Blassingame. Holt provides persuasive evidence that the ruling class had different goals than the rank and file. Yet it is important for historians to remember that blacks were no different from other ethnic groups; they did not comprise a homogeneous mass. To blame the "failure" of Reconstruction on the black elite is present-minded. Why should anyone expect the black middle-class leadership to have acted any differently than politicians do in other communities? They, too, had to operate within the realm of the possible. Moreover, as with all societies, the black middle class had different values from the "peasantry." To expect black political leaders in nineteenth-century South Carolina to have behaved like radical socialists removes them from the context of time and place and ignores the many cooperative efforts among blacks across class lines, well detailed by Blassingame and others.

Historians will continue their research into the black community, its culture, and its class structure in an effort to resolve these conflicts. But what is striking is that scholars are seeking to focus on blacks as actors themselves, not as objects to be discussed and manipulated. Historians continue to seek out sources that will allow them to understand this emerging free community from the perspective of the freed people themselves. And from this effort a more accurate picture of Reconstruction will emerge.

The dispute among historians about the role that northerners, both in Congress and working in the South, played in this drama also needs to be resolved before the full story of life in the South during Reconstruction can be understood. Many scholars continue to stress the limited nature of northern reconstruction efforts: because of the conservative ideology held by northern Republicans, Congress failed to provide blacks with land, sufficient educational opportunities, or even satisfactory protection of their persons and property. Thus, these historians conclude, Reconstruction witnessed struggle but not prog-

---

43. Thomas Holt, *Black over White: Negro Political Leadership in South Carolina During Reconstruction* (Urbana, Ill., 1977).

ress. There were few significant changes in the economic, social, or political structure of southern society. Blacks were little better off than before the war. The white planter class maintained control over the southern economy, the southern political order, and the southern society.[44]

In stressing continuity, these historians miss the drama and significance of emancipation. Although it is certainly true that Reconstruction was an "incomplete revolution" and that black opportunities were severely limited, "*to blacks,* emancipation appeared as a fundamental watershed in their lives." For the first time, the freed people could control their families and their daily lives. Even if they did not own land, sharecropping offered a significant improvement over the old plantation system. Blacks had geographic and occupational mobility, both of which had been denied to them in slavery. They had their own community, their own institutions, and their own culture. Their determination in the face of massive white resistance and a weak northern policy and their achievements in all areas gave them a sense of pride and self-worth that kept them going through the decades of repression that followed Reconstruction.[45]

Those scholars who stress change over continuity have been able to look beyond the political structure and focus on the lives of individuals. In addition, these scholars recognize the importance of judging not by today's standards, but by those of the times being studied—and by using those standards they are able to see the dramatic changes that the Civil War and the Reconstruction era produced for black Americans despite the conservative goals of whites both North and South. Moreover, these scholars can better appreciate how ideas of freedom and equality evolved. They appreciate the varying degrees of commitment or opposition to equality held by different individuals. Thus, by keeping John Hope Franklin's admonitions in mind and striving for objectivity, they can more effectively analyze how federal policy

44. See Dwight B. Billings, *Planters and the Making of a "New South": Class, Politics, and Development in North Carolina, 1865–1900* (Chapel Hill, 1979); James T. Currie, *Enclave: Vicksburg and Her Plantations, 1863–1870* (Jackson, Miss., 1980); Mandle, *Roots of Black Poverty;* Shofner, *Nor Is It Over Yet;* Campbell, *A Southern Community;* and Ripley, *Slaves and Freedmen.* See also the sources cited in notes 10, 11, and 31 above.

45. Quotation from Foner, *Nothing but Freedom,* 6–7, emphasis added. See also Willie Lee Rose, "Jubilee and Beyond: What Was Freedom?" in *What Was Freedom's Price?* ed. Sansing, 3–20; Blassingame, *Black New Orleans;* Williamson, *After Slavery;* Howard Rabinowitz, *Race Relations in the Urban South, 1865–1890* (New York, 1978); Magdol, *Right to the Land;* Gutman, *Black Family;* and Alexander, *North Carolina Faces the Freedmen.*

evolved and the impact that it had on the lives of southerners, white and black. Finally, by examining the full range of activities—social, economic, and cultural as well as political—and the full cast of characters—freed people as well as whites from the North and the South—today's revisionists describe, more clearly than ever before, the continual conflict that characterized Presidential Reconstruction.

When one emphasizes the full fabric of life, rather than merely the political struggles, traditional periodization tends to lose its significance. John Hope Franklin stimulated a new generation of scholars to undertake a serious reexamination of Presidential Reconstruction. In doing so, they have gone well beyond Franklin's original work, making the labels "Presidential Reconstruction" and "reconstruction, Confederate style" nearly obsolete. Tracing the development of the southern economy or the emerging free black community with its new religious, social, and educational institutions, historians today tend to see the entire Reconstruction period as a unit. But this emphasis on the continuity of the Reconstruction era risks minimizing the significance of Congressional Reconstruction and the acquisition of the right of suffrage by black Americans. More work still is needed concerning the effects that the exercise of political rights had on the social, economic, and cultural development of the black community as well as on the South as a whole. Such research should produce a more complete understanding of what the Reconstruction era actually was like for those who lived through those turbulent times.

3

Reform Republicans and the Retreat from Reconstruction

✎ MICHAEL LES BENEDICT

In 1961, John Hope Franklin published one of the earliest and most influential of the studies that completely revised earlier interpretations of the origins of so-called Radical Reconstruction.[1] Most of these works concentrated on the development of reconstruction policy; none analyzed closely the *decline* of Republican radicalism, which decline was attributed variously to the death of radical leaders, northern racism, and commitment to federalism or laissez faire.[2]

Historians long have recognized that the defection of self-consciously reform-oriented Republicans played an important part in the decline of radical Republicanism and the abandonment of southern Republicans in the 1870s.[3] The reformers included academicians

---

1. John Hope Franklin, *Reconstruction: After the Civil War* (Chicago, 1961). Other influential revisionist accounts were Herman Belz, *Reconstructing the Union: Theory and Policy During the Civil War* (Ithaca, N.Y., 1969); Michael Les Benedict, *A Compromise of Principle: Congressional Republicans and Reconstruction, 1863–1869* (New York, 1974); William R. Brock, *An American Crisis: Congress and Reconstruction, 1863–1867* (New York, 1963); John H. Cox and LaWanda Cox, *Politics, Principle, and Prejudice, 1865–1866: Dilemma of Reconstruction America* (New York, 1963); David Donald, *The Politics of Reconstruction, 1863–1867* (Baton Rouge, 1965); Eric L. McKitrick, *Andrew Johnson and Reconstruction* (Chicago, 1960); Kenneth M. Stampp, *The Era of Reconstruction, 1865–1877* (New York, 1965); Hans L. Trefousse, *The Radical Republicans: Lincoln's Vanguard for Racial Justice* (New York, 1969).

2. In recent years Eric Foner, building on the work of David Montgomery, has stressed reaction against labor radicalism in the North as a major cause for the abandonment of southern Republicanism. Eric Foner, *Politics and Ideology in the Age of the Civil War* (New York, 1980), 125–27, 144; Eric Foner, *Reconstruction: America's Unfinished Revolution, 1863–1877* (New York, 1988), 475–84, 512–24, 582–87; David Montgomery, *Beyond Equality: Labor and the Radical Republicans, 1862–1872* (New York, 1967).

3. James Ford Rhodes, *A History of the United States from the Compromise of 1850* (7 vols.; New York, 1904), VI, VII, *passim;* William A. Dunning, *Reconstruction, Social and Eco-*

such as Charles W. Eliot, David A. Wells, Francis Lieber, and Amasa Walker; littérateurs and editors such as Horace White of the Chicago *Tribune,* Edwin L. Godkin of the New York *Nation,* James Russell Lowell and Charles Eliot Norton of the *North American Review,* George William Curtis of *Harper's Weekly,* and Parke Godwin and Charles Nordhoff of the New York *Evening Post;* and intellectually inclined businessmen and lawyers such as Edward Atkinson, John Murray Forbes, Dorman B. Eaton, and Richard Henry Dana. These men identified themselves as an intellectual elite—"the best men"— who bore a special responsibility to the nation but who also were entitled to special deference.[4] During the war and the early years of Reconstruction, most of them had been firm supporters of radical antislavery action, providing an intellectual foundation and political support for radical Republican demands for emancipation and equal rights.[5] As Franklin complained, however, when the final Republican Reconstruction policy took shape, these "former advocates of strong measures against the South turned their fire on those attempting to carry out the strong measures."[6] By 1870, most of the reformers were clearly hostile to much of the leadership of the Republican party and were helping to create the movement, already known as "liberal Re-

---

nomic, *1865–1877* (New York, 1907), 190–202, 238–41; Earle Dudley Ross, *The Liberal Republican Movement* (New York, 1919), 237–39; W. E. Burghardt Du Bois, *Black Reconstruction: An Essay Toward a History of the Part Which Black Folk Played in the Attempt to Reconstruct Democracy in America, 1860–1880* (New York, 1935), 623–24; Paul H. Buck, *The Road to Reunion, 1865–1900* (Boston, 1937), 90–96; James G. Randall and David Donald, *The Civil War and Reconstruction* (2d ed.; Boston, 1961), 658–59; Allen W. Trelease, *Reconstruction: The Great Experiment* (New York, 1971), 177–80; Forrest G. Wood, *The Era of Reconstruction, 1863–1877* (New York, 1975), 84–85; James McPherson, *Ordeal by Fire: The Civil War and Reconstruction* (New York, 1982), 568–72; Patrick W. Riddleberger, "The Radicals' Abandonment of the Negro During Reconstruction," *Journal of Negro History,* XLV (April, 1960), 88–102; Stampp, *Era of Reconstruction,* 190–92; Trefousse, *Radical Republicans,* 454–63.

4. The standard published account of these elite reformers' ideas and activities is John G. Sproat, *"The Best Men": Liberal Reformers in the Gilded Age* (New York, 1968). For an excellent discussion of their attitudes toward and impact on the political process, see Michael E. McGerr, *The Decline of Popular Politics: The American North, 1865–1928* (New York, 1986), 42–68. Their role in Gilded Age politics is also discussed in H. Wayne Morgan, *From Hayes to McKinley: National Party Politics, 1877–1896* (Syracuse, 1969), *passim.* Matthew Thomas Downey offers an excellent assessment of their ideas in "The Rebirth of Reform: A Study of Liberal Reform Movements, 1865–1872" (Ph.D. dissertation, Princeton University, 1963).

5. George M. Fredrickson, *The Inner Civil War: Northern Intellectuals and the Crisis of the Union* (New York, 1965), 113–29. Sproat, in his influential study of the reformers, stresses too much their "moderation" during Reconstruction. In the war years and the early years of Reconstruction, the reformers generally took more radical positions than moderate leaders in the Republican party.

6. Franklin, *Reconstruction,* 198.

publicanism," that would sap the party of much of its intellectual vigor and its crusading spirit.

Liberal Reformers and Laissez-Faire Morality

Historians have recognized the importance of the liberal reformers' defection, but they have not very well explained it. The most common viewpoint attributes the desertion to racism.[7] It is difficult, however, to see how the reformers' racism differentiated them from other Republicans. Few Republicans during the war or Reconstruction believed blacks to be the equals of whites. Republicans had insisted only that the freedmen be secured equality in basic civil and (after some hesitation) political rights, not that they be conceded what was called at the time "social equality." Even Thaddeus Stevens said that he had "never held to that doctrine of negro equality . . . in all things—simply before the law." The radical Republican Ignatius Donnelly expressed the outlook that most Republicans shared: "If it be true . . . that the negro belongs to an inferior race . . . the more reason is there why he should be protected by equal laws." Or as a California Republican legislator put it when he voted to eliminate the state's ban on black testimony, "It is not elevating the negro to give him justice." [8]

To understand what did alienate liberal reformers from Republican reconstruction policy after 1869, one must assess their ideas in the context of the almost idolatrous faith in science that swept European and American intellectuals in the nineteenth century. Science made sense of a physical world that for millennia had been rationalized through superstition or religion. By the mid-nineteenth century, educated men clamored for the application of the same tool to human

7. *Ibid.*, 200–201; Sproat, *"The Best Men,"* 29–44; William Gillette, *Retreat from Reconstruction, 1869–1879* (Baton Rouge, 1979), 366–68; Riddleberger, "Radical Abandonment of the Negro," 98–102; Robert F. Durden, *James Shepherd Pike: Republicanism and the American Negro, 1850–1882* (Durham, N.C., 1957).

8. Stevens in the *Congressional Globe,* 38th Cong., 1st Sess., 125; Ignatius Donnelly Diary, January 14, 1866 (Donnelly Papers, Minnesota Historical Society, St. Paul); Dennis W. Harrington, quoted in Sacramento *Daily Union,* March 6, 1863, p. 1. See also Thomas T. Davis in the *Congressional Globe,* 38th Cong., 2d Sess., 155; John F. Farnsworth, *ibid.,* 1st Sess., 2979; Timothy Otis Howe, *ibid.,* 39th Cong., 1st Sess., 438; *Leslie's Illustrated Newspaper,* December 25, 1869, p. 242. Hans L. Trefousse, "Ben Wade and the Negro," *Ohio Historical Quarterly,* LVIII (April, 1959), 161–76.

relationships. They were convinced that these relationships were subject to laws just as certain as those that governed the physical universe. The new "social science," as it was called, would ferret out these laws. Charles Francis Adams, Jr.'s recollection of his scientific awakening indicates science's almost mystical attraction. The revelation occurred while he lay abed in Europe in 1865, recovering from the rigors of his Civil War service and reading an essay by John Stuart Mill on Auguste Comte. "That essay of Mill's revolutionized in a single morning my whole mental attitude," Adams remembered. "I emerged from the theological stage . . . and passed into the scientific." [9]

In no area were reformers more certain that scientific truth had been discovered than in economics—the "science of wealth," as one of its most influential students called it. Not only did economics (or "political economy," as it also was called) belong "to the same class of sciences with mechanics, astronomy, optics, chemistry, [and] electricity," but its laws already were known and needed only to be applied to specific circumstances. They were laws "like those of other sciences," laws "universal and invariable in their operation." [10]

Most nineteenth-century economists concluded that because natural laws of economics existed, they were beyond human interference. The clergyman-economist Lyman Atwater put it most trenchantly: "Legislation cannot alter the laws of nature, of man, of political economics." [11] Moreover, contemporary economists confused the notion of *interfering* with economic laws with that of *harnessing* them. It was no part of economics, as the reformers understood it, to study how human economic activities might be modified to achieve some social goal. Rather, political economy was, as Godkin put it, the science of "what man, as an exchanging, producing animal, would do, if let

9. Charles Francis Adams, Jr., *Charles Francis Adams, 1835–1915: An Autobiography* (Boston, 1916), 179. For the "worship" of science and the growth of the notion of social science, see Luther L. Bernard and Jessie Bernard, *Origins of American Sociology: The Social Science Movement in the United States* (New York, 1943), *passim*, esp. 45–55, 461–523; Thomas L. Haskell, *The Emergence of Professional Social Science: The American Social Science Association and the Nineteenth-Century Crisis of Authority* (Urbana, Ill., 1977), 65–90; William E. Nelson, *The Roots of American Bureaucracy, 1830–1900* (Cambridge, Mass., 1982), 82–112; Fredrickson, *Inner Civil War,* 199–211.

10. Amasa Walker, *The Science of Wealth* (7th ed.; Boston, 1874), 3–4, originally published in 1866; Gamaliel Bradford, "The Treasury Reports," *North American Review*, CX (January, 1870), 209. See also Richard T. Ely, *Ground Under Our Feet: An Autobiography* (New York, 1938), 58; Sproat, *"The Best Men,"* 142–68.

11. Sidney Fine, *Laissez Faire and the General Welfare State: A Study of Conflict in American Thought, 1865–1901* (Ann Arbor, 1956), 123.

alone." That was "a real science," in Godkin's estimation. Years later his point of view had changed, and he lamented that political economy "has assumed the role of an advisor, who teaches man to make himself more comfortable through the help of his government"; it had "no more claim to be a science than philanthropy." [12] Thus economists, and the reformers who so ardently had popularized their conclusions, laid upon government the famous injunction *laissez-nous faire,* which the influential American astronomer and financial writer Simon Newcomb translated as the "let-alone principle." [13]

As the historian Sidney Fine has observed, "Free trade and liberty were synonymous to the foes of protection." He might have said the same of almost every position the laissez-faire liberal reformers took, whether on the tariff, finances, taxation, or labor legislation. Despite its scientific trappings, the laissez-faire economic theory was in essence a commitment to liberty as the theorists perceived it—that is, to the "right of every man to employ his own efforts for the gratification of his own wants." [14] Therefore, the social science that the reformers worshiped was shot through with value judgments that would be considered inappropriate by modern scientific standards. It was not unusual for a "scientific" reformer to insist, for example, that "any honest man" could understand financial questions "because they are also, and equally, moral questions." [15]

The great threat to liberty lay in the temptation to use the power of the state to promote the interests of one group at the expense of others—that is, to enact "special" or "class" legislation. The struggle against kings and aristocrats had been waged to free the people from the inordinate power that enabled such persons to use the state to levy

12. Rollo Ogden, *Life and Letters of Edwin Lawrence Godkin* (2 vols.; New York, 1907), I, 11. See also Edwin L. Godkin, " 'The Economic Man,' " in Godkin, *Problems of Modern Democracy: Political and Economic Essays of Edwin Lawrence Godkin,* ed. Morton Keller (Cambridge, Mass., 1966), 156–79, originally published in the *North American Review* in 1891.

13. Simon Newcomb, "The Let-Alone Principle," *North American Review,* CX (January, 1870), 1–33.

14. Fine, *Laissez Faire and the General Welfare State,* 65; Arthur Latham Perry, *Elements of Political Economy* (New York, 1870), 80–81.

15. Godkin quoted in Irwin Unger, *The Greenback Era: A Social and Political History of American Finance, 1865–1879* (Princeton, N.J., 1964), 121. Despite his scientism, E. L. Godkin's biographers agree that his judgments on public issues were always based primarily upon his moral values. Edward C. Kirkland, *Business in the Gilded Age: The Conservatives' Balance Sheet* (Madison, Wisc., 1952), 29–33; Morton Keller, introduction to Godkin, *Problems of Modern Democracy,* xxix. See R. Jackson Wilson, *In Quest of Community: Social Philosophy in the United States, 1860–1920* (New York, 1968), 39–40, for a similar judgment.

special, monopolistic exactions from the rest of society.[16] Such power also had been the essence of the slave system in the South, where the entire weight of the state was thrown behind the expropriation of the labor of black workers by white masters. "The highest right of property is the right to freely exchange it for other property," reformers insisted. "Any system of laws which denies or restricts this right for the purpose of subserving private or class interests, reaffirms . . . the principle of slavery."[17]

To the liberal reformers, all efforts specifically to benefit one group, even a group hardly able to protect itself without such intervention, shared this dangerous, antilibertarian tendency. "Wealth gained . . . by means of a protective tariff or a . . . law enforcing the use of paper money . . . [or] the leisure secured by eight and ten-hours laws . . . are all gained at the cost of the mass of consumers," Edward Atkinson insisted, even though demands for these various things came from disparate sources. Indeed, Atkinson identified protectionism with communism. "The two ideas are identical in principle," he insisted, explaining that "protection . . . attempts to enforce an inequitable distribution of our annual product," whereas communism "invokes the force of law under the mistaken idea that a more equitable division may be had."[18] William Graham Sumner, one of the few reformers to have remained a steadfast Democrat, in the 1880s would summarize the laissez-faire, liberal-reform position: "[Whenever] the question is raised, What ought the State to do for labor, for trade, for manufacturers, for the poor, for the learned professions . . . that is [,] for a class or an interest, it really is the question . . . What ought Some-of-us to do for Others-of-us?" In the democratic United States, such government action would establish a tyranny in which "a man's neighbors are his masters."[19]

16. Francis Parkman, "The Failure of Universal Suffrage," *North American Review,* CXXVI (July–August, 1878), 1–20; William Graham Sumner, "State Interference," in Albert G. Keller and Maurice R. Davie, eds., *Essays of William Graham Sumner* (2 vols.; New Haven, 1934), II, 138–40; Michael Les Benedict, "Laissez Faire and Liberty: A Re-Evaluation of the Meaning and Origins of Laissez-Faire Constitutionalism," *Law and History Review,* III (1985), 293–331. Read in this light Sproat, *"The Best Men,"* 205–42.

17. This was the way the publishers distilled David A. Wells's tract *The Creed of Free Trade* (N.p., n.d.) on the pamphlet's cover.

18. Edward Atkinson, "The Inefficiency of Economic Legislation," *Journal of Social Science,* IV (March, 1871), 124; Edward Atkinson, *Revenue Reform: An Essay* (Boston, 1871), 18.

19. William Graham Sumner, *What Social Classes Owe Each Other* (1883; rpr. New York, 1925), 11–12; Sumner, "State Interference," in Keller and Davie, eds., *Essays of William Graham Sumner,* II, 145–46.

Thus at the heart of the reformers' laissez-faire ideology lay a continued adherence to the notion of "equal rights" that had fueled Jacksonian resistance to "special privilege" in economic areas and Republican opposition to privilege based on race. With the establishment of majoritarian democracy by Jacksonian Democrats and radical Republicans, however, the great threat to equal rights no longer seemed to emanate from above, but from below. Weak-minded sentimentalists or corrupt demagogues would promise ignorant or venal voters benefits that could be acquired only by invading the rights of those whose abilities had lifted them above the crowd. "The problem," one reformer wrote, "is, to make men who are equal . . . in political rights and . . . entitled to the ownership of property . . . content with that inequality in its distribution which must inevitably result from the application of the law of justice." [20]

Of course, socialism posed one such threat to liberty, and after the uprising of the Paris Commune in 1871, liberal reformers would be deeply fearful of that threat. Another danger lay in the perceived willingness of corruptionists to harness the ignorance of voters and gain power through out-and-out demagoguery. This problem was especially acute in big cities—populated, the reformers believed, with ignorant immigrants who had no heritage of liberty or training in American democracy. Such people were "the dangerous classes," and the Tammany Hall–like corruption built upon their votes was no more than "organized communism and destruction of property under the guise of taxation." [21]

To the liberal reformers, nothing was more symbolic of the dangers of demagoguery than the political success of the radical Republican Benjamin F. Butler. Butler was the only important Massachusetts Republican ostentatiously to repudiate the doctrines to which the reformers were so firmly committed. Combining adroit use of political patronage with "demagogic" calls for government intervention in the

---

20. Abram S. Hewitt, *Selected Writings of Abram S. Hewitt,* ed. Allan Nevins (New York, 1910), 277. Hewitt, like Sumner, was a lifelong Democrat. But he clearly shared reformers' beliefs and attitudes, working for the supremacy of these in the Democratic party as most reformers did in the Republican. See Allan Nevins, *Abram S. Hewitt: With Some Account of Peter Cooper* (New York, 1935), *passim.*

21. Charles Loring Brace, *The Dangerous Classes of New York, and Twenty Years' Work Among Them* (New York, 1872); Simon Sterne, *Suffrage in Cities* (New York, 1878), 13. See also Parkman, "Failure of Universal Suffrage," 20. Sproat does not discuss the relationship that reformers perceived between urban corruption and threats to liberty, but he describes well their general attitude toward city-dwelling immigrants in *"The Best Men,"* 250–57. See also Downey, "Rebirth of Reform," 113–16.

economy, he defied the efforts of "better" men to mold public opinion and exert political influence. "Butlerism," the reformers fumed, was simply a plan for "the use of Government to carry out the poor and ignorant man's view of the nature of society." For the next thirty years, they would fight its author tooth and nail.[22]

Not surprisingly, the reformers' convictions had serious implications for their attitudes toward democracy. The reformers believed that "the highest allegiance of every man is due to liberty and civilization. . . . The possession of the suffrage by anybody . . . is but a means to these ends," not an end in itself. If this belief alone were not enough to undermine their commitment to democracy, to it was added their conviction that there was a science of society—and the more one perceives measures to govern society to be matters of science, the less they can be matters of public opinion. As Frances Lieber put it while agitating for free trade, "Truth is not settled by majorities."[23] So the reformers did not conceive politics to be the mechanism by which the will of the majority was translated into action. Instead, it was "the art by which the teachings of social science are put into practice." Legislators at all times had to keep in mind the "laws of social order and well-being," laws as "immutable as that of gravitation."[24]

It followed that, as Henry Adams put it, "the great problem of every system of Government has been to place administration and legislation in the hands of the best men"—those with "the loftiest developments of moral and intellectual education."[25] As Adams perceived, this conviction "clash[ed] with our fundamental principle that one man is as good as another." Although Adams admitted, at least at first, that he did not know how to escape this dilemma, most reformers were unabashedly elitist. "It is curious, that, in a country which boasts of its intelligence, the theory should be so generally held that the most

22. New York *Nation,* April 9, 1874, pp. 230–31. See also "The Butler Canvass," *North American Review,* CXIV (January, 1872), 147–70.
23. E. L. Godkin to Charles Eliot Norton, April 13, 1865, in William N. Armstrong, ed., *The Gilded-Age Letters of E. L. Godkin* (Albany, N.Y., 1974), 27; Frances Lieber, *Notes on Fallacies Peculiar to American Protectionists* (4th ed.; New York, 1870), 39. See also Benjamin Pierce, "The National Importance of Social Sciences in the United States," *Journal of Social Science,* XII (1880), xii.
24. New York *Nation,* February 10, 1870, p. 91; George L. Prentiss, *Our National Bane; or, The Dry Rot in American Politics* (New York, 1877), 2. For an insightful assessment of the relationship between the "liberal reform" movement of the 1870s and the era's new, scientific theory of knowledge, see Downey, "Rebirth of Reform," 98–112.
25. Henry Adams to John Gorham Palfrey, February 19, 1869, in Palfrey Papers, Houghton Library, Harvard University; Charles Francis Adams, Jr., "The Protection of the Ballot in National Elections," *Journal of Social Science,* I (1869), 91.

complicated form of human contrivance . . . can be worked at sight by any man able to talk for an hour or two without stopping to think," James Russell Lowell wrote. "Experience would have bred in us a rooted distrust of improvised statesmanship, even if we did not believe politics to be a science, which . . . demands the long and steady application of the best powers of men as . . . [can] master even its first principles."[26] To a reformer like Lowell, democracy was "after all, nothing more than an experiment," to be judged by whether it fulfilled its function of elevating "the best men" to leadership.[27]

Convictions like these naturally led the liberal reformers to endorse proposals to reform the civil service so as to make ability the criterion for appointment and to make tenure independent of politics. Of course, there was a good deal of self-interest in this. Well-educated and certain of their own talents, the liberal reformers could not help but be convinced that under such standards the jobs would go to men like themselves—a conviction reflected in Atkinson's brash affirmation to David Wells: "If you or I or any other honest economist ever seeks office, we should get it." Several historians of the civil service reform movement have noted that liberal reformers' interest in such reform blossomed when they failed to receive appointive offices for which they believed themselves particularly suited.[28]

Other specific policies followed logically from the reformers' scientific understandings and moral convictions. The first of these involved the money question. The reformers were convinced that political economists had demonstrated that the value of goods and services was determined by their supply and the demand for them. That intrin-

26. Henry Adams to Palfrey, February 19, 1869, in Palfrey Papers; James Russell Lowell, "A Look Before and After," *North American Review*, CVIII (January, 1869), 259–60 (I have reversed the order of the sentences). The liberal reformers' elitism is implicit throughout Sproat's exegesis of their ideas. In *"The Best Men,"* 277–78, he draws the same conclusion as Lowell. See also E. L. Godkin, "Legislation and Social Sciences," *Journal of Social Science*, III (1871), 115–32.

27. James Russell Lowell to Joel Benton, January 19, 1876, in *Letters of James Russell Lowell*, ed. Charles Eliot Norton (Cambridge, Mass., 1904), 377–78, Vol. XV of Lowell, *The Complete Writings of James Russell Lowell*, 16 vols. This was a common refrain. See also Henry Adams to Palfrey, February 19, 1869, in Palfrey Papers; Charles Francis Adams, Jr., "The Protection of the Ballot in National Elections," 91–92; William Graham Sumner, "The Challenge of Facts," in *Essays of William Graham Sumner*, ed. Keller and Davie, II, 119–20; William Graham Sumner, "Politics in America, 1776–1876," *North American Review*, CXXII (January, 1876), 87.

28. Edward Atkinson to David A. Wells, July 17, 1871, in David A. Wells Papers, Library of Congress; Ari Hoogenboom, *Outlawing the Spoils: A History of the Civil Service Reform Movement, 1865–1883* (Urbana, Ill., 1961), 21, 51–52, 62–63; Ari Hoogenboom, "Civil Service Reform and Public Morality," in *The Gilded Age*, ed. H. Wayne Morgan (Syracuse, N.Y., 1970), 77–95; Downey, "Rebirth of Reform," 117–21.

sic value could not be affected by changes in how it was measured. To insure a stable economy, however, people needed a stable standard, free of fluctuation, by which to measure value so that they could compare the value of one kind of goods with that of another. In the opinion of nearly all American economists—and of the liberal reformers—experience had proved "scientifically" that only gold could serve that function, although a few believed silver also might do. "Money," the medium of exchange, therefore had to be based on gold, or perhaps gold and silver, in order to reflect the real value of goods.[29]

To repeat, one could not alter the intrinsic value of goods, that is, the value determined by supply and demand, by changing the standard by which it was measured—for example, by inflating the amount of money in circulation irrespective of the availability of gold to back it. Such artificial inflation was no different from trying to change the weight of goods by altering the scales, "as if more hay scales would mean more hay," the liberal reformer-businessman John Murray Forbes scoffed. Such an effort would make people uncertain of the value of the money, not increase the value of the goods, and thus it would introduce serious instability into the economy.[30]

As always with the reformers, however, beyond the question of the expediency of tampering with the standard of value was that of its morality. Speculative fever associated with inflation would lead to "the diffusion of a taste for luxury, dissipation, and excess," not to mention "gambling . . . scoundrelism and effrontery."[31] Moreover, as the supply of money grew, its purchasing power would depreciate. Creditors, who in good faith had lent money to those seeking it, would be repaid in currency of less value. Thus, a policy of inflation was a dangerous example of state action that threatened liberty. When debtors pressed for such a policy, they were seeking to use state power to benefit themselves at the expense of creditors, since inflation amounted to an appropriation of the property of one group for the use of another. Following this reasoning, the liberal reformers perceived currency based

29. Julian M. Sturtevant, *Economics; or, The Science of Wealth* (New York, 1877), 69–75; Francis Bowen, *American Political Economy* (New York, 1870), 257–72; Perry, *Elements of Political Economy*, 34–35, 209–35. See also Walter T. K. Nugent, *The Money Question During Reconstruction* (New York, 1967), 52–58; Unger, *Greenback Era*, 127–29.

30. John Murray Forbes to Carl Schurz, January 23, 1874, in Carl Schurz Papers, Library of Congress; Bowen, *American Political Economy*, 325–45; Walker, *Science of Wealth*, 124–223; Sturtevant, *Economics*, 89–90, 96–97; Perry, *Elements of Political Economy*, 248–59; Nugent, *Money Question*, 52–58.

31. Bowen, *American Political Economy*, 342.

on gold to be "honest money" or even "moral money." During the Civil War, the government had been forced to issue "legal tender notes"—the so-called greenbacks—backed by no more than a promise to repay them in gold or silver someday. After the war, the reformers favored steady "contraction" of the currency—that is, a steady reduction in the amount of greenbacks circulating—and they believed deeply that those who agreed with them were "the friends of sound money and sound morals."[32] Those who pressed for "easy money" presented "the bald issue whether the nation shall be a liar and a thief or not."[33]

Closely linked to the currency question was the issue of how to repay the national debt incurred in suppressing the rebellion. Those who pressed for inflation also generally urged that the debt be repaid in the paper currency in which it had been incurred. Of course, this policy would keep paper money in circulation, as the inflationists wanted, and therefore would violate the same fundamental economic laws that inflation did, in the opinion of the liberal reformers. Moreover, the reformers thought that the moral question was put even more starkly on this issue than on inflation. They insisted that refusal to repay the debt in gold amounted to its repudiation.[34]

Another violation of scientific principles and republican liberty was the protective tariff. Laissez-faire economists and their liberal reformer allies were certain that, if left alone, people would exchange those goods they could produce at least cost for other goods produced more cheaply elsewhere. The "great laws of human nature which are the natural forces of the science" of economics would accomplish this as surely as "universal gravitation will construct the solar system as it is." Such free trade would benefit both parties and permit the widest

32. Francis O. French to Elihu B. Washburne, December 31, 1877, in Elihu B. Washburne Papers, Library of Congress. The letters and writings of the liberal reformers were replete with such moralistic phrases. See, for example, Charles Francis Adams, Jr., "The Currency Debate of 1873–1874," *North American Review*, CXIX (1874), 115–16; "The Legal Tender Decision," New York *Nation*, February 17, 1870, p. 100; Carl Schurz, "Honest Money," in Frederic Bancroft, ed., *Speeches, Correspondence, and Political Papers of Carl Schurz* (6 vols.; New York, 1913), III, 161–214; and Amasa Walker, "Governmental Interference with the Standard of Value," *Bankers' Magazine*, III (1867), 738.

33. John Hay to Whitelaw Reid, September 24, 1875, quoted in William Roscoe Thayer, *The Life and Letters of John Hay* (2 vols.; Boston, 1915), I, 426.

34. Unger, *Greenback Era*, 81–83, 122–23; Walter T. K. Nugent, *Money and American Society, 1865–1880* (New York, 1968), 106–109; Chester McArthur Destler, *American Radicalism, 1865–1901: Essays and Documents* (New York, 1963), 32–49; Robert P. Sharkey, *Money, Class, and Party: An Economic Study of Civil War and Reconstruction* (Baltimore, 1959), 99–107, 168–69.

distribution of goods, since goods always would be produced where this could be done most cheaply, thereby keeping prices low.[35]

Besides flatly scorning arguments that protective duties were necessary to promote American industrial development, laissez-faire economists and liberal reformers once again raised an even more compelling moral objection: protection imposed higher prices on American consumers so that the capitalists and laborers of a particular industry might survive foreign competition. Like inflationary schemes, the protective tariff was but an effort to use the power of government to enrich one group in the community at the expense of another. A petition for tariff protection, wrote Atkinson, ought to read as follows: "Whereas we, the undersigned, are desirous of establishing certain branches of industry . . . for which we have not neither the capital nor the skill, we ask that our countrymen shall be compelled to purchase our products at such prices as it may be found necessary for us to impose, while we are learning our trade and accumulating wealth at the cost of our said neighbors."[36]

Reformers and Radicals

Historians generally have perceived the defection of the reformers to have begun after the restoration of most of the southern states to normal relations in the Union and the election of Ulysses S. Grant to the presidency in 1868, culminating in the Liberal Republican bolt of 1872. Yet on all counts, from general principles to specific policies, future liberals began to drift away from their radical allies and toward the more conservative elements of the party as early as 1867. In doing so, the reformers robbed radical politicians of one of the strongest elements of their appeal, for the alliance with the reformers had given radicals something of a cachet, of somehow being more

35. Sturtevant, *Economics*, 118; Bowen, *American Political Economy*, 480–95; Perry, *Political Economy*, 347–63.

36. Atkinson, *Revenue Reform*, 10. See also Perry, *Political Economy*, 85, 280; Sturtevant, *Economics*, 83; Abraham L. Earle, *Our Revenue System and the Civil Service: Shall They Be Reformed?* (6th ed.; New York, 1878), *passim*, originally published 1871; David A. Wells, "The Meaning of Revenue Reform," *North American Review*, CXIII (July, 1871), 145, 148; William Graham Sumner, *Protection and Revenue in 1877* (New York, 1878), 7; William Graham Sumner, "What Is Free Trade?" in Keller and Davie, eds., *Essays of William Graham Sumner*, II, 393; James Russell Lowell, in *Complete Writings of James Russell Lowell*, VI, 217.

than "mere" politicians. By the 1870s, the more radical Republicans seemed no more virtuous than any other politicos—less so, in fact, than those who had replaced them in the reformers' affections.

The reformers' conviction that one can arrive at a science of society was, as Godkin recognized, "based on the theory that society is not an artificial arrangement regulated by contract like a business partnership, but an organism that grows in accordance with certain laws." [37] This evolutionary sociology approximated the central principle of Burkean conservatism, and the statement itself embodied a none-too-subtle slap at the traditional American notion, rooted in the nation's Lockean heritage, that men enter into society by free acts of will, which in turn implies equality of rights within society. Thus, the radical Republican argument that all men, including black men, had certain rights by virtue of their entering society was nonsense. A community's understanding of what rights individuals and groups possessed grew naturally out of its earlier development, and no one had an abstract right to anything more. Within the framework of American development, individual liberty had become a paramount value, and the extension of legal and political equality to the former slaves had been an appropriate method of securing liberty to them. But this was a matter of expedience and egalitarian tradition, not of right, and if the consequences were evil, no theory of abstract rights could stand in the way of a different solution to the problem of the freedmen's status.[38]

The reformers' commitment to new "scientific" ideas about social relations made enthusiasm for any major social or economic reform suspect. For if society was governed by natural laws, there were distinct limits to the possibilities of social improvement through drastic "artificial" changes imposed by human will. Reformers scoffed at the "inordinate belief, common among the half-educated, in the potency of legislation." Thus the new social science was profoundly conservative. "Social science," Godkin wrote, "seeks to convince people that in sociology, as in medicine, all vendors of panaceas are quacks, that anybody who goes about saying that either equality, or freedom, or female suffrage, or prohibition, or common schools, or the ballot will make

---

37. New York *Nation*, February 10, 1870, p. 90.
38. Godkin to Norton, April 13, 1865, in Armstrong, ed., *Gilded-Age Letters of E. L. Godkin*, 27; New York *Nation*, November 14, 1867, pp. 396–97; William Graham Sumner, "Republican Government," in Keller and Davie, eds., *Essays of William Graham Sumner*, II, 195–96; Sproat, *"The Best Men,"* 254–55.

the world what it ought to be, should no more be listened to than the patent pill-man." [39]

Their disagreements with radical politicians over specific issues disturbed reformers even more than the growing divergence between the two groups' general understanding of society and reform. By 1867, Republicans were engaged in a bitter struggle over financial and tariff policy, barely hidden by the facade of unity imposed by their battle with President Johnson and the Democrats over reconstruction. Manufacturing interests in developing industries, bankers who had not joined the newly established national banking system, western bankers, capitalists who were inclined to aggressive investment program, railroad promoters, agrarians, and labor reformers pressed for easy money and high tariffs. Merchants involved in international trade (and their local agents and independent wholesalers), manufacturing interests in established industries, and leading bankers urged contraction of the currency and reduction of tariff rates.

Blind to the economic self-interest that motivated the hard-money, low-tariff forces, the liberal reformers allied with them as a matter of "scientific" and moral principle. The reformers were dismayed, however, to find the most important Republican radicals among the leading proponents of soft money and high tariffs. Thaddeus Stevens, Benjamin F. Butler, William D. Kelley, Benjamin F. Wade, and Zachariah Chandler all were tainted. Many of the reformers shared the feelings of the Ohio Republican congressman Rufus P. Spalding, who complained: "It would seem that no man can come fully up in these days to the standard of radicalism unless he be prepared to put a tariff upon foreign goods that shall amount to a prohibition, and to open and extend the paper circulation of the country without limitation." [40]

In fact, the reformers' fear was misplaced; radical Republicans were not united on these issues. But the identification of key radical leaders with soft money and high tariffs was so strong that the differences among less prominent radicals were overlooked. Even Charles

39. Henry Reed, "Some Late Efforts at Constitutional Reform," *North American Review,* CXXI (July, 1875): 35; New York *Nation,* February 10, 1870, p. 90. William Graham Sumner, the most influential popular American sociologist of the late nineteenth century, consistently warned that efforts to modify the existing social order through legislation risked unforeseen consequences because of unconsidered interaction with general social laws. Appropriately, he named one of his most widely read popular essays "The Absurd Effort to Make the World Over," *Forum,* XVII (March, 1894), 92–102.

40. *Congressional Globe,* 39th Cong., 2d Sess., 290.

Sumner came under suspicion until he proved his financial orthodoxy in 1868, and several historians have suggested that there was an implicit radical Republican "ideology" in which soft money, high tariffs, and racial liberalism were manifestations of an underlying egalitarianism.[41]

The liberal reformers were shocked by the early successes of the soft-money, high-tariff forces. In 1867 the soft-money, protariff lobby persuaded Congress to repeal the authority under which Secretary of the Treasury Hugh McCulloch had been restricting the circulation of greenbacks since 1866. Congress also had come close to passing a general upward revision of tariff rates and had succeeded in increasing the tariff on wool and wool products. Support seemed to be growing for a proposition to pay the national debt in greenbacks. Early in 1867 the worried special commissioner on revenue, David A. Wells, wrote an intimate, "I am afraid the extremists and inflationists will have it pretty much their own way." [42]

Aware of the reformers' concern, conservative Republicans worked assiduously to widen the break. "There is not a man who fought against us in the rebellion in whom I have not more confidence and for whom I have not more respect than I have for Mr. B. F. Butler ... [and] Thad. Stevens is no better than Butler," Iowa's conservative Republican senator, James W. Grimes, wrote Atkinson. "The great question in American politics today is the financial question," he insisted, and he believed that this question "ought to override . . . reconstruction." As radicals attacked Republican conservatives such as William Pitt Fessenden, senator from Maine, as "clogs and obstructions"

41. Sharkey, *Money, Class, and Party,* 281–83; Montgomery, *Beyond Equality,* 85–89. The relations between Sumner and the reformers may be seen in his correspondence with Edward Atkinson. By April, 1868, Atkinson expressed anger at the silence of the New England congressional delegation in the face of the inflationists' pressure, and Sumner answered curtly. Charles Sumner to Edward Atkinson, April 24, 1868, in Edward Atkinson Papers, Massachusetts Historical Society, Boston. When Sumner finally came out openly and forcefully for contraction in a major Senate speech, his closest political lieutenant, Edward L. Pierce, wrote him: "You can hardly tell how much easier the work of your reelection is made by that speech. I was exceedingly anxious to have you make it, and . . . was in great fear that it might not come." Edward L. Pierce to Charles Sumner, July 31, 1868, in Charles Sumner Papers, Houghton Library, Harvard University. See David Donald, *Sumner and the Rights of Man* (New York, 1970), 346–47. For evidence that there was no ideological connection between radicalism on Reconstruction issues and support for high tariffs and inflation, see Benedict, *Compromise of Principle,* 40–54.

42. David A. Wells to Edward Atkinson, January 15, 1867, quoted in Herbert Donald Ferleger, *David A. Wells and the American Revenue System, 1865–1870* (New York, 1942), 168–69. See also *ibid.,* 143–75; Stanley Coben, "Northeastern Business and Radical Reconstruction: A Re-examination," *Mississippi Valley Historical Review,* XLVI (June, 1959), 67–90; Sharkey, *Money, Class, and Party,* 82–88; 107–15.

to a thoroughly just reconstruction program, Grimes warned, "Let . . . 'clogs and obstructions' be removed from Congress and Thad. Stevens and Butler be in controul [sic] as they then would be with their revolutionary and repudiating idea in the ascendancy and our government would not last 12 mos."[43]

The implications of a radical victory within the Republican party for its position on financial and tariff issues drove the reformers into a de facto alliance with Republican conservatives. On the money question, the reformers joined the conservatives in praising the contractionist policies of Secretary McCulloch, in a campaign that culminated in highly publicized plans for a testimonial dinner in McCulloch's honor in Boston. The movement was a public rebuke to the radicals, who bitterly opposed extending honors to anyone openly supporting Johnson's reconstruction policy. As arranged, McCulloch declined the invitation but used the opportunity to defend his hard-money policies in a letter that was then broadcast by the Boston group.[44]

The reformers' cooperation with McCulloch cooled their ardor for one of the most important radical proposals, the impeachment of Andrew Johnson for his obstruction of congressional reconstruction policies. If Johnson were removed from office, the high-tariff, inflationist Ben Wade, president *pro tem* of the Senate, would succeed him. McCulloch certainly would lose his position as secretary of the treasury, and an inflationist just as surely would replace him. Moreover, the circumstance would give Wade a crucial boost in his quest for the 1868 Republican presidential nomination.[45]

The radicals' flirtation with a policy of land confiscation and redistribution in the South, along with southern radicals' endorsement of former Confederate disfranchisement and courtship of black voters through promises of further change, also alienated the reformers. Land confiscation and redistribution was, of course, the quintessential case of using state power for the benefit of one group at the expense of another. When radicals justified such a policy on the grounds that "a

43. James W. Grimes to Edward Atkinson, September 15, October 14, 1867, in Atkinson Papers.
44. David A. Wells to Henry L. Dawes, September 21, 1866, in Dawes Papers, Library of Congress; David A. Wells to Arthur L. Perry, March 11, 1867, quoted in Ferleger, *Wells*, 181; Benedict, *Compromise of Principle*, 263.
45. Michael Les Benedict, *The Impeachment and Trial of Andrew Johnson* (New York, 1973), 66–67, 133–35; Joseph Logsdon, *Horace White, Nineteenth-Century Liberal* (Westport, Conn., 1971), 151–54.

landed aristocracy is fatal to the advance of the cause of liberty and equal rights," the hitherto sympathetic, reformer-linked Boston *Advertiser* asked: "Why a *landed* aristocracy? This mode of argument is two-edged. For there are socialists who hold that any aristocracy is 'fatal to the advance of the cause of liberty and equal rights'—socialists who would not hesitate to say that . . . large income places [one] . . . in the ranks of an aristocracy." Driving the same point home, the conservative Cincinnati *Commercial* gleefully began to refer to Butler and Stevens as the "Red Rads." [46]

The liberal reformers also felt threatened by southern radicals' appeals to the former slaves for their main support and by their desire to disfranchise large numbers of formerly Confederate southern whites. The reformers shared the certainty of nearly all white Americans that blacks were incapable of the intellectual achievements of whites, or at least of Anglo-Saxon and Germanic whites. Therefore, black enfranchisement, although just and necessary, was dangerous. As James Russell Lowell put it, "What is bad among ignorant foreigners in New York will not be good among ignorant natives in South Carolina." Like lower-class white northerners, especially Irish immigrants, southern blacks easily might be subject to manipulation. Charles Francis Adams, Jr., was expressing a common concern among reformers when he wrote that Americans were lifting voting restrictions despite the development of a "Celtic proletariat on the Atlantic coast, an African proletariat on the shores of the Gulf, and a Chinese proletariat on the Pacific." [47] Disfranchisement of the white southern "intelligent class" would only make things worse.

As they pondered these prospects, reformers found southern radicals themselves something less than attractive. The radicals' campaigns for black support on such issues as confiscation, civil rights laws, expanded public services, and hostility to the white "upper class" seemed the obvious counterpart to those of such freebooters as Ben Butler and the Tammany Hall Democrats in the North. Godkin thought it was "plain" that the freedmen were "in danger of falling into the hands of demagogues who will use them without scruples for

46. Boston *Daily Advertiser,* June 13, 1867, p. 2; Cincinnati *Daily Commercial,* June 15, 1867, p. 4.
47. Lowell, "A Look Before and After," 71; Charles Francis Adams, Jr., "Protection of the Ballot," 108–109.

purposes which will finally prove disastrous to the race," and he demanded that "the national leaders of the party . . . find some means of liberalizing the party managers at the South."[48]

To counter the danger, Massachusetts reformers organized the Massachusetts Reconstruction Association at about the same time they endorsed Johnson's treasury secretary McCulloch. The association's purpose was to "prevent the creation of an exclusive black men's party and to kill the scheme of confiscation," Atkinson informed McCulloch. Not coincidentally, its organizers also hoped "to secure the election of a southern [congressional] delegation who shall not be under Thad Steven[s'] lead on tariff and currency questions." The New York *Nation* quickly endorsed the effort. "We need not urge such men to see to it that nothing is done to excite the freedmen to feelings of revenge or with delusive hopes of direct benefits from Government," Godkin noted with satisfaction. What the freedmen needed, and what the Reconstruction Association would provide, was a crash course on the laws of political economy. "The more demagogues rave and rant, the more car-loads of teachers and books we ought to send off," Godkin urged.[49]

Thus, by the summer of 1867, Republican conservatives and liberal reformers were allied in a bitter war upon the radicals. As the conservative organs blasted radical "one idea men, fanatics," Godkin's *Nation* echoed them, in its genteel way, with a new definition of "True Radicalism": "Many well-meaning persons . . . are so anxious to be considered 'radical' in their views that they fear to stop even when they have attained all that is really desirable or practicable." Efforts to transform southern society overnight by further radical legislation were doomed to failure because social science taught that social institutions evolve naturally. "The wise radical is content to wait . . . and slowly to build up when the work of pulling down is properly over."[50] Henry Adams began to refer to himself, Richard Henry Dana, and their allies as representing the "conservative liberalism of New England." By late August, the Chicago *Tribune* editor Horace White also found himself in an anamolous position. "I call myself a Radical," he

48. New York *Nation*, October 31, 1867, p. 354.
49. Edward Atkinson to Hugh McCulloch, August 7, 1867, in Hugh McCulloch Papers, Library of Congress; New York *Nation*, July 18, 1867, p. 50; July 25, 1867, p. 70.
50. Indianapolis *Daily Journal*, August 2, 1867, p. 4; New York *Nation*, July 18, 1867, p. 51.

mused, "and yet find myself more in harmony with those . . . style[d] Conservatives than with any other branch of the party."[51]

At this same time the *Nation,* recognized as the reformers' organ, leveled its guns at Stevens, Butler, and especially Wade, the radical, high-tariff, easy-money candidate for the 1868 Republican presidential nomination. The reformer-linked Boston *Advertiser* chimed in, charging that Wade's ideas on these issues and his criticism of labor-capital relations were "simply and wholly . . . an avowal of agrarian sympathies." The *Nation* sarcastically asserted that Wade exemplified the undertrained "self made man in politics" who "takes any bull by the horns, mounts the stump, and disposes of the most troubling problems . . . in a few sentences."[52]

This attack on Wade's training leads to the question of just what the reformers' goals were, as they opened fire upon their former allies. They always insisted that they wanted only to purify the American political system and upgrade its leaders, and they recoiled with horror from the manipulation and boss-rule that they perceived to be implicit in back-room politics. Yet they themselves continually engaged in similar conduct, attempting to control policy and fix appointments from behind the scenes.[53]

Sincerely believing that they were more honest and more capable than those in power, the reformers were ambitious men. "A man can have no truer satisfaction than in knowing that he has made himself a power," Lowell wrote Godkin in 1868, congratulating the editor on his influence; Lowell knew this would be taken as a compliment. In seeming contrast, Henry Adams wrote his brother Charles in 1869: "You like strife in the world. I detest and despise it. You work for power. I work for my own satisfaction." Yet Henry's insight into his brother's character may have been better than his insight into his own,

51. Henry Adams to Charles Francis Adams, Jr., May 8, 1867, in Worthington C. Ford, ed., *Letters of Henry Adams (1858–1891)* (Boston, 1930), 128; Horace White to Zachariah Chandler, August 20, 1867, in Zachariah Chandler Papers, Library of Congress.

52. New York *Nation,* July 4, 1867, pp. 10–11; July 11, 1867, p. 22; August 1, 1867, pp. 90–92; August 15, 1867, p. 122; September 12, 1867, pp. 20–21; September 19, 1867, p. 221; October 10, 1867, pp. 286, 294–96; November 14, 1867, p. 386; Boston *Daily Advertiser,* June 17, 1867, p. 2; New York *Nation,* July 4, 1867, p. 11.

53. For reformers' political ambitions and desire for appointive office, see Downey, "Rebirth of Reform," 118–21; Geoffrey Blodgett, "Reform Thought and the Genteel Tradition," in *Gilded Age,* ed. Morgan, 66; Hoogenboom, "Civil Service Reform and Public Morality," in *Gilded Age,* ed. Morgan, 77–95; Hoogenboom, *Outlawing the Spoils,* 34–35, 62–63, 77; Edward C. Kirkland, *Charles Francis Adams, Jr., 1835–1915: Patrician at Bay* (Cambridge, Mass., 1965), 38–41; Samuel Shapiro, *Richard Henry Dana, Jr., 1815–1882* (East Lansing, Mich., 1961), 106–63 *passim;* Ferleger, *Wells,* 220–54 *passim.*

considering the obvious pleasure with which he informed a friend a few months later that "I am . . . winding myself up in a coil of political intrigue and getting the reputation of a regular conspirator. . . . I am on the side which has the strongest men, and Reform is always a sure card." [54]

What ailed Henry Adams, his fellow reformer Oliver Wendell Holmes, Jr., wrote later, was his failure to get public office "handed to him on a silver platter." The reformer-economist Amasa Walker was disturbed by similar traits in two other reform leaders: he found David A. Wells "distracted by vanity and want[ing] to be at something sensational"; the Chicago *Tribune's* liberal editor, Horace White, was "not free from the same complaint." [55]

They may have wanted it for the best of reasons, but what the reformers wanted was power. "I fear there is little hope for reform from regular politicians," Godkin wrote Charles Eliot Norton privately in 1867. "If the country is to be saved and purified it must be by some force outside their ranks." Godkin thought the reformers needed to organize for "the hunting down of corrupt politicians, the stoppage of unscrupulous nominations." By "corrupt politicians," however, he did not mean actual crooks; he meant those who got their nominations through political manipulation—that is, by the common methods of the day. And "unscrupulous nominations" were, of course, in the eye of the beholder. [56]

Repelled by political ambition in others, Godkin perhaps was psychologically incapable of admitting that such a political revolution as he advocated inevitably would mean the elevation of men like himself. A similar combination of righteousness and ambition is detectable in Richard Henry Dana's lament, "There will be no more politics for me in Massachusetts until this set, who now rule us . . . of low toned, ill taught men pass aside." Charles Nordhoff made the connection plainer still. "It belongs to us to be recognized as the true leaders of the Repub-

54. James Russell Lowell to E. L. Godkin, November 5, 1868, quoted in Ogden, *Godkin*, II, 77; Henry Adams to Charles Francis Adams, Jr., December 9, 1869, quoted in Ford, ed., *Letters of Henry Adams*, I, 60; Henry Adams to Charles Milnes Gaskell, December 7, 1869, ibid., 173–74.

55. Ernest Samuels, *Henry Adams: The Major Phase* (Cambridge, Mass., 1964), 193; Amasa Walker to Jacob D. Cox, December 5, 1870, in Jacob D. Cox Papers, Library of Congress.

56. E. L. Godkin to Charles Eliot Norton, April 23, 1867, quoted in Ogden, *Godkin*, I, 299–300. One must not be misled by the actual corruption that would be discovered during the Grant administration into thinking that Godkin meant financial peculation at this time. He merely meant the corruption that he thought was inherent in the spoils system and in emphasis on party discipline. For an excellent discussion, see Downey, "Rebirth of Reform," 94–98.

lican party," he wrote Carl Schurz in 1870. "If we are not that we are nothing." [57]

Newly allied with the conservative elements of the Republican organization, the reformers aimed for nothing less than the elimination of radicals from the party's leadership. The argument that future leaders must be capable of applying the teachings of social science to government was the lever with which they hoped to dislodge them. The moral issue of slavery had required radical leadership, the reformers admitted. "People came to look upon fidelity to the antislavery cause, and a generally philanthropic tendency as the one test of statesmanship, and under cover of this feeling a large number of gentlemen have won their way to places in public life"; however, "circumstances have . . . so changed, and the problems presented for solution are so different, that they are fit to fill them no longer." Meanwhile, "the state and nation are constantly injured by their chosen servants, who lack the simplest rudiments of knowledge . . . of the principles essential to the public welfare." [58]

This argument could carry weight only if Republicans agreed that the great moral issue was settled. The radicals' firmness on that issue had secured them their power, the reformers recognized, and so long as Republicans perceived the war issues to be paramount, the radicals could not be dislodged. On the other hand, as Atkinson wrote McCulloch, "Let the reconstruction matters be once settled, and the fight between Protection and Free Trade will be upon us, and Free-Trade views will win." [59] Therefore, the scope of the great Civil War issues had to be narrowed. As the radicals proposed land redistribution, nationally supervised education, and long-term congressional control as means by which to secure real equality in the South, the reformers urged Republicans to be content with the elimination of unequal laws. "Let us be content with securing equal justice in the South, and then combine to attack corruptions nearer home," they urged. [60]

---

57. Richard Henry Dana to James Russell Lowell, June 12, 1869, quoted in Shapiro, *Dana*, 154; Charles Nordhoff to Carl Schurz, December 21, 1870, in Schurz Papers. See Downey, "Rebirth of Reform," 76–127 for an insightful discussion of the relationship between "reform" and power after the Civil War.

58. New York *Nation*, August 1, 1867, pp. 91–92; Andrew D. White, quoted *ibid.*, July 4, 1867, p. 11.

59. Edward Atkinson to Hugh McCulloch, May 28, 1867, quoted in Harold Francis Williamson, *Edward Atkinson: The Biography of an American Liberal, 1827–1905* (Boston, 1934), 81.

60. New York *Nation*, July 18, 1867, p. 51.

The reformers understood that the radical Republicans had secured their positions by appealing to the antislavery sentiment of the Republican rank and file. The reconstruction issue was the natural outgrowth of the antislavery movement, and it tapped the same underlying sentiment. The reformers and their conservative allies understood very well that if they could eliminate the "Negro question" from politics, they would deprive the radicals of the vehicle by which they had driven to power in the party. With the restoration of all but three of the southern states to normal status in the Union in 1868, the election of Ulysses S. Grant to the presidency in the same year on a platform of "Let Us Have Peace," and the passage in 1869 of the Fifteenth Amendment, securing black suffrage, the reformers insisted that the old issues were dead and would be superseded by questions of finance, taxation, and reform in government administration. The implications for the future leadership of the Republican party were plain, as James Russell Lowell made clear in a January, 1869, article designed to serve as the keynote of the reformers' campaign for power. In the fight over slavery and equal rights, Lowell observed, "ethics have been called on to perform the function of jurisprudence and political economy"; consequently, "an easy profession of faith is getting to be the highest qualification of a legislator." But the times dictated a change: "The Republican party, so long accustomed to deal largely with problems into which morals entered largely and directly, is now to be tried solely by its competency for other duties." [61] The point was clear. The new problems required the expertise of the reformers rather than the sentimental moralism of the radicals.

All this implied a new attitude toward southern whites. As early as 1866, Horace White had looked forward to a post-Reconstruction, free-trade alliance between West and South, a prospect apparently endangered by what conservatives thought was the protariff bias of southern Republican radicals. [62] Moreover, hostility toward the former rebels played into the hands of the radical southern "demagogues" who were courting black support by stressing the differences between the interests of southern blacks and whites. As a result, by 1867 reformers and conservative Republicans already were urging Republican

61. Lowell, "A Look Before and After," 261–66. See also New York *Times*, November 12, 1868, p. 4; New York *Nation*, January 28, 1869, pp. 64–65.
62. Logsdon, *White*, 119. See also Edward Atkinson to Henry Charles Carey, November 11, 1867, quoted in Williamson, *Atkinson*, 79–80.

leaders to conciliate white southerners by stressing the moderation of Republican Reconstruction policy and by disavowing radical demands for further change. Reconciliation with white southerners remained a staple of the liberal-reform program throughout the 1870s.[63]

The liberal reformers' sympathy for southern whites was based on more than political calculation, however. It was reinforced by their perceptions of politics in the South under Republican governments— and in this connection the reformers' racism came into play. It was not that the reformers' growing sympathy with conservative white southerners was founded on race hatred, nor did racism ever lead them, as it did most white southerners and northern Democrats, to justify legal discrimination against black people. Rather, the reformers' belief in black intellectual and moral inferiority led them to perceive the freedmen as posing the same threat to liberty in the South that the so-called "dangerous classes" of whites posed in the North—the threat of oppressive "class legislation." Having slight faith in blacks' political intelligence or political integrity, the reformers were quick to respond to the pleas of southern whites, who as early as 1868 were charging that the reformers' fears already had come true.

By the 1870s, most southern Conservatives—particularly those moderate Conservatives with whom the liberal reformers most closely identified—no longer framed their criticism of Republican Reconstruction in terms of white supremacy. That was the coin of the White League and color-liners, whose extremism more moderate whites claimed to resist. Promising acquiescence in the political and legal equality guaranteed by the Reconstruction amendments, moderate Conservatives lambasted scalawags and carpetbaggers, who "control the politics of the State through the control which they have obtained over the colored man." [64] The result of this control, they charged, was a massive system of class legislation. Penniless blacks elected governments that taxed whites to support bloated payrolls, expensive and corrupt building and internal-improvement programs, inefficient and largely black schools, and unnecessary public services. Whereas "all

---

63. Springfield *Daily Illinois State Journal*, July 3, 1867, p. 2; Springfield (Mass.) *Daily Republican*, March 29, 1867, p. 2; New York *Tribune*, May 20, 1867, p. 4; May 28, 1867, p. 4; Boston *Daily Advertiser*, July 6, 1867, p. 2; Benedict, *Compromise of Principle*, 259–60; Buck, *Road to Reunion*, 90–96, 265–68; McPherson, *Ordeal by Fire*, 563–64, 568–70; Downey, "Rebirth of Reform," 267–71, 364–87, 433–41.

64. *Hinds County Gazette* (Raymond, Miss.), quoted in the Jackson (Miss.) *Weekly Clarion*, June 30, 1873, p. 1.

persons in the community who receive the benefits of government ought to contribute equally according to their means," southern Republicans "boast that one class of the population is required to bear only a small share of the burdens of taxation," the Conservatives claimed. "Taxation is robbery, when imposed for private gain, or to build up monopolies for the benefit of the few at the expense of the many."[65] No complaint could have been better framed to win the reformers' sympathy.

Controlling the nation's leading intellectual organs, the liberal reformers ultimately had an immense influence upon the intellectual currents of the United States, and their distaste for the redistributive policies of the southern Republican regimes spread through the North. By the mid-1870s, it would be a common sentiment that, in the words of the conservative Republican New York *Times*, "these freedmen must be convinced that public affairs must not be managed solely for pillage and oppression."[66] Many Republicans came to believe that even black suffrage and Republican control of the South were at best necessary evils, justified only by the threat southern Conservatives posed to freedmen's civil rights and to the Union. To stress that threat, Republican leaders desperately employed the rhetoric that came to be known as "waving the bloody shirt." But as southern Conservatives pledged to protect black rights under Conservative regimes and as charges that white southerners continued to nurture treasonous designs against the nation became ever more fatuous, national Republican support for southern Republicanism became less and less tenable.

The change seriously affected power relationships within the Republican party. During the Civil War and Reconstruction years, ambitious Republicans had sought to harness the radicalism of most party activists and the rank and file in order to advance their party careers. Pressure from such radicals often had forced intraparty rivals toward radicalism in self-defense.[67] But under the reformers' attack, radicalism lost much of its appeal to activists and rank and file. Moreover,

---

65. Jackson (Miss.) *Weekly Clarion*, June 29, 1871, p. 2; November 23, 1871, p. 2. See also Michael Les Benedict, "The Problem of Constitutionalism and Constitutional Liberty in the Reconstruction South," in *An Uncertain Tradition: Constitutionalism and the History of the South*, ed. James W. Ely and Kermit L. Hall (Athens, Ga., 1989).

66. New York *Times*, February 17, 1874, p. 4.

67. Benedict, *Compromise of Principle*, 58–69. For a general discussion of nineteenth-century political factionalism and its effect on party positions on issues, see Michael Les Benedict, "Factionalism and Representation: Some Insight from the Nineteenth-Century United States," *Social Science History*, IX (1985), 361–98.

many established leaders were identified thoroughly with the results of radical Reconstruction and, as the reformers had recognized earlier, could hardly be dislodged on that issue. By the 1870s, liberalism was a more attractive position from which to attack factional rivals than radicalism. Allying with the reformers, ambitious challengers insisted that Republicans had to replace the reconstruction issue with others that would mobilize the rank and file and reconcile "the best men" to the party.[68]

Just as established leaders had been pushed toward radicalism by such challenges in the 1860s, many were pushed toward conservatism in the 1870s. While some hard-liners urged firmness, the more flexible of the Republican leaders searched for new issues. After the terrible Republican defeats in the elections of 1874, that search became desperate. In the state elections of 1875, some Republican candidates experimented with a mix of support for hard money, anti-Catholicism, and attacks on agrarian and labor radicalism—all of which resonated with the laissez-faire morality of the liberal reformers. The experiment proved especially successful in the key state of Ohio. There Republicans demonstrated how to win victories on new issues, electing a governor who by virtue of his triumph came to be perceived as the embodiment of the possibilities—the flexible Rutherford B. Hayes.

68. Morton Keller, *Affairs of State: Public Life in Late Nineteenth-Century America* (Cambridge, Mass., 1977), 277–78; Downey, "Rebirth of Reform."

4

Segregation and Reconstruction

❧ HOWARD N. RABINOWITZ

Reconstruction: After the Civil War devoted little attention to segregation. Indeed, the word does not appear in the index, although there is an entry for separate schools and reference to separate Negro churches. Such neglect was common at the time. In 1961 the origins of segregation in the South had not yet emerged as a controversial issue. Although John Hope Franklin had written on the subject in his essays "History of Racial Segregation in the United States" (1956) and "Jim Crow Goes to School" (1959), he had been concerned primarily with the post-Reconstruction years except in the area of education.[1] In addition, his book was intended mainly as a rebuttal to the Dunning school, which had concentrated on political and economic matters and slighted social relations between the races. Franklin's references to segregation were thus only incidental to the discussion of related issues, such as Reconstruction's considerable achievements in education.

Yet the foundation for the future controversy over the timing and extent of segregation already had been laid six years before the appear-

This essay was completed while the author was a fellow at the Center for Advanced Study in the Behavioral Sciences. I am grateful for financial support provided by the National Endowment for the Humanities and the Andrew W. Mellon Foundation. I also thank Peter Kolchin for reading an early version of the essay.

1. John Hope Franklin, "History of Racial Segregation in the United States," *Annals,* CCCIV (March, 1956), 1–9; John Hope Franklin, "Jim Crow Goes to School: The Genesis of Legal Segregation in Southern Schools," *South Atlantic Quarterly,* LVIII (Spring, 1959), 225–35. The latter was a product of Franklin's "association with Counsel for the plaintiffs" in *Brown* v. *Board of Education,* service that indicated Franklin's personal as well as professional interest in the subject. John Hope Franklin, "Mirror for Americans: A Century of Reconstruction History," *American Historical Review,* LXXXV (1980), 11.

ance of *Reconstruction* with the publication in 1955 of C. Vann Woodward's *Strange Career of Jim Crow,* a work well known to Franklin, who had read it in manuscript and been influenced by it, although he did not cite it in his bibliography.[2] *Strange Career* had originated as the James W. Richard Lectures, which Woodward wrote during the summer months immediately following the *Brown v. Board of Education* decision and presented at the University of Virginia in October, 1954. Woodward's primary aim was to demonstrate that segregation was not a longstanding southern "folkway," but a relatively recent development and therefore more vulnerable to change than commonly believed. In a 1971 essay, "The Strange Career of a Historical Controversy," Woodward defined what by then had become known as the "Woodward Thesis." This was, "first, that racial segregation in the South in the rigid and universal form it had taken did not appear with the end of slavery, but toward the latter years of the century and later; and second, that before it appeared in this form there transpired an era of experiment and variety in race relations of the South in which segregation was not the invariable rule."[3] Or as Woodward put it in the original and subsequent editions of *Strange Career,* it was not until the post-1890 period that a rigid segregation code "lent the sanction of law to a racial ostracism that extended to churches and schools, to housing and jobs, to eating and drinking. Whether by law or by custom, that ostracism eventually extended to virtually all forms of public transportation, to sports and recreations, to hospitals, orphanages, prisons, and asylums, and ultimately to funeral homes, morgues, and cemeteries."[4]

Woodward stated that previous observers had assumed the prevalence of segregation in the postwar period, but he failed to mention specific names in the text. Among the few possibilities listed in *Strange Career's* brief bibliography, the most likely candidate was Gilbert Ste-

2. C. Vann Woodward, *The Strange Career of Jim Crow* (New York, 1955). In the preface, Woodward thanks Franklin for reading the manuscript. Franklin did cite Woodward's *Origins of the New South, 1877–1913* (Baton Rouge, 1951), which contained the seeds of the *Strange Career* argument.

3. C. Vann Woodward, "The Strange Career of a Historical Controversy," in Woodward, *American Counterpoint: Slavery and Racism in the North-South Dialogue* (Boston, 1971), 237. Woodward reaffirmed this definition and discussed the background for the writing and presentation of *Strange Career* in C. Vann Woodward, *Thinking Back: The Perils of Writing History* (Baton Rouge, 1986), 82–83.

4. Woodward, *Strange Career,* 8. *Cf.* the same work in its Oxford University Press Galaxy Edition (1957), 8, and in its 1966 and 1974 New York editions, p. 7. All subsequent references are to the 1966 and 1974 editions.

phenson, who in *Race Distinctions in American Law* (1910) had argued that in train travel, "the 'Jim Crow' laws . . . coming later, did scarcely more than to legalize an existing and widespread custom." In fact, segregation was not a major issue in the study of the postbellum South prior to the appearance of *Strange Career*. Woodward thus opened an entire new field for study. In doing so, however, he focused on the period between the end of Reconstruction and the proliferation of Jim Crow legislation around the turn of the century. Like others, he devoted scant space to Reconstruction itself. Although in subsequent editions he acknowledged the greater presence of segregation in certain areas of southern life during Reconstruction, it was assumed that integration or at least fluidity was the more common experience during those years.[5]

Woodward's interpretation was quickly accepted by historians, especially those sympathetic to the aims of the civil rights movement then gathering momentum. In his 1956 article on the history of segregation, Franklin was probably the first scholar to employ the Woodwardian framework. Although careful to acknowledge the existence of earlier de facto and even de jure segregation, he argued that "it was not until the final quarter of the nineteenth century that states began to evolve a systematic program of legally separating whites and Negroes in every possible area of activity. And it was not until the twentieth century that these laws became a major apparatus for keeping the Negro in 'his place.' "[6] Some conservatives, such as E. Merton Coulter, were restrained in their reactions to *Strange Career,* and most southern state historical journals chose not to review it, but southern white liberals and blacks were laudatory in initial reviews.[7]

This pattern reappeared in the first wave of articles and monographs aimed at testing the Woodward Thesis. The southern white liberal Charles Wynes, in *Race Relations in Virginia, 1870–1902* (1961),

5. Gilbert Thomas Stephenson, *Race Distinctions in American Law* (London, 1910), 214. For the modifications and the restrictions of the Woodward Thesis over the course of its various editions, see Howard N. Rabinowitz, "More Than the Woodward Thesis: Assessing *The Strange Career of Jim Crow,*" *Journal of American History,* LXXIX (1988), 842–48.

6. Franklin, "History of Racial Segregation," 1 and *passim.*

7. Most academic journals used black reviewers. See, for example, Rufus E. Clement, *Journal of Southern History,* XXI (1955), 557–59; James Bonner McRae, *Phylon,* XVI (1955), 472–73; W. M. Brewer, *Journal of Negro History,* XL (July, 1955), 379–82; Rayford W. Logan, *American Historical Review,* LXI (1955), 212–13. For the views of a white liberal, see George B. Tindall, Review of Woodward's *Strange Career,* in *Louisiana Historical Quarterly,* XXXVIII (October, 1955), 100–102. See also the unsigned review—almost certainly Coulter's in a journal edited by him—in *Georgia Historical Quarterly,* XXXIX (December, 1955), 417–18.

and the black historian Frenise Logan, in *The Negro in North Carolina, 1876–1894* (1964), gave the thesis its earliest and most important support. Both scholars emphasized the flexibility of Reconstruction-era race relations and the presence of at least occasional integration. According to John W. Graves, Woodward's view also held true for Arkansas. Graves's 1968 study of the 1891 separate-coach law concluded that "for many years a degree of racial intermingling prevailed that would be unthinkable in later times." His subsequent dissertation on the broader aspects of race relations in Arkansas between 1865 and 1905 was justifiably more restrained, but concluded that although considerable discrimination existed, "ambiguity and confusion characterized the Reconstruction legacy in the sphere of civil rights." [8]

In "Race Relations in Louisiana, 1877–1898" (1968), Henry C. Dethloff and Robert P. Jones used evidence similar to Graves's to present an even stronger endorsement of the Woodward Thesis for the Bayou State. Implicit support also could be found in John Blassingame's *Black New Orleans, 1860–1880* (1973), Dale Somers' "Black and White in New Orleans" (1974), and Louis Harlan's narrower study of school desegregation in New Orleans during Reconstruction. Although Joseph H. Cartwright's *Triumph of Jim Crow* (1976) depicted a profound shift toward Jim Crow in Tennessee as early as the beginning of the 1880s, Cartwright believed, like the others, that a significant degree of integration existed during Reconstruction. [9] Advocates of such a view also could enlist George Tindall's *South Carolina Negroes, 1877–1900* (1952). Writing before the appearance of *Strange Career,* Tindall had anticipated many of its findings, albeit for only one state. He subsequently endorsed Woodward's general assess-

8. Charles E. Wynes, *Race Relations in Virginia, 1870–1902* (Charlottesville, Va., 1961), *passim,* esp. 149; Frenise A. Logan, *The Negro in North Carolina, 1876–1894* (Chapel Hill, 1964); John W. Graves, "The Arkansas Separate Coach Law of 1891," *Journal of the West,* VII (1968), 531–41; John W. Graves, "Town and Country: Race Relations and Urban Development in Arkansas, 1865–1905" (Ph.D. dissertation, University of Virginia, 1978), 61. Although it is often misleading, see also John W. Graves, "Jim Crow in Arkansas: A Reconsideration of Urban Race Relations in the Post-Reconstruction South," *Journal of Southern History,* LV (1989), 421–48.

9. Henry G. Dethloff and Robert P. Jones, "Race Relations in Louisiana, 1877–1898," *Louisiana History,* IX (1968), 301–23; John W. Blassingame, *Black New Orleans, 1860–1880* (Chicago, 1973); Dale A. Somers, "Black and White in New Orleans: A Study in Urban Race Relations, 1865–1900," *Journal of Southern History,* XL (1974), 19–42; Louis R. Harlan, "Desegregation in New Orleans Public Schools During Reconstruction," *American Historical Review,* LXVIII (1962), 663–75; Joseph H. Cartwright, *The Triumph of Jim Crow: Tennessee Race Relations in the 1880s* (Knoxville, 1976).

ment for the rest of the South, doing so in a review that called for further studies but asserted that "it is not likely that they will alter substantially the conclusions of Professor Woodward."[10]

By the mid-1970s, then, a consensus on segregation had emerged, substantiated in several state studies and enshrined in college survey texts. According to this consensus, segregation as a rigid, legalized system was a product of the 1890s along with increased lynching and disfranchisement, and at least by implication was less common than integration during Reconstruction. Most significantly, segregation was a relatively recent phenomenon.[11]

This opinion did not go unchallenged, however. Leon Litwack, in *North of Slavery* (1961), had pointed to the widespread existence of segregation in the antebellum North. Richard Wade's *Slavery in the Cities* (1964) depicted an entrenched system of segregation in antebellum southern cities, raising doubts about the fate of this system during Reconstruction. Ten years later Ira Berlin's study of antebellum southern free Negroes, *Slaves Without Masters,* extended Wade's conclusion to include the nonurban areas of the South, although Berlin demonstrated some ambivalence toward the Woodward Thesis itself.[12]

More direct attacks on the thesis were already under way, drawing inspiration in part from Vernon Wharton's earlier documentation of extensive segregation in *The Negro in Mississippi, 1865–1890* (1947). The pivotal work was Joel Williamson's *After Slavery: The Negro in South Carolina During Reconstruction, 1861–1877* (1965), the first work in the debate to focus on Reconstruction per se. Rather than assuming that integration was the norm during Reconstruction and then tracing its alleged demise in subsequent years, as his predecessors had done, Williamson sought to establish its initial extent. In doing so, he gave equal status to customs and laws, unlike earlier historians. His

10. George Brown Tindall, *South Carolina Negroes, 1877–1900* (Columbia, S.C., 1952); Tindall, Review of Woodward's *Strange Career,* 102. For an explicit endorsement of the Woodward Thesis, albeit one based on limited evidence for a border state that did not undergo Reconstruction, see Margaret Law Callcott, *The Negro in Maryland Politics, 1870–1912* (Baltimore, 1969), esp. ix, 134–38.

11. See, for example, Rebecca Brooks Gruver, *An American History* (2d ed.; Reading, Mass., 1976), 547; John Garraty, *A Short History of the American Nation* (2d ed.; New York, 1977), 274–75; John D. Hicks, George E. Mowry, and Robert Burke, *A History of American Democracy* (4th ed.; New York, 1970), 367.

12. Leon Litwack, *North of Slavery: The Negro in the Free States, 1790–1860* (Chicago, 1961); Richard C. Wade, *Slavery in the Cities: The South, 1820–1860* (New York, 1964); Ira Berlin, *Slaves Without Masters: The Free Negro in the Antebellum South* (New York, 1974), esp. 326–27, 383–84.

findings for South Carolina—the state in which blacks had the most power—directly challenged those of Woodward and his defenders. Although Williamson acknowledged examples of integration, he found de facto segregation to be so prevalent that by the end of Reconstruction there existed a crystallized "duo-chromatic order" in South Carolina.[13] Soon after, Roger A. Fischer began a series of frontal attacks on the Woodward Thesis over ground that had proved fertile for Woodward's supporters. In "Racial Segregation in Ante Bellum New Orleans" (1969) and "The Post–Civil War Segregation Struggle" (1968), Fischer argued for the early appearance and persistence of segregation in the Crescent City. In *The Segregation Struggle in Louisiana, 1862–1877* (1974), he expanded his argument to include the entire state; in the process, he removed some of his previous ambivalence about the value of the Woodward Thesis in order to stress even more the relative importance of segregation during the Reconstruction.[14] Although less systematic in their investigations of segregation in Florida, Joe M. Richardson, in *The Negro in the Reconstruction of Florida, 1865–1877* (1965), and Jerrell H. Shofner, in *Nor Is It Over Yet* (1974) found evidence similar to Fischer's. As Shofner concluded, "The Jim Crow legislation [of the 1890s] reinforced existing social customs which had remained unchanged by post–Civil War developments."[15]

By the mid-1970s, there seemed to be a stalemate. Various studies had appeared that supported the Woodward Thesis, but the works most directly concerned with the extent of segregation during Reconstruction had argued for the practice's prevalence and for an essential

13. Vernon L. Wharton, *The Negro in Mississippi, 1865–1890* (Chapel Hill, 1947); Joel Williamson, *After Slavery: The Negro in South Carolina During Reconstruction, 1861–1877* (Chapel Hill, 1965), esp. 198–99. For an amplification of his views and a convenient summary of the initial stages of the debate, see Joel Williamson, ed., *The Origins of Segregation* (Lexington, Ky., 1968), esp. the introduction.

14. Roger A. Fischer, "Racial Segregation in Ante Bellum New Orleans," *American Historical Review,* LXXIV (1969), 926–37; Roger A. Fischer, "The Post–Civil War Segregation Struggle," in *The Past as Prelude: New Orleans,* ed. Hodding Carter et al. (New Orleans, 1968), 288–304; Roger A. Fischer, *The Segregation Struggle in Louisiana, 1862–1877* (Urbana, Ill., 1974). For a similar emphasis on the essential continuity in Louisiana's pattern of segregation, but without reference to Woodward, see Joe Gray Taylor, *Louisiana Reconstructed, 1863–1877* (Baton Rouge, 1974), esp. 434, 438–39.

15. Joe M. Richardson, *The Negro in the Reconstruction of Florida, 1865–1877* (Tallahassee, 1965); Jerrell H. Shofner, *Nor Is It Over Yet: Florida in the Era of Reconstruction, 1863–1877* (Gainesville, 1974), *passim* (quotation, 344). For a study of the state's post-Reconstruction experience that focuses on de jure segregation but sees a general tightening of de facto practices by 1880, see Wali R. Kharif, "Black Reaction to Segregation and Discrimination in Post-Reconstruction Florida," *Florida Historical Quarterly,* LXIV (October, 1985), 161–73.

continuity in social relations between 1865 and 1900. In "A Strange Chapter in the Career of 'Jim Crow'" (1969), August Meier and Elliott Rudwick had sought to reconcile the opposing views by pointing to an alleged cyclical pattern in the segregation of streetcars. Segregation appeared initially soon after the Civil War and persisted in some places during Reconstruction before being eliminated until its reappearance around the turn of the century.[16] The article was suggestive and demonstrated further the complexity of the issue, but no one followed its lead and it did not resolve the conflict. Not surprisingly, a number of state studies of southern blacks published during these years ignored the controversy and simply made passing reference to the mixture of segregation and integration.[17] Yet textbooks continued at least implicitly to endorse Woodward's position, and in the 1966 and 1974 revisions of *Strange Career,* while modifying some of his earlier remarks, Woodward gently but authoritatively dismissed the criticisms by Litwack, Williamson, and Wade.[18]

In large measure the state of the debate over the extent and role of segregation during Reconstruction reflected the fact that Woodward had been allowed to dictate the ground rules, which both disciples and critics seemed to accept. The most basic agreement involved the relative importance of law and custom. Although Woodward had briefly acknowledged the relevance of custom, his argument centered on the absence of laws requiring segregation prior to the 1890s. Supporters agreed with this emphasis; detractors, although admitting the later appearance of laws, argued that de facto segregation was present much earlier and was firmly in place even during Reconstruction.

Woodward also was permitted to decide which laws would count. After all, during Reconstruction several states had antimiscegenation statutes, and most had laws permitting or requiring separate schools, cemeteries, militia units, and welfare services. Moreover, de jure seg-

---

16. August Meier and Elliott Rudwick, "A Strange Chapter in the Career of 'Jim Crow,'" in *The Black Community in Modern America,* ed. Meier and Rudwick (New York, 1969), 14–19, Vol. II of *The Making of Black America: Essays in Negro Life and History,* 2 vols. See also August M. Meier and Elliott Rudwick, "The Boycott Movement Against Jim Crow Streetcars in the South, 1900–1906," *Journal of American History,* LX (1969), 756–75.

17. Peter Kolchin, *First Freedom: The Responses of Alabama's Blacks to Emancipation and Reconstruction* (Westport, Conn., 1972); Lawrence D. Rice, *The Negro in Texas, 1874–1900* (Baton Rouge, 1971). For a later study that takes a similar approach, but seems to emphasize the greater importance of segregation and continuity, see James M. Smallwood, *Time of Hope, Time of Despair: Black Texans During Reconstruction* (Port Washington, N.Y., 1981), esp. 122, 127.

18. Woodward, *Strange Career,* 12–29.

regation did not depend only on the passage of laws explicitly requiring segregation. As Charles A. Lofgren argued in *The Plessy Case* (1987), prior to the 1890s courts commonly held that existing legislation permitted racially separate public accommodations, provided they were equal.[19]

Woodward governed the terms of the debate in yet another way in that only certain areas of southern life were included in the argument over segregation. Although Woodward at times had cast a wide net, the Woodward Thesis covered much less ground than either its proponents or opponents seemed to appreciate. Whole areas of southern life were written out of the debate. For example, Woodward granted the early and rigid appearance during Reconstruction of segregation in militia service, public education, religion, and a broad range of social welfare provisions. One might also add fraternal organizations, clubs, and other voluntary associations. What was at issue, therefore, was the relative degree of segregation in public accommodations, especially public conveyances. Even such a staunch defender of the thesis as Charles Wynes admitted its weakness when it came to places like restaurants, hotels, and theaters.[20]

The debate was narrowed further owing to the organization of the books that appeared. Typically, there would be one chapter called "The Color Line" or "Race Relations" that focused on segregation in public accommodations. Other chapters might consider education, justice, and religion. Segregation in those areas would be mentioned, certainly, but basically would be taken for granted and not included in the broader debate. In this process, the extent and meaning of racial separation in southern society became distorted.

In addition, the segregation debate placed too much emphasis on the white majority. Because *Strange Career* was so much a product of the civil rights era, and because segregation was seen as a "bad thing," Woodward concentrated on white attitudes and behavior. Segregation was something done to blacks by hostile and vindictive southern whites. Most scholars embraced this view, even when their own evidence suggested a more complex reality. Neither white Republicans

---

19. *Ibid.*; Charles A. Lofgren, *The Plessy Case: A Legal-Historical Interpretation* (New York, 1987), esp. pp. 9, 147, and chap. 6.

20. See Woodward, *Strange Career*, 24–25; Wynes, *Race Relations*, 149–50. For a fuller discussion of the limits of the Woodward Thesis, see Rabinowitz, "More Than the Woodward Thesis," 846–48.

nor blacks were seen as playing critical roles in the emergence of Jim Crow, except perhaps as its tragically overmatched opponents.

Most limiting of all, however, was the confinement of the debate to the alternatives of integration or segregation, with the concomitant unthinking linkage of the various forms of oppression that increasingly plagued blacks by the turn of the century. In the first instance, scholarship sometimes degenerated into a "Can you top this?" contest between examples of segregation and integration, with competing assertions about whether the glass of discrimination was half full or half empty. Each side acknowledged the existence of both alternatives prior to the 1890s but differed as to their relative importance, a judgment often dependent on one's political orientation. The advantage, of course, was with the proponents of the Woodward Thesis. No one could deny that integration was at least occasionally a fact of life for some southern blacks under some circumstances. And for those who linked Jim Crow laws with disfranchisement and the increase in lynching, there was no question about there being a decline in status for blacks during the 1890s.

In any case, by the mid-1970s there was growing interest in going beyond the initial terms of the segregation debate. This change resulted partly from an overdue awareness that blacks were not simply objects of history but subjects as well. Inspired both by the role of blacks in current events and by changes in scholarly inquiry, scholars began to carve out a place for blacks as actors, rather than passive victims, in accounting for the development of segregation. James McPherson, for example, in "White Liberals and Black Power in Negro Education" (1970), noted that by the end of Reconstruction, blacks had accepted segregated higher education but were pressing for their own black instructors to replace whites. In "Half a Loaf: The Shift from White to Black Teachers in the Negro Schools of the Urban South" (1974), I pointed to a similar and even more pronounced pattern below the college level. Sociologists such as E. Franklin Frazier earlier had noted the vested interest that some blacks had in segregated institutions, and historians now began, especially in light of the black power and black nationalist movements, to question the commitment of blacks to integration.[21]

---

21. James M. McPherson, "White Liberals and Black Power in Negro Education, 1865–1915," *American Historical Review,* LXXV (1970), 1357–86; Howard N. Rabinowitz, "Half a Loaf: The Shift from White to Black Teachers in the Negro Schools of the Urban South, 1865–

While examining the nature of race relations in five southern cities, I noticed that blacks and their white Republican allies often accepted or actually requested segregated facilities. In a series of articles and in *Race Relations in the Urban South* (1978), I argued that they did so either because provisions were expected to be equal or because even inferior provisions often represented an advance over a previous policy of exclusion. Not only was this frequently the case with theaters, public conveyances, hotels, and other staples of the segregation controversy, but also—and even more significantly—in such previously neglected areas as public education, welfare policy, and militia service. Viewed in this light, segregation might actually have worked as an advance for blacks—especially when couched in terms of equal treatment—because it replaced exclusion. As such, it could be presented and endorsed by both black leaders and their white allies without completely alienating the mass of hostile southern whites. Segregation therefore could be seen as an achievement of Reconstruction rather than as an example of Redeemer or post-Redeemer oppression. Thus, although providing ample evidence of the extent of de facto and even de jure segregation well before the 1890s across a wide spectrum of southern life, I sought to redirect attention not only to new alternatives, but also to the question of *why* segregation emerged, and not simply how much there was or when it appeared.[22]

The concept of a shift from exclusion to segregation has been received favorably by southern historians, including proponents and opponents of the Woodward Thesis.[23] In an effort to go beyond the nar-

---

1890," *Journal of Southern History,* XL (1974), 565–94; E. Franklin Frazier, *Black Bourgeoisie: The Rise of a New Middle Class in the United States* (New York, 1957).

22. Howard N. Rabinowitz, *Race Relations in the Urban South, 1865–1890* (New York, 1978). See also Howard N. Rabinowitz, "From Exclusion to Segregation: Health and Welfare Services for Southern Blacks, 1865–1890," *Social Service Review,* XLVIII (1974), 327–54; Rabinowitz, "More Than the Woodward Thesis"; and Rabinowitz, "Half a Loaf."

23. See esp. the reviews of Rabinowitz, *Race Relations in the Urban South,* by Joel Williamson, in *American Historical Review,* LXXXIV (1979), 857–58, and George B. Tindall, in *Civil War History,* XXV (1979), 179–81, and even the more critical one by Charles Wynes, in *Florida Historical Quarterly,* LVII (1978), 236–38. For C. Vann Woodward's positive reaction—with certain reservations concerning public conveyances—see his foreword to the paperback edition of *Race Relations in the Urban South, 1865–1890* (Urbana, Ill., 1980); his review in the *Journal of Southern History,* XLIV (1978), 476–78; and Woodward, *Thinking Back,* 96–97. Although the exclusion-to-segregation framework has not been tested systematically for additional southern cities or states, surprising corroboration of it came in Lawrence O. Christensen, "Race Relations in St. Louis, 1865–1916," *Missouri Historical Review,* LXXVIII (1984), 123–36. Less surprisingly, examination of another community outside the South produced mixed results in Joanne Wheeler, "Together in Egypt: A Pattern of Race Relations in Cairo, Illinois, 1865–1915,"

row terms of the initial debate, some historians have turned to comparative history. Again, it was Woodward who led the way, this time in his 1971 essay about the debate over his thesis. After a thorough review, he concluded that on the whole, the existing literature had supported his essential interpretation concerning the relatively late appearance of a rigid system of segregation and proscription. He then sought to transcend the old debate in an effort to explain the post-1890 transformation in southern race relations. Rejecting evolutionary, cyclical, and industrialization models, he embraced Pierre L. van den Berghe's race-relations typology, which posited "paternalistic" and "competitive" models based on a comparison of the racial histories of Mexico, Brazil, the United States, and South Africa. To define status, paternalistic systems relied on social distance; competitive systems sought physical distance. Still taking for granted widespread integration during Reconstruction and a transitional post-Reconstruction period, Woodward ascribed the shift during the 1890s to a region-wide change from paternalism to competitiveness.[24] Given disagreements over the actual extent of segregation prior to the 1890s, this analysis was interesting but nonetheless unsatisfying. It has received little support. It did, however, help to direct attention to the comparative dimensions of Jim Crow.

South Africa proved to be an especially productive laboratory for racial comparisons. In *White Supremacy: A Comparative Study in American and South African History* (1981), George Fredrickson emphasized the differences in the origins and institutionalization of segregation in the two countries "in terms both of underlying structures and patterns of historical development." Fredrickson sought to stake out a middle position on the pervasiveness of segregation in the South during Reconstruction, but he fully sided with Woodward on the importance of legal actions during the 1890s, especially with regard to disfranchisement. John Cell, however, in *The Highest Stage of White Supremacy: The Origins of Segregation in South Africa and the American South* (1982), found greater similarity between the two countries. Like Fredrickson, Cell employed the exclusion-to-segregation frame-

---

in *Toward a New South? Studies in Post–Civil War Southern Communities,* ed. Orville Vernon Burton and Robert C. McMath, Jr. (Westport, Conn., 1982), 103–35.
24. Woodward, "Strange Career of a Historical Controversy," 234–60.

work and granted the significance of post-1890 developments, but he was more impressed by the extent of de facto segregation during Reconstruction. What was important, he argued, was not a shift in behavior, but changes in rhetoric and the law—changes that served to institutionalize existing social arrangements. And unlike Fredrickson, Cell found South African moderates, who favored intermediate steps, to be similar to the South's advocates of segregation over exclusion, or separate but equal treatment.[25]

The basic points remained at issue. Comparative history revealed a good deal about the formal institutionalization of racial segregation but was less useful in illuminating the impact and extent of the less formal de facto practices of the Reconstruction years. At this point, a leader in the original debate, Joel Williamson, announced that it was time "to move to one side, and begin again." Now less concerned than previously about the amount of segregation during Reconstruction, Williamson pointed to the "Great Changeover" after 1889, with the rise of white extremists advocating lynching, disfranchisement, and legalized segregation, as much for psychological as political or economic reasons. Nevertheless, in *The Crucible of Race* (1984), Williamson argued that whether through law or custom, "during Reconstruction and for some years thereafter, the essential pattern of life of the great mass of black people precluded any significant mixing of the races."[26] This assessment was, of course, the same as the one he had made for South Carolina twenty years earlier. What had changed was his appreciation of the importance of the post-1890 developments.

Published almost thirty years after *Strange Career,* Williamson's *Crucible of Race* provides an excellent opportunity for taking stock. What remains most constant is the need to view Reconstruction within a broader context. Yet surprisingly little of the segregation controversy has focused on the Reconstruction era itself. Far more is known about the pattern of racial relations before and after Reconstruction, especially if the period is defined narrowly as that of Radical Reconstruc-

25. George M. Fredrickson, *White Supremacy: A Comparative Study in American and South African History* (New York, 1981), 250 and *passim;* John Cell, *The Highest Stage of White Supremacy: The Origins of Segregation in South Africa and the American South* (New York, 1982), chaps. 4–7 and *passim.* For an earlier appeal for a compromise between the Woodward and anti-Woodward positions based solely on the American context, see George M. Fredrickson, *The Black Image in the White Mind: The Debate on Afro-American Character and Destiny, 1817–1914* (New York, 1971), esp. 202.

26. Joel Williamson, *The Crucible of Race: Black-White Relations in the American South Since Emancipation* (New York, 1984), viii, 252, and *passim.*

tion, or even as the years between 1865 (or 1862) and 1877. More emphasis has been placed on conditions after Reconstruction than during it. The questions are what we now know and where we go from here.

The key point is that unlike 1961 when *Reconstruction: After the Civil War* appeared, today the degree of segregation in southern society has become a major subject for historical inquiry. Rare indeed is an index without the topic's presence. For this, of course, we can thank *Strange Career* and the civil rights movement. Yet segregation has become such an accepted subject that scholars are beginning to take it for granted as trendier topics, such as the transformation of the white yeomanry or other class-related matters, take center stage. This is unfortunate, for there is still much to do in the study of segregation, although the Woodward Thesis itself is no longer the issue: scholars are now in a position to ask what actually happened rather than which historian was right.

To begin with, a consensus of sorts (although often unacknowledged) has been reached as to the facts about segregation.[27] It is clear that during Reconstruction segregation was a widespread factor in southern life; as even two of Woodward's defenders recently put it, segregation was the "dominant tendency" of the period.[28] Much of this segregation, moreover, was the result of voluntary action on the part of blacks, as found in churches and an impressive array of associations. Other instances, as in public schools, welfare institutions, cemeteries, and militia units often were agreed upon mutually by whites and blacks, although such separation frequently was enforced by law. Still other examples of separation, as in public conveyances, restaurants, hotels, theaters, and the like, were the result of de facto arrangements that had a greater degree of flexibility in some cases— although by no means in very many, especially given the tendency of courts to uphold separate, ostensibly equal arrangements. Whatever its source, segregation often constituted an improvement over a previ-

27. See esp., in a series edited by John Hope Franklin, a survey of the Reconstruction period by a student of his, Michael Perman, *Emancipation and Reconstruction, 1862–1879* (Arlington Heights, Va., 1987), 81–82, and a penetrating survey of the literature in the field in LaWanda Cox, "From Emancipation to Segregation: National Policy and Southern Blacks," in *Interpreting Southern History: Historiographical Essays in Honor of Sanford W. Higginbotham*, ed. John B. Boles and Evelyn Thomas Nolen (Baton Rouge, 1987), 250–52. See also Eric Foner, *Reconstruction: America's Unfinished Revolution, 1863–1877* (New York, 1988).

28. J. Morgan Kousser and James M. McPherson, eds., *Region, Race, and Reconstruction: Essays in Honor of C. Vann Woodward* (New York, 1982), xxvi.

ous policy of excluding blacks from the area in question. Within this environment, the several state civil rights acts and the 1875 federal civil rights act (already stripped of proposed coverage of schools and cemeteries) were, as Franklin noted in *Reconstruction* and elsewhere, essentially dead letters; at best, they served to assure blacks separate but equal access to facilities.[29]

Furthermore, there is general agreement that something very important happened at the end of the 1880s. Although de jure segregation was more of a factor before the 1890s than Woodward and others have recognized, there is no denying its significant increase at the end of the century. The segregation laws were important, however, for different reasons from those Woodward argued. The laws did not represent a shift in the actual degree of segregation between the races, but rather, as Cell and Williamson argued, a shift in rhetoric and white attitudes. The essential question should not be why the South went from a fluid to a rigid system of race relations in the 1890s, but why it became necessary to legalize customary practices.

Historians must consider the possibility, which I have suggested elsewhere, that the altered attitudes and especially the behavior of some blacks themselves might have helped force such changes.[30] Woodward, of course, has argued that the transformation in the 1890s was caused entirely by the actions of whites—for example, by the withdrawal of northern support for blacks, the disillusionment of white insurgents after the failure of the Populist movement, and a capitulation to racism by Conservatives. Other scholars have followed Woodward's lead in focusing on whites but have identified different groups and factors. Cell, for example, pointed to the economic developments of the 1890s and the role of the white upper classes (although, ironically, he did this in a chapter noting the important role black actions played in the white push for apartheid in South Africa).

29. John Hope Franklin, *Reconstruction: After the Civil War* (Chicago, 1961), 141, 201–202, 223; John Hope Franklin, "The Enforcement of the Civil Rights Act of 1875," *Prologue*, VI (1974), 225–35. See also Lofgren, *Plessy Case*, 132–37, and Rabinowitz, *Race Relations in the Urban South*, 186–89, 195–96.

30. Rabinowitz, *Race Relations in the Urban South*, epilogue and *passim*. See also Rabinowitz, "From Exclusion to Segregation," 350. For a relatively strong endorsement of this view, see Lofgren, *Plessy Case*, 25–26; for a more tentative one, see Cox, "From Emancipation to Segregation," 251–52. On the role of white fears of the "new Negro," for a brief mention that does not give enough credence to the justification for such fears, see Linda M. Matthew, "Keeping Down Jim Crow: The Railroads and the Separate Coach Bills in South Carolina," *South Atlantic Quarterly*, LXXIII (1974), 117–29.

Williamson considered the key to be the extreme white racialists he called "Radicals," who used a threatening economic and political environment to fulfill their psychological need to subdue the black population. With less documentation, David Donald has taken a generational approach: having arrived at "middle adulthood," Civil War veterans in their fifties allegedly sought to safeguard their legacy of white supremacy through legalized segregation and disfranchisement. Clearly, the last word has not been written about white Democratic motives for supporting segregation in either its de facto or de jure forms.[31]

Whatever the motivating factors, any discussion of segregation during Reconstruction and its aftermath must assess not only the relative importance of de facto and de jure segregation, but also the mixture of voluntary and involuntary segregation. De jure segregation was unquestionably the work of whites, but too often historians have assumed implicitly that de facto segregation also must have been entirely the responsibility of whites. In fact, much of the segregation during and after Reconstruction was initiated or supported by blacks. Most obvious—and often quite troubling to whites—was the black withdrawal from white churches, a movement that began even before Reconstruction. Together with new churches, blacks often established their own schools, welfare institutions, political organizations, and benevolent and fraternal societies, all within increasingly segregated black neighborhoods.[32] Sometimes this self-segregation was in response to white neglect or hostility, but often it was simply a statement of black communal identity. Any discussion of segregation, therefore,

31. Woodward, *Strange Career* (1974), 51–64; Cell, *Highest Stage,* chaps. 6, 8; Williamson, *Crucible of Race,* chap. 4 and *passim;* David Donald, "A Generation of Defeat," in *From the Old South to the New: Essays on the Transitional South,* ed. Walter J. Framer, Jr., and Winfred B. Moore, Jr. (Westport, Conn., 1981), 3–20. See also Fredrickson, *Black Image in the White Mind,* 203, 266–67, for an earlier version of Cell's argument, which stresses upper-class manipulation of the concept of "*Herrenvolk* democracy." For the limitations of Williamson's psychological approach, see Howard N. Rabinowitz, "Psychological Disorders, Socio-Economic Forces, and American Race Relations," *Slavery and Abolition,* VII (1986), 188–94. For a fuller discussion of what has been done and needs to be done to account for the post-1890 Jim Crow statutes, see Rabinowitz, "More Than the Woodward Thesis," 849–51.

32. Clusters of black settlement, formed around the basic institutions of black life, were fixtures of the urban landscape in the years immediately following the war. Indeed, many of these settlements had originated in the antebellum period as areas for free Negroes and hired-out slaves. See Rabinowitz, *Race Relations in the Urban South,* chap. 5. Some historians view residential segregation as having been less pronounced. See, for example, Harold D. Woodman, "Economic Reconstruction and the Rise of the New South," in *Interpreting Southern History,* ed. Boles and Nolen, 298–99.

must go beyond the narrow limits of white-enforced segregation in public accommodations if it is to illuminate the reality of the cultural urges that southern blacks shared with other American ethnic groups.

Scholars also need to keep in mind the distinction between segregation and other forms of discrimination. A major source for the initial appeal of the Woodward Thesis was its linkage of segregation, disfranchisement, and proscription as phenomena of the 1890s. There was, after all, no disputing the increase in lynching and the almost complete denial of the vote to southern blacks after 1890. Joel Williamson and John Cell, among others, also linked these different forms of discrimination even though disagreeing with Woodward over the reasons for, or the degree of, the transformation in race relations.[33] It must be remembered, however, that segregation has a history of its own and that racial separation was widespread during Reconstruction even though blacks voted in large numbers. Segregation also thrived in the supposedly transitional 1880s and, for that matter, in much of the twentieth-century North. What was important about the 1890s for southern segregation was not the newness of Jim Crow laws and customs, but the relentless confirmation of them.

Finally, in approaching the issue of segregation during Reconstruction, scholars need to do more than examine the attitudes, motivations, and behavior of blacks and southern white Democrats. A great deal remains to be learned about the white Republicans who were, it needs to be emphasized, the critical policy makers and implementers on the local, state, and national levels during Reconstruction. In *Reconstruction: After the Civil War,* Franklin noted the division of opinion on racial matters within this group. As he put it, "Many of the native whites who held office were as opposed to the equality of Negroes as were many of the disfranchised former Confederates." He added that "it was the native whites who insisted on segregated schools and laws against intermarriage."[34] In the years since 1961 most historians have rejected the traditional depiction of congressional radicals, "carpetbaggers," and "scalawags" as all being unremitting miscegenationists and undifferentiated advocates of "social equality." A substitute view of these men is only beginning to emerge,

33. See esp. Cell, *Highest Stage,* 14. For a fuller discussion of Cell's approach, see Howard N. Rabinowitz, "The Not So Strange Career of Jim Crow, "*Reviews in American History,* XII (1984), 58–64.

34. Franklin, *Reconstruction,* 196.

however, and so far it has focused mainly on a handful of leaders or the most radical faction.[35]

Reflecting the frustrations of the 1960s, historians such as Forest Wood and Lawrence J. Friedman found little difference between Republicans and Democrats with respect to racial discrimination. In Wood's opinion, "One of the most obvious facts about race relations in the 1860s and 1870s was that the vast majority of Americans, white and black, took racial separation for granted." Friedman, arguing that "segregation and integration are not vital issues," saw no need to distinguish among whites as he focused on their drive for Negro "servility."[36] Those who have singled out white Republicans for special treatment usually have been more concerned with other issues and seemingly have taken acceptance of segregation for granted. One partial exception is Ted Tunnell, whose *Crucible of Reconstruction* (1984) provides a thoughtful analysis of the range of racial ideas among Louisiana's Unionists, emphasizing their desire to avoid offending potential white voters and their lack of commitment to racial equality.[37] More typical is Sarah Woolfolk Wiggins' study *The Scalawag in Alabama Politics* (1977), which showed that this much-maligned group of white southerners was better off, more honorable, and more respected than the stereotype allowed, but which noted their belief in white supremacy only in passing and without providing a detailed explanation.[38] Still others, such as Michael Les Benedict in *A Compromise of Principle* (1974) and Herman Belz in *Emancipation and Equal Rights* (1978), concentrated on suffrage and broader civil rights issues and on

35. See, for example, Kenneth M. Stampp, *The Era of Reconstruction, 1865–1877* (New York, 1965), 101–105.

36. Forrest Wood, *Black Scare: The Racist Response to Emancipation and Reconstruction* (Berkeley, 1970), 134; Lawrence J. Friedman, *The White Savage: Racial Fantasies in the Postbellum South* (Englewood Cliffs, N.J., 1970), vii and *passim*. See also Forrest G. Wood, *The Era of Reconstruction, 1863–1877* (New York, 1975). For a criticism of this new tendency to blur distinctions among whites and denigrate the contributions of reconstructionists, see Herman Belz, "The New Orthodoxy in Reconstruction Historiography," *Reviews in American History,* I (1973), 106–13.

37. Ted Tunnell, *Crucible of Reconstruction: War, Radicalism, and Race in Louisiana, 1862–1877* (Baton Rouge, 1984), esp. 53–65, 117–20, 123–28, 167–69. Tunnell divides the Unionists into conservatives, radicals, and reactionaries but argues that even most radicals did not always favor integration. As a result, Tunnell concludes, even after passage of the state's 1869 civil rights law "segregation in Louisiana remained virtually unchanged."

38. Sarah Woolfolk Wiggins, *The Scalawag in Alabama Politics, 1865–1881* (University, Ala., 1977). For a study concerned primarily with the economic attitudes and behavior of one type of carpetbagger and arguing that these northern Republicans accepted a generalized racism comparable to that of white southerners despite an avowed dedication to an ideology of free labor, see Lawrence N. Powell, *New Masters: Northern Planters During the Civil War and Reconstruction* (New Haven, 1980), esp. 31, 121, 142–43.

the Republicans' constitutionally inspired conservatism (or moderation), which limited the degree to which they would use the federal government to support black rights.[39]

What clearly is needed is a study of white Republicans that examines their attitudes not only toward civil and political rights in general, but also toward the relative desirability in social relations of exclusion, segregation, and—the period's least favored option—integration.[40] Further examination of white Republicans and segregation will help to place in focus the meaning of Reconstruction in general and the ways in which racial policy compared with preceding and subsequent periods. I would argue that Reconstruction was primarily about securing black suffrage and civil rights such as the right to contract, to perform jury service, and the like. With respect to social rights, there was no integrationist thrust, either as a goal or as a reality. The basic aim, as in the rest of Reconstruction policy—indeed, as in American reformist ideology throughout the nation's history—was equal access or opportunity, not equality of condition.

A growing body of work, for example, suggests an essential continuity between the Civil Rights Act of 1875 and the *Plessy* v. *Ferguson* Supreme Court decision in 1896, legal entities once seen as antithetical. As early as 1967, in "Racial Segregation in Public Accommodations," Alfred Avins argued that with the exception of a few radicals, congressional Republicans sought to end unequal treatment of blacks rather than segregation per se, an assessment that I subsequently endorsed and expanded upon. More recently, Charles Lofgren's *Plessy Case* (1987) and Stephen J. Riegel's "Persistent Career of Jim Crow" (1984) have argued that as designed by the framers of the era's civil rights legislation and as interpreted by the courts, *equality* of accommodation did not necessarily mean *identity* of accommodation, and that *distinction* was not the same as *discrimination*.[41]

---

39. Michael Les Benedict, *A Compromise of Principle: Congressional Republicans and Reconstruction, 1863–1869* (New York, 1974); Herman Belz, *Emancipation and Equal Rights: Politics and Constitutionalism in the Civil War Era* (New York, 1978).

40. For a modest beginning, see Rabinowitz, *Race Relations in the Urban South*, esp. 185–86.

41. Alfred Avins, "Racial Segregation in Public Accommodations: Some Reflected Light on the Fourteenth Amendment from the Civil Rights Act of 1875," *Western Reserve Law Review,* XVIII (1967), 125–83; Rabinowitz, *Race Relations in the Urban South;* Lofgren, *Plessy Case,* 70–76, 132–37, and *passim;* Stephen J. Riegel, "The Persistent Career of Jim Crow: Lower Federal Courts and the 'Separate but Equal Doctrine,' 1865–1896," *American Journal of Legal History,* XXVIII (1984), 17–40. See also Jonathan Lurie, "The Fourteenth Amendment: Use and Application in Selected State Court Civil Liberties Cases, 1870–1890—A Preliminary Assess-

Thus, segregation can be seen as an improvement over exclusion or absence of equal access. White southerners reluctantly accepted this shift and continued it into the post-Reconstruction years. The real issue was not segregation as such, but equal treatment within a segregated society. There were times during Reconstruction when this goal was achieved, especially with regard to school appropriations, but by the 1890s such treatment was clearly unequal. When joined to disfranchisement, to the failure of courts to demand truly equal separate accommodations, to increased violence and inflammatory racial rhetoric, and to the expansion of laws into spheres not previously covered, segregation became part of a significant shift in the nature of southern racial relations. Simple physical separation of the races, never *complete* in the South even after 1900, had been the norm at least since Reconstruction, particularly outside the limited sphere of train and streetcar travel.[42] Ironically, in a South committed to Negro inferiority and submission, the idea (and occasionally the reality) of separate but equal treatment was actually one of the few achievements of Reconstruction.

---

ment," *American Journal of Legal History,* XXVIII (1984), 295–313. For an interpretation of the Civil Rights Act of 1875 that stresses the act's equalitarian intent despite its minimal impact, see James M. McPherson, "Abolitionists and the Civil Rights Act of 1875," *Journal of American History,* LII (1965), 493–510.

42. For a discussion of the incompleteness of the shift after 1890, see Rabinowitz, "More Than the Woodward Thesis," 848. By accepting Woodward's depiction of a rigidly discriminatory twentieth-century South, his critics provided still another example of how they allowed him to determine the terms of the debate over segregation.

5

The Failure of Southern Republicanism, 1867–1876

❧ CARL H. MONEYHON

The congressional plan for Reconstruction of the South left many crucial issues to be decided in the arena of state politics. In the unreconstructed southern states, all adult males (except for those few whites specifically disfranchised for rebellion) would form an electorate. That biracial electorate would choose delegates to state constitutional conventions and form governments acceptable to Congress. Thus, the region's future was placed in the hands of coalitions of white and black voters who organized state Republican parties throughout the South. The Republicans produced the necessary constitutions and, in every state except Virginia, took over the first restored governments. Although state party goals varied, everywhere Republicanism represented a commitment to changing significant aspects of southern society, and modern historians have seen in these parties the potential for a South with a greater commitment to equality in race relations and economic opportunity. Yet despite early successes, by 1877 the Republicans had been driven from power in every southern state, and the possibilities for the different South that they had promised had disappeared with them.

The failure of Reconstruction to accomplish the changes that appeared to be inherent in it continues to interest historians. The role of the Republican party, and particularly of the state Republican parties, has always been considered central to any understanding of the outcome of Reconstruction and has been the object of much scholarly attention.

The earliest historical assessment of southern Republicanism provided a simple analysis of the parties and their fate. Usually called the "Dunning interpretation," this view concluded that the Republicans represented the worst elements of society: ignorant blacks, malicious southern whites, and "carpetbaggers"—northerners who had come south to plunder the region. Given power by a radical Republican Congress interested in punishing the South, these people governed with tyranny and corruption. They provoked the hostility of all the better elements of southern society, who eventually rose up and struck down these travesties. The Dunning interpretation was already in trouble by the 1930s as the result of research that showed many of its generalizations not to be true. Still, a new overview taking into account early revisionist work was slow to emerge.[1]

A revisionist synthesis finally challenged the Dunning interpretation in the 1960s. The publication of two major books marked the development of this new analysis: John Hope Franklin's *Reconstruction: After the Civil War* (1961) and Kenneth M. Stampp's *The Era of Reconstruction* (1965).[2] With regard to southern Republicanism, the central revisionist idea was that the coalition of blacks, northern immigrants, and native white "scalawags" that constituted these parties was not one of ignorance, greed, and opportunism, as portrayed by earlier historians. In fact, the new synthesis showed that the Republican governments, although not totally devoid of corruption and bad leadership, did a much better job of dealing with the problems that confronted the southern states after the war than the Dunningites had charged.

Franklin's work, in particular, changed the traditional portrayal of black Republicans. In no state, not even among those with black majorities, he concluded, had there been "Negro rule." Black leaders pursued a remarkably moderate course in their public roles, demonstrating little vindictiveness toward whites. While they sought equal rights, they did not attempt a revolution in the social relations between the races. Nor were they economic radicals, seeking instead to pro-

---

1. For a discussion of the traditional interpretation of Reconstruction and the emergence of revisionist studies see Bernard A. Weisberger, "The Dark and Bloody Ground of Reconstruction Historiography," *Journal of Southern History*, XXV (1959), 427–47; John Hope Franklin, "Whither Reconstruction Historiography?" *Journal of Negro Education*, XVII (1948), 446–61.
2. John Hope Franklin, *Reconstruction: After the Civil War* (Chicago, 1961); Kenneth M. Stampp, *The Era of Reconstruction, 1865–1877* (New York, 1965).

mote stabilization of their communities' economic life. Franklin's characterization of those blacks who managed to secure office paralleled the comments of James G. Blaine: "The colored men who took their seats in both Senate and House did not appear ignorant or helpless. They were as a rule studious, earnest, ambitious men, whose public conduct . . . would be honorable to any race." [3]

The northern men who joined southern Republican parties also were presented in a new light. Franklin placed their coming to the South in the context of the traditional migrations of the American people. Some carpetbaggers may have come south seeking political opportunities, but the majority came immediately following the war to seek business opportunities in a region they perceived as an economic frontier. With a real interest in the economic future of the South, these men had a stake in the region's government. Franklin observed two specific goals common to these northern immigrants. They wanted law and order to protect their investments, and they wanted state and local government allied with the business community. They became Republicans because they believed that party offered the best chance to secure these goals. [4]

As for the final element in the Republican coalition, the southern white scalawags, Franklin concluded that most of these individuals came from that part of the population that had been excluded from the benefits of government in antebellum times. Their principal goal was to build southern society on a broader base than the plantation aristocracy. The scalawags were not radicals, however, especially on measures expanding and sustaining the rights of blacks. Stampp added to this picture the support of prewar Whigs, observing that the scalawags were an "absurd coalition of class-conscious poor whites and yeoman farmers who hated the planters, and class-conscious Whig planters and businessmen who disliked the egalitarian Democrats." [5] Ultimately, as Franklin observed, the scalawags' alliance with blacks and carpetbaggers was simply "expedient." [6]

Once in power, the Republicans drafted policies and carried out

3. Blaine quoted in Franklin, *Reconstruction*, 137–38. See also *ibid.*, 133, 102, 89–92, and Stampp, *Era of Reconstruction*, 167–68.
4. Franklin, *Reconstruction*, 92–96.
5. *Ibid.*, 98–101; Stampp, *Era of Reconstruction*, 165.
6. Franklin, *Reconstruction*, 101.

CARL H. MONEYHON

programs that not only reformed and expanded participation in government in the South, but also increased government's role in the region. Although concluding that the Republican constitutions drafted
in 1868 did not embrace revolutionary doctrines regarding economics
or government, Franklin recognized that they did contain provisions
that were radical in a southern context. These provisions included universal adult male suffrage, free public education, and a variety of social
welfare programs. Republican governments were as moderate as the
constitutional conventions, even if aspects of their programs, particularly efforts at protecting the civil rights of blacks and securing equal
access to public facilities, were at variance with the desires of most
whites in the South. Although the Republican regimes provided some
instances of corruption, the revisionist synthesis concluded that "the
radical governments were by far the most democratic the South had
ever known. They were the only governments in southern history to
extend to Negroes complete civil and political equality, and to try to
protect them in the enjoyment of the rights they were granted." [7]

Revisionism presented a major interpretive problem. If the southern Republicans were not the despicable creatures portrayed in earlier
historical works, historians still had to account for their ultimate, decisive defeats. Here the works of Franklin and Stampp diverged, reflecting the failure of revisionism to produce a consensus on this issue—or, indeed, a conclusive assessment of the significance of the
Republican experience. Both men recognized that a variety of factors
played a part in Republican failure in the South; abandonment by the
northern Republicans, local factionalism, corruption, and racism all
were important. Stampp and Franklin disagreed, however, over the
relative influence of these elements.

Stampp's analysis emphasized the dominant importance of racism
in defeating southern Republicanism. He suggested that racism
worked against these parties in two ways. First, it made impossible the
formation of a class-based party of poor blacks and whites that could
have been the basis for a Republican majority. Stampp observed: "In
the South the fact that the radical governments were committed to
equal civil rights for the two races and were supported by Negro votes
was enough to arouse most white farmers and mechanics to vigorous

7. Ibid., 118, 106–16, 139–51; Stampp, Era of Reconstruction, 184–85.

opposition.... For lower-class whites the most readily available means of achieving personal prestige was a caste system designed to keep the Negro 'in his place' and give them a superior and privileged position as members of the white race." [8]

Given the basic opposition of a majority of whites to Republicanism, the only chance these governments had was to maintain strength by protecting their existing voters and by preventing their opponents from regaining access to the political process. Here, however, by hindering the party's development of programs to achieve either result, racism worked against Republicanism in a second way. In the South itself, scalawags were always reluctant allies with blacks, and disagreements between whites and blacks over policy and office led to significant internal divisions within the Republican party structure. Factionalism, born of these racial suspicions along with other factors, dissipated Republican strength in the face of growing Democratic opposition. At the same time, the Grant administration's abandonment of southern Republicans and blacks, motivated in part by a loss of idealism and by the North's own racist assumptions, deprived the Republican regimes of their last possible source of support. Unable to block the resurgence of a white majority, the southern Republicans collapsed. [9]

Franklin's conclusions varied from Stampp's largely in emphasis. Without denying the importance of racism as a political tool, Franklin saw the roots of failure in the economic and social policies of the reconstructionists. Internal divisions based on factors other than race diverted Republicans from the essential task of party building. The leaders early abandoned real concern for the black voters who gave them power, and turned instead to securing their own personal political ambitions or participating in the politics of economic development. They never produced the changes, particularly redistribution of land, that might have made possible a permanent Republican majority. As a result, constituents—especially blacks—began drifting away from the Republican party even before the Democrats struck violently at the radical governments. "It was the absence of effective machinery for sustaining the political organization and for developing some eco-

8. Stampp, *Era of Reconstruction*, 195–96.
9. *Ibid.*, 192, 205–13.

nomic independence that served to bring about the eventual downfall of the Republican party, and, consequently, of the new governments in the South," wrote Franklin.[10]

By pursuing policies that left economic and social power in the hands of the antebellum southern oligarchy and failed to build alternative bases of power in southern society, the Republicans left their constituents and themselves in the hands of the enemy. Franklin concluded that Reconstruction could have ended even without any violence, since too much power had been left in the hands of the former Confederates, who could use their control over the southern economy to starve both Republican voters and Republican governments. "By political pressure, economic sanctions, *and* violence," he noted, "they brought Radical Reconstruction crashing down almost before it began."[11] Implicit in Franklin's analysis, however, was the idea that it might have been possible to build a successful Republican coalition that would have survived the force of racism.

Franklin's and Stampp's works, focusing on the detrimental impact of factional strife and the effect of party policy on voters, set the agenda for two decades of research and writing on Republican failure. The greater emphasis has been on factionalism, in particular the struggles among party leaders. The literature on this issue has developed along two different lines. One approach has been an assessment of the causes and importance of differences between northern and southern party leaders. The second line of development has been a continuing effort to evaluate the importance of internal differences that beset the local parties. New conclusions have been reached regarding the relationship between the southern and national Republicans, but no universally accepted generalizations have been produced regarding the exact dynamics of local factionalism.

Several studies of northern Republicanism have produced new understanding of the forces that limited northern interest in and concern with the plight of the southern parties. Scholars continue to see such factors as northern racism, a waning of interest in the southern problem, and changing political conditions in the North as components of the decision-making process used by northern leaders. The

10. Franklin, *Reconstruction*, 126.
11. *Ibid.*, 123.

principal recent works, however, have emphasized other factors as being of broader consequence in producing problems for southern Republicanism. In particular, scholars have demonstrated the importance of, first, the leaders' limited view of the central government's role, and second, their inability to develop a clear idea about what a reconstructed South should be like.

Central to the new interpretation of the relationship of northern Republicans to their southern brethren was the work of Michael Les Benedict. His 1974 book, *A Compromise of Principle,* concluded that in implementing Congressional Reconstruction, the Republicans in Congress were limited by a basically conservative view of what they could do in the South. Not racism, then, but a political philosophy that narrowly circumscribed the course of action considered possible produced the rules for Reconstruction that prevented Republican success in the South. Republican policy left conservative or moderate men in charge in the South, encouraged a too-rapid restoration, and ignored basic problems of education and land reform. Benedict wrote of Congress and its plan: "Its radicalism lay in one provision: black suffrage. But by ignoring the other elements of the radical program, Republicans would learn that they had minimized the effectiveness of the one element they had accepted." [12]

Benedict's conclusion regarding the basic structure of congressional policy was pushed further by William Gillette in *Retreat from Reconstruction* (1979), which examined the continued relationship between northern politicians and the South after the readmission of southern states to the Union. While accepting the role of racism in the ultimate retreat from Reconstruction by the North, Gillette also concluded that administrative inefficiency and constitutional conservatism helped to cripple the process. As a result of indecision by the president and Congress, the federal government never formulated a coherent policy of support for the southern Republican regimes and never developed the administrative machinery to produce or enforce such a policy. This problem was exacerbated by a constitutional view that idealized local autonomy and precluded centralizing efforts that might

---

12. Michael Les Benedict, *A Compromise of Principle: Congressional Republicans and Reconstruction, 1863–1869* (New York, 1974), 243; Michael Les Benedict, "Preserving the Constitution: The Conservative Basis of Radical Reconstruction," *Journal of American History,* LXI (1974), 65–90.

have aided the reconstruction process. Congressmen, Gillette concluded, "preferred to write new laws rather than to oversee the proper enforcement of existing laws." [13] Given this context, the changing political climate of the 1870s led northern Republicans to an easy abandonment of their southern colleagues.

Complementing the critical role played by conservative political ideology in undermining southern Republicanism, two recent books have suggested, was the failure of northern Republicans to achieve a consensus as to what they expected from the South. Examining southern Republicans in Congress, Terry Seip discovered that conflicting sectional economic interests often pitted southern Republican against northern. A viable southern party required sectional cooperation, but discord overcame the sources of party unity, and "even open enmity marred their relationship." Seip cited Zachariah Chandler of Michigan, considered a radical Republican, as holding ideas typical of those encountered by the southerners. Chandler fought the southern members of his own party at almost every turn, objecting to the funding of levee construction, blocking appropriations for southern river and harbor improvements, opposing a refund of the cotton tax, and ignoring pleas for campaign funds and speakers. "With such friends," Seip concluded, "it is hardly surprising that southern Republicans experienced difficulties in Congress." [14]

Richard Abbott's investigation of the national Republican party's southern policy showed that the entire northern leadership lacked a clear idea of what to do about the South. Abbott believed that the southern parties' chances were never good, but that they would have been improved if southern Republicans had ever been encouraged or supported by northern party members. He observed that at the heart of northern ambivalence about the South was the fact that national Republican leaders never really believed that it was possible to build a Republican organization in the region. They could not even agree on what groups in the South they might appeal to. As a result, they proved unwilling to give to the southern parties anything that might alienate their own northern constituencies or restrict their ability to manipulate northern voters. National policies designed to influence the north-

13. William Gillette, *Retreat from Reconstruction, 1869–1879* (Baton Rouge, 1979), 363–80.
14. Terry L. Seip, *The South Returns to Congress: Men, Economic Measures, and Intersectional Relationships, 1868–1879* (Baton Rouge, 1983), 6, 278.

ern electorate—for example, the use of bloody-shirt propaganda—continued to be applied even though they alienated potential white voters in the South. Northern leaders failed to give positive incentives to white southerners to support the local parties, and they did nothing to help maintain black voting strength. Their actions turned the limited chances for Republican success into no chance.[15]

One effect of scholarship in this vein has been to focus attention more directly on the southern state parties in efforts to explain party weaknesses. Success by southern Republican parties had to be achieved locally, and if in fact there was a chance for success, the sources of failure have to be discovered locally. There was no possibility that the national party would back long-range intervention in the South by the national government. After assuring black voter participation, national leaders were paralyzed by their basic political philosophy and their own lack of agreement on policy.

Scholars examining the dynamics of Republican politics at the state level all have concluded that factional struggles were an integral part of the life of these parties. By fighting with each other, Republican leaders divided their forces in the face of strong and hostile enemies and appeared to deprive their parties of all ability to act decisively. Most work on this subject has attempted to explain why party leaders would engage in such obviously suicidal behavior. A variety of factors has been suggested: racism, carpetbagger-scalawag rivalries, regional political struggles, alternative political strategies, and class conflicts. Scholars largely agree as to the destructive influence of factionalism, but there is little agreement on which particular forces prompted the struggles that even contemporary party leaders concluded undermined their power.

Two characteristics of the studies of local Republicanism appear to have limited historians' efforts to produce a general explanation of why factionalism persisted and how it contributed to the failure of the local parties. The first has been the general trend in Reconstruction literature to carry out what Howard Rabinowitz, analyzing the development of black political history during Reconstruction, has called "rehabilitation" history. Rather than explaining southern politics, historians have spent much of their time disproving the traditional characterizations of the groups constituting the southern Republican party.

15. Richard H. Abbott, *The Republican Party and the South, 1855–1877: The First Southern Strategy* (Chapel Hill, 1986), 238–43.

This focus has reinforced the basic revisionist assessment but has not contributed to a more systematic analysis of the central problem presented by the history of these parties—their failure.[16]

The second limitation on such analysis has been an emphasis on the particular rather than the general as historians have tried to explain the politics of the ten different states that underwent Congressional Reconstruction. As Otto Olsen pointed out in a 1980 essay, "Variations in the history of each state have always served to hinder an effective general synthesis."[17] Each state had its own unique economy, society, and political history. The relative strengths of the black, scalawag, and carpetbagger elements of the party varied in each state. Biographical studies and analyses of specific components of the party coalition have added to this particularist fragmentation.

Nonetheless, the work done on factionalism has produced a great broadening of knowledge about the kinds of issues that provoked dissent among Republican supporters and helped produce ultimate failure. The importance of racism, both in terms of provoking general opposition to the Republican regimes and in producing internal dissent, has been recognized by all who have written on southern Republicanism, and particularly emphasized by some. In one of the earliest state studies completed after the appearance of the revisionist synthesis, Alan Conway suggested that in Georgia not even radical white Republicans believed in the right of blacks to participate in politics, even though that very right was essential to Republican victory. Reluctant to force blacks as political equals upon the white South, white Republicans refused to take even the steps essential for survival.[18] Based on her investigation of Alabama scalawags, Sarah Woolfolk Wiggins suggested that in that state, racism restricted the development of party policy because state party leaders found it impossible to satisfy their black constituents without alienating whites, who were unwilling to see full equality granted. Jerrell H. Shofner's works on Florida also have emphasized the role of race. The importance of racism as a destructive force has been emphasized particularly in studies of Louisi-

16. Howard N. Rabinowitz, ed., *Southern Black Leaders of the Reconstruction Era* (Urbana, Ill., 1982), xvii. In this essay I focus on those works that address the problem of Republican failure most directly; consequently, I do not cite numerous otherwise excellent studies that have expanded our knowledge of blacks, scalawags, carpetbaggers, and individual Republican leaders.

17. Otto H. Olsen, ed., *Reconstruction and Redemption in the South: An Assessment* (Baton Rouge, 1980), 2.

18. Alan Conway, *The Reconstruction of Georgia* (Minneapolis, 1966), 225.

ana politics. Charles Vincent's work on black legislators concluded that they could not surmount the barrier of white racism either in the general population or among their Republican allies, who deserted them on all efforts to secure fundamental reforms. Ted Tunnell's study of Louisiana Reconstruction showed that in the face of White League attacks, the state's Republican leadership proved incapable of protecting the state's majority of black voters and refused to take steps that would have kept blacks united and in the party. Most white Republicans were never comfortable in the party, and in the face of Conservative assaults they "often acted as if they preferred a White League victory to the consequences of successful black resistance." [19]

The emphasis upon racism as the principal factor producing party lethargy has been integrated into many general studies on Reconstruction. Typically, in his recent investigation of Reconstruction violence, George Rable concluded that racial differences proved critical in promoting internal divisions that sapped party strength and prevented its resistance to violence. Basically, whites—especially scalawags—were never willing to concede full black political equality; thus, they opened themselves up to disputes with black leaders and white leaders willing to expand black rights. Possibly more important in producing political failure was the fact that the race issue prevented any real success in attracting enough white voters to make the party genuinely biracial and a viable contender for office.[20]

The racial hypothesis has not completely carried the field, however. All scholars have recognized the importance of racism, but many have emphasized other divisive forces as having even greater impact. Several studies have suggested the importance of divisions between

---

19. Sarah Woolfolk Wiggins, *The Scalawag in Alabama Politics, 1865–1881* (University, Ala., 1977), 125; Sarah Woolfolk Wiggins, "Democratic Bulldozing and Republican Folly," in *Reconstruction and Redemption,* ed. Olsen, 73; Jerrell H. Shofner, "A Failure of Moderate Republicanism," in *Reconstruction and Redemption,* ed. Olsen, 19–20, 43; Joe Gray Taylor, "Louisiana: An Impossible Task," in *Reconstruction and Redemption,* ed. Olsen, 202–36; Ted Tunnell, *Crucible of Reconstruction: War, Radicalism, and Race in Louisiana, 1862–1877* (Baton Rouge, 1984), 218. See also Joe M. Richardson, *The Negro in the Reconstruction of Florida, 1865–1877* (Tallahassee, 1965); Charles Vincent, *Black Legislators in Louisiana During Reconstruction* (Baton Rouge, 1976); Merline Pitre, *Through Many Dangers, Toils, and Snares: The Black Leadership of Texas, 1868–1900* (Austin, 1985), 199–203.

20. George C. Rable, *But There Was No Peace: The Role of Violence in the Politics of Reconstruction* (Athens, Ga., 1984), 102–103. For a discussion of the pervasiveness of this thesis, see J. Mills Thornton III, "Fiscal Policy and the Failure of Radical Reconstruction in the Lower South," in *Region, Race, and Reconstruction: Essays in Honor of C. Vann Woodward,* ed. J. Morgan Kousser and James M. McPherson (New York, 1982), 391 n. 2. For examples of this idea in general Reconstruction studies, see Rembert W. Patrick, *The Reconstruction of the Nation* (New York, 1967), 149–62, and Allen W. Trelease, *Reconstruction: The Great Experiment* (New York, 1971), 148–49.

CARL H. MONEYHON

outside and native whites—carpetbaggers and scalawags. Works by Richard Current, Jack Scroggs, and William C. Harris typify this view. Implicitly or explicitly, these studies conclude that carpetbaggers generally were willing to concede more to blacks, and were also more progressive, than their native white colleagues. This put them into conflict with southern white Republicans who attempted to minimize the changes in southern society, especially changes in race relations. The conflict involved racial views, but race was only one component of the broad ideological differences that separated the two sides. Concerning Mississippi carpetbaggers, for example, Harris wrote that they possessed the "intense Republican idealism that swept the North during the Civil War era."[21]

Seeking to create a general view of carpetbaggers, Richard Hume and Peter Kolchin both have written group biographies in an effort to overcome the limitations of studies devoted to individuals or narrow groups. Their conclusions, however, have been the same as those reached by the earlier scholars. Hume's study of 159 carpetbagger delegates to the "Black and Tan" conventions of the South concluded that the generalizations provided by Current and Harris, although based on smaller samples, were essentially true. In a more direct comparison of the careers of scalawags and carpetbaggers in Congress, Peter Kolchin suggested that carpetbaggers were the driving elements within the Reconstruction governments and possessed a political philosophy advocating a more positive role for government in areas ranging from economics to race. This philosophy provoked a competition with scalawags, who seldom were committed to Republicanism or radicalism as understood by carpetbaggers and blacks, being unwilling to carry out even the policies essential for Republican success. Scalawag leadership, according to Kolchin, was a clear sign of Republican disintegration.[22]

21. William C. Harris, "The Creed of the Carpetbaggers: The Case of Mississippi," *Journal of Southern History*, XL (1974), 202; Jack B. Scroggs, "Carpetbagger Constitutional Reform in the South Atlantic States, 1867–1868," *Journal of Southern History*, XXVII (1961), 475–93; Richard N. Current, "Carpetbaggers Reconsidered," in *Festschrift for Frederick B. Artz*, ed. David H. Pinkney and Theodore Ropp (Durham, N.C., 1964), 139–57; Richard N. Current, *Three Carpetbag Governors* (Baton Rouge, 1967), 25, 54–55, 97.
22. Richard L. Hume, "Carpetbaggers in the Reconstruction South: A Group Portrait of Outside Whites in the 'Black and Tan' Constitutional Conventions," *Journal of American History*, LXIV (1977), 330; Peter Kolchin, "Scalawags, Carpetbaggers, and Reconstruction: A Quantitative Look at Southern Congressional Politics, 1868–1872," *Journal of Southern History*, XLV (1979), 75, 76.

This interpretation has found an important advocate in Carl Degler, who in *The Other South* concluded that although party failure derived from many sources, including the hostility of white southerners to the political equality of blacks and the northern refusal to protect black political rights, the carpetbagger-scalawag split played a major role in dooming Republicanism to minority status. Although neither group was ready for full acceptance of black equality, the place of blacks in society was at the heart of the differences between them: northern whites were willing to define more equitably the place of blacks in southern society.[23]

More recently, however, another explanation of the carpetbagger-scalawag split has been developed by Lawrence Powell. In his examination of Deep South carpetbaggers, Powell argued that most northerners became involved in politics not because of their feelings of public altruism and patriotic duty, but because they were in economic trouble by 1867, and Congressional Reconstruction opened up employment opportunities for them. In effect, their very livelihood depended on their control over the machinery of politics; consequently, their willingness to open opportunities for southern white Republicans to displace them was limited. Economic necessity, not ideology, thus gave the factional quarrels between outside and native white Republicans an uncompromising quality and helped thwart the cooperation essential for the party to expand or even to hold its own against resurgent Conservatives.[24]

Another explanation of the intense internal struggles among Republicans has emphasized regional rivalries among whites. Allen Trelease suggested in his work on southern scalawags that most native white Republicans came from the hill country of the South, and that for them affiliation with the Republican party was a continuation of prewar political conflicts, as reflected in their support of reform legislation of an egalitarian character and programs of economic development. This did not mean that they consistently supported all Republican policies, particularly when it came to radical racial policies. They were willing to work with blacks, but unwilling to go further than

23. Carl N. Degler, *The Other South: Southern Dissenters in the Nineteenth Century* (New York, 1974), 256–63.

24. Lawrence N. Powell, "The Politics of Livelihood: Carpetbaggers in the Deep South," in *Region, Race, and Reconstruction*, ed. Kousser and McPherson, 318–19.

necessary in recognizing black rights. This recalcitrance promoted friction between them and blacks, as well as with the white proponents of black rights.[25]

In my study of Texas Republicanism, I offered another variation on the regional-conflict idea. Disputes among regionally based white party leaders produced constant internal party turmoil. What sustained this conflict was the refusal of all of these white leaders to accept full political equality for blacks. Thus, groups out of power could always attempt to gain control of the party by offering more to blacks than the dominant faction did. As long as white leaders failed to deal with blacks equitably, they could not count on black votes, and this insured that no one group could maintain control over the party, since there was always the possibility of undercutting black support. This struggle, which took place between scalawag groups, produced a slow but steady expansion of the place white leaders were willing to accept for blacks in society and in politics, but it also undermined their efforts to attract white voters who had not been so radicalized.[26]

Class divisions also have been seen as critical to the production of party strife. Generally, the studies that emphasize class divisions have begun with the idea that a coalition of lower-class whites and blacks was possible after 1867 and have questioned why Republican leaders failed to make an appeal aimed at creating this coalition. The general conclusion has been that the masses were betrayed by their leaders. In his 1966 article on North Carolina scalawags, Otto Olsen observed that the differences between the poor or yeoman farmers who provided the backbone of white Republican voting strength and the former Whigs and merchants who assumed leadership roles in the local parties prevented the party from pursuing programs that would have consolidated the Republican position. Party leaders were moderates who were unwilling (or unable) to pursue the radical, reformist stand that was their only chance of success. Olsen believed that it might have been possible to create a program to retain the masses of white voters, perhaps anticipating the methods and goals of the Populists, but the orthodoxy and business orientation of party leadership prevented that. Although less precise about the reasons why Georgia Republican

25. Allen W. Trelease, "Who Were the Scalawags?" *Journal of Southern History,* XXIX (1963), 467–68.
26. Carl H. Moneyhon, *Republicanism in Reconstruction Texas* (Austin, 1980), 196.

leaders failed to work early to build a class-based coalition, Elizabeth S. Nathans concluded in a 1969 study that such a coalition was initially the only chance for success. State leaders ultimately took that path, but by the time they did, it was too late.[27]

Several recent works on black Republican leaders have uncovered the same moderate or conservative bent among them and support a class analysis. Thomas Holt's study of black leaders in South Carolina described these men as "bourgeois" in their origins and ideology. Like Olsen's North Carolina scalawags, they pursued policies that were not in the interests of the majority of their constituents. Edmund L. Drago, examining black politicians in Georgia, observed a similar conservatism, although he attributed it to the domination of black politics by preachers whose ideological roots in the ideals of Christian mercy caused them to back away from legislation that would have protected themselves and their constituents. August Meier, in summing up the findings of a collection of essays on black politicians and politics throughout the South, concluded that across the region, the typical black political leader was a moderate. Meier went even further to suggest a potentially useful generalization that could be the basis for understanding all Republican political activity: that the American political system itself, requiring politicians to emerge out of a milieu of personal, class, and race conflicts, made the rise of moderate individuals inevitable and the survival of radicals unlikely.[28]

Drawing particularly on the works of Olsen, Nathans, and Holt, among those of other revisionists, Armstead L. Robinson in a 1981 essay examined the whole South and attempted to assess the entire Reconstruction experience within the context of class conflict. Although arguing against simple reductionism, Robinson found that class, obviously apparent in party rhetoric, was more important than race in determining the splits that destroyed Republicanism. Class not only separated the yeomen from the white elites, but also produced divisions among black leaders. Robinson concluded: "It seems clear

27. Otto H. Olsen, "Reconsidering the Scalawags," *Civil War History,* XII (1966), 318; Elizabeth Studley Nathans, *Losing the Peace: Georgia Republicans and Reconstruction, 1865–1871* (Baton Rouge, 1969), 225.
28. Thomas Holt, *Black over White: Negro Political Leadership in South Carolina During Reconstruction* (Urbana, Ill., 1977), 3–4; Edmund L. Drago, *Black Politicians and Reconstruction in Georgia: A Splendid Failure* (Baton Rouge, 1982), 161–62; August Meier, "Afterword: New Perspectives on the Nature of Black Political Leadership During Reconstruction," in *Southern Black Leaders,* ed. Rabinowitz, 402.

that class tensions were the fundamental impediment to the success of southern Republicanism." [29]

Michael Perman developed an explanation of Republican failure centered on the party leadership's view of politics. Perman assumed that the only chance for Republican success was a class appeal that failed to materialize, and his work focused on why Republican leaders refused to pursue this appeal. He concluded that party leadership was divided into two groups, regulars and centrists. The regulars derived their influence from black voters and had little interest in developing a rival power base among poor or disadvantaged whites. Centrists saw the party's future in attracting old Whigs or Unionists, but the centrist leaders pursued political power along historic and conservative lines; that is, they perceived politics as coalitions of individuals rather than coalitions of interests. Thus, they tried to bring individual politicians into the party in order to attract more voters. They ignored grass-roots electoral mobilization and made few mass appeals. This elitist approach to politics was fatally flawed. It failed to bring in the kind of voters that the party had to have. It also challenged the Democratic-Conservatives on precisely the terrain where they possessed the greatest advantage. [30]

Historians' inability to produce general conclusions about Republican factionalism has helped produce alternative approaches to the problem. Recent literature, sometimes called "postrevisionism," has produced a different explanation of Republican failure. Like the Dunning interpretation, but also similar to Franklin's emphasis on party machinery and programs, this new view examines Republican programs and their impact and reaches negative conclusions without attacking the motives and abilities of the Republican leaders. According to this model, the real failure by the southern Republicans was their inability to produce a program that could overwhelm the negative influences working against it. Such a program might have been developed, and it would not have had to rest on an appeal to class. The reasons that no such program was put in place have to do in many ways with bad choices and bad luck rather than factional divisions.

---

29. Armstead L. Robinson, "Beyond the Realm of Social Consensus: New Meanings of Reconstruction for American History," *Journal of American History*, LXVIII (1981), 276–97.
30. Michael Perman, *The Road to Redemption: Southern Politics, 1869–1879* (Chapel Hill, 1984), 106–107.

Scholars holding this view have suggested that Republican leaders became victims of uncontrollable forces, primarily an economic collapse that destroyed economic opportunity and the tax base in the South. The leaders pinned their hopes on programs of economic development that, had they worked, might have benefited all southerners. Unfortunately for the South, they did not work. Republican leaders tragically misassessed the impact on their constituencies of their programs, particularly those involving fiscal policy and railroad development. The implications of this failure for the party's effort to create a biracial coalition were severe. Implementing programs that overlooked or actually harmed the interests of the white as well as the black lower classes, the Republicans drove away potential voters.

One of the earliest books that advanced this interpretation was William C. Harris' work on Mississippi. Harris concluded that the roots of Republican failure must be seen in Republican fiscal policy. The Mississippi Republicans, he indicated, gravely misunderstood the financial situation and prospects of postwar Mississippi. As a result, they placed excessive demands upon the tax resources of the state, hoping for a restoration of the economy that never came. Their policies were poorly conceived and badly carried out. The Republicans failed to distribute taxes equitably, refused to go beyond the property tax, could not efficiently collect revenues, could not control peculation, and in the end resorted to a disastrous issuance of warrants to fund operations. "Perhaps more than any other reason," wrote Harris, "including the endemic race issue and the emotionalism generated by Reconstruction politics, the problem of finance proved the undoing of the Republican dream."[31]

Mills Thornton, in an essay on Republican fiscal policy in the Deep South states, carried this idea further with his argument that Republican fiscal policy actually may have driven the much-sought-after white yeomanry away from the Republican party. Comparing Reconstruction taxes with antebellum taxes, Thornton showed that the shift of the tax burden from personal to real property placed a particular burden on small landholders, to the extent that in Alabama and Mississippi small farmers were paying 2 to 4 percent of their total cash

31. William C. Harris, *The Day of the Carpetbagger: Republican Reconstruction in Mississippi* (Baton Rouge, 1979), 333, 352. See also William C. Harris, "Republican Factionalism and Mismanagement," in *Reconstruction and Redemption*, ed. Olsen, 78–112.

income, and from 8 to 10 percent of their discretionary income, in taxes. These taxes might have been borne had the taxpayers seen any resulting increase in state services, but Thornton concluded that there was none. Examining disbursements for education, Thornton found an actual reduction of per capita expenditures on the schoolchildren in all states except Florida. Although not denying the existence of racism, Thornton suggested that the nature of the tax situation offered a "persuasive" alternative explanation to the failure of the Republican governments.[32]

Mark Summers' examination of Republican efforts at railroad development presented an equally damaging account of the effectiveness and impact of the party's policies. Republicans had tied their aim of creating a majority party to the construction of railroads that would produce economic prosperity for all. In the end, the South had railroads but no railroad system, and the laws that shaped construction produced inefficiency and outright corruption, preventing the roads from creating the hoped-for prosperity. Rather than making the Republicans the economic saviors of the South, the railroads helped to bring down the party. Summers concluded: "If failure of Republican railway programs did not wreck them politically, it certainly contributed to their ruin, gave respectable Conservatives a powerful issue complementing that of race, and aggravated the divisions already present in the Republican ranks. Railroad aid, then, neither gave birth to Republicanism nor wrecked it, but made its passage into power easier, its factionalism more bitter, and its downfall more devastating than it might otherwise have been." [33]

The shift of focus apparent in these analyses of Republican programs adds a new dimension to the picture of the forces at work in the southern Republican experience, but as in the studies of factionalism, the new approach does not produce completely satisfactory results. It shows more clearly what the Republican policies were and what impact they had on the community. Obviously, the majority of voters rejected those policies and the party itself. What remains unclear, however, is whether the voters were in fact influenced by the inadequacy of Republican programs any more than by racism or other factors.

32. Thornton, "Fiscal Policy and the Failure of Reconstruction," 381, 371.
33. Mark W. Summers, *Railroads, Reconstruction, and the Gospel of Prosperity: Aid Under the Radical Republicans, 1865–1877* (Princeton, N.J., 1984), x–xi, 299–301.

I suggest that in addition to its "rehabilitation" focus and its particularism, recent work faces a third barrier to its ability to reach a broader view of the history of southern Republicanism. That barrier is the failure to identify clearly the concerns and interests of the mass of white and black voters within which the parties operated. The studies discussed here have been views from the top down, usually making broad assumptions about the motivations of individual voters—assumptions that then inform conclusions about the cause or causes of Republican failure. In fact relatively little is known about the nature of the general electorate, and almost nothing is known about the real and potential Republican voters. Until there is a better understanding of these people, conclusions concerning what flaws within the Republican parties produced failure will remain highly speculative.

There is no easy way to discover what was taking place among the political masses. Traditional sources, ranging from public documents to correspondence, have been used generally to understand the ideas of leaders. Statistical analyses of voting patterns are limited by the nature of the data, which usually prove intractable to disaggregation below the county level; as Allen Trelease pointed out twenty-five years ago, such information can reveal areas of Republican voting strength, but not who voted Republican.[34] Yet a look at the southern voter is essential to a proper assessment of the results of Reconstruction.

One way of developing a clearer idea of the interests and concerns of the individual voter is to look more closely at local politics. My own research on local party leaders in Arkansas suggests the potential of such an approach. An analysis of Republicans who gained local political office showed how these individuals were tied much more closely to the local communities than those who achieved state or federal offices. Whereas a good many carpetbaggers rose to state power, scalawags dominated the local level, especially in 1868. A comparison of the lowland counties of the southeastern half of the state with the highland counties, traditionally considered bastions of white Republican strength, showed that 87 percent of office holders were local whites in the southeast, compared with 90 percent elsewhere. This evidence suggests support for the party throughout the state. It also suggests men rooted in the community, who perhaps better reflected the ideas that

34. Trelease, "Who Were the Scalawags?" 467.

attracted southern whites to Republicanism than did officeholders at the state level.[35]

The property and wealth of these individuals, compared with that of prewar officeholders, suggested that they represented a new class that had come to power. They were farmers, for the most part, but with little property. Their speeches and the few letters that they wrote indicated the change even further. These men considered themselves the backbone of the state, but crushed by the old political and social elites. One criticized the "gentlemen" who had sent the farmer and mechanic to war, "leaving their farms uncultivated; their graneries exhausted; their wives and daughters forced to transfer their energies from the house to the field ... while these gentlemen were at home wallowing in their riches."[36] The new men were ready for a radical change that would bring down the old elite through taxes and other policies.

If these men do represent the potential strength of Arkansas Republicanism among whites, the implications for interpreting the failure of Republicanism in the state are clear. Although they may have been racists (that is not clear), local whites were willing to cooperate in a biracial coalition to obtain their goals; thus, racism per se should not have defeated their efforts. What is particularly apparent is that the state Republican party never produced a program that offered them the radical changes they sought. The state leaders failed to offer what their constituents wanted, although it is unclear whether this was because, as Franklin suggested, they turned to the fulfillment of personal political ambitions or economic development, or because they represented a moderate, bourgeois class. Whatever motivated the leadership, actual and potential constituents quickly drifted away.

Analysis of local political leaders and politics represents just one possible approach to discovering the roots of southern Republicanism. There are obvious problems with it. The relative lack of local black politicians in Arkansas, for example, frustrates efforts at getting deeper into the views of black voters. It is impossible, perhaps, to prove that local Arkansas Republican politicians, few if any of whom were black, were actually representative of potential groups of voters.

35. These results originally were reported in a paper entitled "Republican Reconstruction at the County Level: Arkansas as a Case Study," delivered at the annual meeting of the Southern Historical Association, New Orleans, November, 1987.
36. Little Rock *Republican*, February 2, 1868.

Despite such difficulties, analysis of the southern electorate is critical, whatever means is used to do it. If one can understand whom the Republicans could have appealed to, then it will be possible to evaluate the forces that brought about the rejection of Republican ideas and programs.

Possibly the Republican effort never had a chance to survive in a racist white society. Perhaps it had the potential of being a successful class-based party but could not transcend the moderation of its leadership. For whatever reason, except in a few areas of the South, it did not secure the support essential for survival. In order to understand that failure, however, scholars must move beyond a political analysis of leaders and policies alone, and place political activity in a thoroughly researched social and economic context. Only then might they resolve the revisionist and postrevisionist dilemma of causation.

6

Counter Reconstruction
The Role of Violence in
Southern Redemption

∾ MICHAEL PERMAN

The erosion and eventual overthrow of Reconstruction in the South was accomplished, to a considerable extent, by violence and intimidation. Few historians would disagree with this assertion, yet because these kinds of activities were often sporadic, localized, and anonymous, it has been difficult to describe and quantify them, let alone calculate precisely how much they contributed to the downfall of the Reconstruction governments themselves. As a result, the significance of violence during Reconstruction has been as shadowy as the acts themselves.

John Hope Franklin's *Reconstruction: After the Civil War* was one of the first studies of the Reconstruction era to be quite categorical about the importance of violence. The chapter that examined the nature and the methods of the opposition to Reconstruction was called "Counter Reconstruction," and it was devoted entirely to violence and the Ku Klux Klan. Arguing that violence long had been endemic in southern whites' responses to any threat to their institutions and way of life—threats, for example, in the form of abolitionism or slave revolts—Franklin wrote that "it was only natural" that violence also would be "a prime factor in any move to oppose the [postwar] order administered by those whom the former Confederates regarded as natural enemies."[1] Indeed, violence and force were at the heart of the counterattack on Reconstruction. Not merely accessories or incidentals, they were its essence. And the Klan was the organizational form

1. John Hope Franklin, *Reconstruction: After the Civil War* (Chicago, 1961), 153.

that the counterattack assumed. Although Klan organizations had emerged soon after the war as a means of frightening blacks back into line, Franklin argued that it was the onset of Reconstruction, and with it "the apparent determination of Negroes and their Radical [Republican] friends to assume and wield political power," that caused the proliferation of the Klan and gave it "respectability and a dignity that it had not anticipated." Therefore, in Franklin's view, the objectives of the Klan were political. Accordingly, he could assert rather conclusively that when the Republican party began to lose control in the early 1870s, "counter reconstruction was everywhere an overwhelming success."[2] The violence against the Republicans' supporters and officials had made it impossible for the party to maintain its hold on power in the South. Moreover, even the attempts by the federal government in 1871 to suppress the Klan had failed to secure many convictions and had simply caused the organization to go underground. Thus, the violence could not be eliminated or its perpetrators punished.

The interpretation of the defeat of Reconstruction that was offered in *Reconstruction: After the Civil War* focused more on the role of organized violence than did any study that had been presented before. Even more significant, it asserted that the violence had been successful. In Franklin's opinion, therefore, Reconstruction had been overthrown by an effective campaign of racially and politically motivated terror. Although at the very end of the chapter, the author added a caveat or two suggesting that "the former Confederates relied on no one method" but employed "political pressure, economic sanctions, *and* violence," his devotion of virtually the entire chapter to organized violence left the reader with the inescapable impression that other tactics were of less significance.[3]

Prior to the publication in 1961 of Franklin's revisionist interpretation, the role of the Klan and violence in the postwar South had been

---

2. *Ibid.*, 156, 172.

3. The relative significance and impact of the violence is, in Franklin's treatment, ultimately rather unclear. The remark quoted here suggests that violence was not, among many tactics, the single most important one. Furthermore, it is not clear whether the actions of the opposition to Reconstruction within the South were of greater consequence than developments outside the region. After concluding that the violent counterreconstruction was "everywhere an overwhelming success," the author observes (p. 176) that "it is now clear that Reconstruction could have been overthrown even without the use of violence." He mentions lack of support in the North for Reconstruction as the alternative cause he has in mind. Indeed, chapter 10 examines this subject in some detail. Obviously, many factors contributed to the downfall of Reconstruction; the question is the relative weight that should be given to each—and this is left imprecise.

treated rather differently. Historians of the Dunning (or "New South") school acknowledged the widespread existence of the Klan but argued that it had arisen for defensive and quite understandable reasons, and not as part of a politically inspired campaign to subvert the Republican party. As William A. Dunning himself put it in *Reconstruction, Political and Economic* (1907), "the Ku-Klux movement was in large measure but the unorganized and sporadic expression of social demoralization" and "was ridiculously remote from any purpose that could be fairly called 'rebellion' against the United States."[4]

Yet Dunning's stance toward the Klan was really quite ambivalent. On the one hand, he was prepared to characterize the organization's mode of operation as "manifest and merciless" and little short of "terrorism"; on the other, he was remarkably hesitant about providing details of its activities, resorting instead to innocuous and vague phrases about "proceedings" and "familiar methods," or about "means that were of but slight consequence compared to the end" in the view of their users. Dunning's ambivalence was also evident in his claim that there was a divergence between the leadership and the rank and file over methods, the former wanting to apply "moral suasion" and the latter physical force. This contrast within the organization was further developed in Dunning's assertion that the Klan had been initiated by "the less sober and substantial class of whites" but later, once the Reconstruction governments had been established in 1868, had come under the control of those who were "serious and respectable."[5] All of this suggests that Dunning either could not make up his mind about the real nature of the Klan or wanted to keep its personnel and its actions ambiguous.

A far less equivocal approach was taken by two of the best-known historians of the Dunning school—James W. Garner in his study *Reconstruction in Mississippi* (1901), and Walter Lynwood Fleming in *Civil War and Reconstruction in Alabama* (1905). Unlike Dunning, they each devoted an entire chapter to the Klan and dwelt in great detail on the secret rituals of the organization and the violent deeds of its members. There was no attempt to mitigate the activities of the Klan. Indeed, far from expressing outrage, both historians argued that there was sufficient provocation to justify the Klan as an understand-

4. William A. Dunning, *Reconstruction, Political and Economic, 1865–1877* (New York, 1907), 187–89.
5. *Ibid.*, 187, 122–23.

able response. As Garner saw it, a policy by which "political power in the South was transferred from the hitherto dominant class to a race emerging from slavery" was not only "one of the most dangerous experiments ever undertaken," but "no intelligent man [could] for a moment expect" that it could be "carried through, unattended by social and political disorders."[6] Furthermore, the form that the resistance took was not as extreme as it might have been. Starting out as a counter to the Union League and a successor to the antebellum slave patrol, the Klan had been intended "simply to scare the superstitious blacks into good behavior and obedience." Only later had it fallen into the hands of less respectable men who were prepared to engage in violent acts—an interesting reversal of the sequence suggested by Dunning. Even at that, Garner maintained that there had never been "armed and organized resistance" aimed at overthrowing Reconstruction; the Klan had engaged merely in "secret retaliation upon its agents, and especially favored beneficiaries, regardless of race, color, or nativity."[7]

A similar source of provocation was cited by Fleming, but he gave the resultant organization a clearly racial objective. The Klan, he said, represented "an understanding among southern whites, brought about by the chaotic condition of social and political institutions between 1865 and 1876." Its purpose was "to recover for the white race control of society and destroy the baleful influence of the alien among the blacks."[8]

Such differences of emphasis aside, the Dunning school's pro-southern interpretation of the period never lavished on the Klan the praise and honor that were soon to become widespread elsewhere in American culture: as a result of Thomas Dixon's novel *The Clansman*, with its subsequent adaptation for the cinema in D. W. Griffith's 1915 epic, *The Birth of a Nation*, the Klan began to be hailed as the heroic and essential agency of southern deliverance from the scourge of Reconstruction. The more cautious and scholarly Dunningite version was also a good deal less eulogistic than Stanley Horn's treatment of the Klan in *Invisible Empire* (1939). Applauding the organization for

6. James W. Garner, *Reconstruction in Mississippi* (New York, 1901), 353.
7. *Ibid.,* 338–39, 353.
8. Walter L. Fleming, *Civil War and Reconstruction in Alabama* (New York, 1905), 653.

its "heroic illegal methods," Horn extolled it in chivalric terms as "clad in shining armor, *sans peur et sans reproche.*"[9]

While this extreme view of the Klan was becoming widely accepted, a direct counter to it was launched by Francis B. Simkins. Alarmed at the enthusiasm and respect being accorded the Reconstruction-era Klan, and concerned about the emergence in the 1920s of a new, although organizationally unrelated, Klan in the North as well as the South, Simkins sought to demythologize the earlier Klan and show how limited in fact had been its impact and significance. In a 1927 article on the Klan in South Carolina, he aimed "to prove how truly indefinite and undramatic, and even unimportant" the organization had been.[10]

In this article and in his 1932 book on South Carolina during Reconstruction (coauthored with Robert H. Woody), Simkins claimed that until 1871 the Klan had been quite marginal. The violence that had occurred before then was not its responsibility and had not even been inflicted by men in disguises, the hallmark of the Klan. After the opposition to the new Reconstruction government failed to carry the state election in 1870, however, the organization began to become a force. Even then, it was confined essentially to three up-country counties: York, Spartanburg, and Union. Furthermore, it was not centrally organized, and its membership was "for the most part, composed of low-type men," thereby making it unworthy of serious consideration. Finally, the Klan did not emerge as a justifiable, reasonable response to bad government and black lawlessness, as the Dunning school and others had claimed. Instead, it was intended to counter the assertiveness of blacks in voting and in organizing in militias and Union League chapters; its ultimate aim was to force blacks into "a position of political impotence and social subordination similar to that which the race had occupied previous to Reconstruction."[11] According to Simkins, the Klan succeeded in this only "in the limited area in which it operated," although this area might have been more extensive if the federal government had not intervened at the end of 1871. Thus, the Klan

9. Stanley Horn, *Invisible Empire: The Story of the Ku Klux Klan, 1866–1871* (Boston, 1939), 376–77.

10. Francis B. Simkins, "The Ku Klux Klan in South Carolina, 1868–1871," *Journal of Negro History,* XII (1927), 606.

11. Francis B. Simkins and Robert H. Woody, *South Carolina During Reconstruction* (Chapel Hill, 1932), 460–61.

experience may have "reaffirmed [whites'] belief that when force was resorted to, the freedman was no match for the former master." Nevertheless, the organization had failed, for it had been unable "to overthrow the reconstruction state government." [12]

The only deviation from this pattern of scholarly interpretations that either downplayed or excused the Klan was W. E. B. Du Bois's discussion of the role of violence in "Back Toward Slavery," the penultimate chapter of his *Black Reconstruction in America* (1935). For Du Bois, lawlessness and violence were at the heart of the effort to defeat Reconstruction. In fact, Reconstruction was overthrown as a result of "a civil war in the South" that was intended to "reduce black labor as nearly as possible to a condition of unlimited exploitation and build a new class of capitalists on this foundation." Although "spasmodic and episodic" from 1865 to 1868, the lawlessness became organized thereafter as the planters utilized fear and terror "to deprive the Negroes, by force, of any real weapon for economic bargaining." Moreover, through the employment of "the shibboleth of race," they "frustrated any mass movement toward union of white and black labor." [13] These were the primary means whereby what Du Bois called "the counter-revolution of property" was accomplished.

Seen in this perspective, violence was not provoked but was an instrument consciously employed by the property-holding elite—which was undergoing major upheaval and reorganization within its own ranks—in order to beat back and dominate labor. Franklin may not have shared Du Bois's assessment of the forces behind the violence, but he certainly concurred in Du Bois's estimation not only of the centrality but also of the success of that violence. Indeed, his chapter title "Counter Reconstruction" bears some similarity to Du Bois's chapter title "Counter-Revolution of Property."

In the 1950s and 1960s, the strength of southern resistance to desegregation gave credence to the approach taken by Du Bois and Franklin. This resistance also gave rise to several studies that stressed the importance of its Reconstruction counterpart. Herbert Shapiro's 1964 article on the Klan in South Carolina was an avowed refutation of Simkins' earlier minimalization of the Klan's impact. Shapiro ar-

12. Simkins, "Ku Klux Klan in South Carolina," 637, 647.
13. W. E. Burghardt Du Bois, *Black Reconstruction: An Essay Toward a History of the Part Which Black Folk Played in the Attempt to Reconstruct Democracy in America, 1860–1880* (New York, 1935), 670, 674, 680.

gued that the Klan was far from a negligible force in that state. Not only did it create "a virtual reign of terror in the up-country," but it also undermined the confidence of northerners about the viability of Reconstruction and forced them to try to appease the opposition by offering amnesty, rather than to attempt to challenge and defeat it.[14] In other words, the Klan phenomenon revealed to northern policy makers the extent of the resistance and compelled them to reconsider.

This kind of evaluation is, of course, very difficult to demonstrate with any precision—a problem that besets all studies of violence, since the broad effects of violent acts and a climate of fear are hard to demonstrate. A less debatable feature of Shapiro's reassessment was the establishment of a connection between the Klan and the Democratic party. Shapiro showed that numerous Democrats either were members of the organization or were involved in outrages it committed. Indeed, several leading Democrats actually were brought before the courts in the federal prosecution of the Klan, and some were convicted and jailed. This evidence confirmed Otto Olsen's 1962 finding that prominent Democrats were very much involved in the North Carolina Klan. In fact, as Olsen pointed out, several of these men had been among the conspirators who had assassinated John W. Stephens and Wyatt Outlaw, leading Republicans in Caswell and Alamance counties, where the Klan was very active.[15]

Shapiro and Olsen provided concrete instances of the Klan being closely tied to the local Democratic party. Their purpose was not to show how respectable the Klan was by this affiliation, but rather to indicate how influential a political role the organization played. Quite a different matter, however, is the question of how successful it was as a political force. Neither historian argued that the Klan's activities won political victories for the Democrats in the Carolinas. Both were, in fact, rather circumspect on this point, claiming that the impact of Klan terror was essentially indirect. Olsen, for instance, concluded that the Klan's ability to establish "Conservative political control" was "somewhat uncertain." The Klan was active, he found, in ten of the fifteen North Carolina counties that swung to the Democratic-Conservatives in 1870 and helped the party to carry the state assembly.

14. Herbert Shapiro, "The Ku Klux Klan During Reconstruction: The South Carolina Episode," *Journal of Negro History,* XLIX (1964), 48.
15. Otto H. Olsen, "The Ku Klux Klan: A Study in Reconstruction Politics and Propaganda," *North Carolina Historical Review,* XXXIX (1962), 340–62.

But this swing resulted not so much from Klan actions themselves as from "the indignant public response to the Republican military movement" to put down the disorders, because in so doing the authorities had proclaimed martial law and suspended civil liberties. Olsen concluded that the Klan was "not so much a necessity" as an indication that the "antebellum ruling gentry" of the state was unable to accommodate to black equality or to the "modern democratic political process." [16] In effect, the Klan was a manifestation of political and social dysfunction rather than a premeditated political maneuver.

With the appearance in 1971 of Allen Trelease's *White Terror* there was at last a scholarly, book-length study of the Klan. Trelease concurred in the view that the organization was not minimal and sporadic in its operation; it was focused in its objectives and political in thrust. As evidence of its role, he reported that local and even state Democratic politicians either were involved directly in Klan activities or at least countenanced them. Moreover, the incidence of Klan activity was focused on those districts, mainly in the Piedmont or up-country areas where, according to Trelease, "the two parties or the two races were nearly equal, or where there was a white minority large enough to intimidate the freedmen." These were regions where the Democrats were in a position to tip the balance and gain the ascendancy. Nevertheless, Trelease concluded that despite the existence of Klan-induced terror throughout the southern states, the organization could not be "credited with overthrowing Republican control" in any state, "although it was a contributory factor in all of them," especially Georgia in 1870 and, to some extent, Alabama and North Carolina the same year. The Klan's most important effect, he decided, was not actually to end Reconstruction anywhere, but rather "to weaken Negro and Republican morale" by showing that the Republican governments were unable to contain the terror and protect their supporters. [17]

Despite his extensive documentation of the Klan's operations, Trelease was less convincing in his explanation of why the Klan arose in some areas of the region and not in others. There were flaws in his suggestion that Klan activity was concentrated in districts with a racial balance that was nearly equal and a Republican majority that was slim and therefore reversible by intimidation. He himself qualified this sug-

16. *Ibid.*, 360.
17. Allen W. Trelease, *White Terror: The Ku Klux Klan Conspiracy and Southern Reconstruction* (New York, 1971), 64, 419.

gestion, first by noticing that some Klan districts were solidly black or white, and then by observing—of South Carolina, for example—that the Klan counties were more equally balanced than elsewhere in the state. This was a rather different criterion from his initial formulation, as J. C. A. Stagg noted in his 1974 article on Klan violence in the South Carolina up-country. Indeed, Stagg went on to point out that twelve of the fifteen counties where the Klan was most active were "predominantly" either black or white. (According to Stagg's definition, predominantly white counties had populations over 50 percent white; predominantly black counties contained populations over 60 percent black. Thus, only York, Laurens, and Union counties had racially "balanced" populations of 50 to 60 percent black.)[18] Because of this, he concluded that an explanation that went beyond political motives was needed.

According to Stagg, the Klan areas were those where problems of land tenure and labor control were most acute. Up-country landowners had far less control than they wanted, because black laborers there worked under various sharecropping arrangements rather than on a "two-day" wage system, as in the rest of the state. In Stagg's view, attempts to coerce black renters to work on "acceptable" terms gave rise to the Klan. Thus, it had its origins in "labor troubles"—although this friction became politicized once the new Republican governments began, after 1868, to enact and enforce laws regulating labor. From these beginnings, Stagg found, Klan violence soon became a general occurrence that was approved by whites of all classes and aimed at restricting blacks in their attempt to rise up from dependency and subordination. With this outcome, what Stagg had begun as an effort to bring precision to the explanation of the emergence of the Klan became somewhat vague and diffuse.

If there is still, at this late date, considerable uncertainty about the genesis and function of the Klan, there at least is little doubt that the Klan was not the agency that dethroned Reconstruction. Whatever political aims it espoused, its accomplishments were not decisive. In his 1984 study of violence in Reconstruction politics, *But There Was No Peace,* George Rable noted that "the Ku Klux Klan brought the southern states only a short distance down the road to 'redemption.'" This

---

18. J. C. A. Stagg, "The Problem of Klan Violence: The South Carolina Up-Country, 1868–1871," *Journal of American Studies,* VIII (1974), 306–307, 304 n. 3.

opinion corroborated similar conclusions arrived at by Simkins, Olsen, and Trelease, although it ran counter to those of Du Bois and Franklin. Rable went on to explain that although the Klan may have weakened Republican voting strength in many counties and contributed to a paralyzing sense of fear, its "lack of organization beyond the local level made it a weak instrument to attack Republican state governments." [19] If that is so, then what did bring about the collapse of Reconstruction? Olsen had surmised that with the fading away of the Klan in North Carolina after 1870, the final defeat of the Republicans was "dependent upon less terroristic procedures." [20] Although other methods than violence indeed were employed, evidence suggests that it was the redirection of violence after 1873, accompanied by the politicalization of race, that actually brought Reconstruction crashing down.

The Klan-initiated violence of the years 1866 through 1871 had emerged from the dislocations and friction of the aftermath of emancipation and military defeat. Even when this social and economic violence had been directed toward political objectives, it had remained local and uncoordinated as well as covert. But in the mid-1870s, its shape and function changed dramatically as the Democratic party searched for a new strategy to end Republican rule in the Deep South, where such rule was still entrenched. The Democrats had won control in Georgia and Alabama in 1870 (only to lose Alabama again in 1872) and had gained effective influence in North Carolina and Virginia, but since then only Texas (in 1873) had been redeemed.

The states still under Republican control could be divided into two groups, in which two different kinds of political situations prevailed. The first group consisted of states like Florida and Arkansas where the Republicans, lacking a sizable black electoral base, were split into two competing but vulnerable factions of whites who thus had to deal with the Democratic opposition in order to gain the initiative within their own disunited party. Under these circumstances, the Democrats were confident that in time, once they became better organized themselves, they could win an electoral majority and gain control. The second group was more problematic, for it consisted of those Deep South

19. George C. Rable, *But There Was No Peace: The Role of Violence in the Politics of Reconstruction* (Athens, Ga., 1984), 111. For a somewhat different interpretation, see Eric Foner, *Reconstruction: America's Unfinished Revolution, 1863–1877* (New York, 1988), 426, 442.
20. Olsen, "Ku Klux Klan," 361.

states with significant, if not majority, black constituencies capable of sustaining the Republican party in power. Here, there was no guaranteed method or imminent prospect for ending Republican control through normal political processes. It was in these states where a new approach was needed that the Democrats devised an alternative political formula for seizing power.

In this emerging strategy, many of the ingredients that had been involved in the earlier Klan episode reappeared. For this reason, perhaps, John Hope Franklin mistakenly elided the two phases: he included in his discussion of Klan violence several later incidents, such as the assassination in 1874 of the black Mississippi Republican leader Charles Caldwell and the ambush and killing of Joseph Crews, a white organizer of South Carolina's black state militia, in 1875. Yet after 1873 the nature and context of the violence in fact had changed decisively. Violence was at the heart of the new strategy, but it was carried out in the open by organized bands or by paramilitary detachments. Furthermore, it received the active encouragement of the Democratic party leadership at the highest level. A third characteristic of this new phase was that the violence was inflicted not so much on individuals as on the structures and institutions of Reconstruction government—on the courthouses, jails, and militia units in those counties that were in Republican hands.

Assaults of this kind were numerous in Louisiana in 1873 and 1874, in such places as Colfax, Coushatta, and even New Orleans in the battle of Liberty Place, but they also occurred in Vicksburg, Mississippi, in 1874 and in Hamburg, South Carolina, in 1876. In addition, racial incidents or riots were provoked and then followed up by manhunts against any blacks who were in the vicinity, as happened in Eutaw, Alabama, in 1874; Clinton, Mississippi, in 1875; and Ellenton, South Carolina, in 1876. Finally, intimidation rather than physical assault was carried out in the election campaigns in Alabama in 1874, Mississippi in 1875, and South Carolina in 1876, when mounted detachments of former Confederate soldiers, dressed in ghostly gray, accompanied Democratic speakers to political rallies and paraded through the black sections of small towns and villages. This was violence on a scale and of a kind that was totally unknown in the earlier Klan era. As I have shown in *The Road to Redemption: Southern Politics, 1869–1879* (1984), it was this coordinated campaign of physical and psychological intimidation that actually overthrew Reconstruction and transferred political control to a truculent, revitalized Democracy.[21]

There is an aspect of these campaigns that cannot be overlooked, or else a distorted view will result. From start to finish, this reign of violence was carried out within a clearly defined political context that shaped the entire maneuver. The objective was not simply to destroy the Republican governments by attacking and dispersing their supporters, but to enable the Democrats to regain power by winning elections. Ironically, the intention was to use violent and illegal means to win power legitimately, through the electoral process. In every case the violence was called off several weeks before the election actually took place, and on polling day the balloting occurred in an atmosphere of relative calm and without significant interference. Of course, this seeming tranquillity would give the federal government no justification for intervening to insure a fair election or for declaring an election invalid. But it was also evident that this procedure was not conceived as a counterrevolutionary move or coup d'état, or even as a violation of the legitimate electoral process, which the Democratic party was eager to uphold. One of the more frequently quoted statements from this episode is the injunction to the Mississippi Democrats in 1875: "Carry the election peaceably if we can, forcibly if we must." What is interesting is the rather squeamish concern about the election at all. This is not counterrevolutionary scheming, but a concern for legality expressed by desperate yet traditional politicians, preoccupied with form as much as outcome. If, as James McPherson has posited, these events have to be interpreted as either "Redemption or counterrevolution," then it seems clear that, in view of the overarching political and electoral context within which they were conceived, the former term more accurately describes the entire episode.[22]

There remains still the question of what strategic political thinking went into these election campaigns—with little doubt, the ugliest in American history. While an open and coordinated campaign of violence was the means envisaged, the issue that was to dominate, even animate, the canvass was race. And the decision to introduce race marked a dramatic departure from the strategy pursued since the Re-

21. Michael Perman, The Road to Redemption: Southern Politics, 1869–1879 (Chapel Hill, 1984), chap. 7.
22. James M. McPherson, "Redemption or Counterrevolution? The South in the 1870s," Reviews in American History, XIII (1985), 545–50.

construction governments had been set up in 1868. In the intervening years race was, of course, ever-present, but it was not made an issue or the focus of a Democratic election campaign. By 1873, however, it appeared to be not merely possible, but actually necessary, to inject race into the center of party politics. At this point, the two parties were based on racially exclusive constituencies, the Democrats having failed in their somewhat desultory attempt to win black support, and the Republicans having proved unable to keep, let alone increase, the white voters they had attracted when their party was founded in 1868. The parties had distinctive racial identities, and race was the most evident difference between them. The trouble was that a campaign based on race could be disastrous for the Democrats in states where blacks were a voting majority. In those Deep South states, the Democrats' hopes of victory were negligible unless considerable numbers of blacks could be coerced into either voting Democratic or not voting at all.

There was great risk involved in a campaign strategy aimed at intimidating the opposition's supporters; for one thing, such a strategy might simply be ineffective. Nevertheless, the Democratic leadership realized that an appeal based on race could galvanize and increase the white vote even if it did not entirely succeed in intimidating black voters. This calculation, as I argued in *The Road to Redemption,* was the essential ingredient, the overriding concern, when the Democrats decided, between 1874 and 1876, to embark on an electoral strategy based on white supremacy and the "white line." By appealing directly to whites' race pride and giving them a feeling of power through the encouragement of antiblack aggression, the party leadership anticipated that those whites who had stayed away from elections in droves during the early years of Reconstruction would finally be made to see what was at stake and thus be stimulated into vigorous action capable of carrying their state in the critical upcoming elections. And indeed, revitalized white participation proved to be the decisive element in the Democratic victories in the state campaigns of 1874 to 1876.

Despite the dramatic decrease of black votes in some locations, such as the oft-cited drop in Yazoo County, Mississippi, from 2,499 Republican votes in 1873 to 7 in 1875, the statewide Republican counts did not decline markedly, and sometimes even increased. In Mississippi, Republicans cast 70,462 votes for state treasurer in 1873; two years later, in the white-supremacy campaign of 1875, the total was reduced only slightly, to 67,171, while thirty-five of the state's seventy-two counties actually increased their Republican vote, although by only slim margins.[23] In South Carolina, the Republican vote for governor in 1874 was 80,403; in 1876, it increased to 86,216 or 91,127, depending on whether the Democratic or Republican figures are accepted in the disputed election.[24] In Alabama, Republicans gave 89,878 votes to David P. Lewis for governor in 1872 and increased their vote to 93,928 when he ran for reelection in 1874. The defeat of the Republicans in the second set of elections, despite their strong showing, was accounted for simply by a vast outpouring of support for the Democrats by whites who had stayed away earlier. The Democratic vote in Alabama increased by 26,000.[25] In Mississippi, a Republican majority of 22,976 in 1873 was transformed into a Democratic majority of 31,544 two years later. In South Carolina, the pattern was the same: a vote of 68,818 in 1874 expanded in 1876 to either 83,071 or 92,261, according to the differing estimates of the two parties.[26]

Clearly, the violence and intimidation inflicted on black voters in the predominantly black counties depressed their vote, sometimes with horrifying ruthlessness. All the same, thousands of black Republicans demonstrated remarkable courage and determination by still appearing on election day to support their beleaguered and demoralized party. This was a display of extraordinary loyalty and political involvement that historians of Reconstruction have never fully appreciated or understood. But the tenacity of black Republicans was more than offset by the votes cast by white Democrats whose racial instincts had been aroused. These ballots made the difference, but they would not have been cast in such numbers without the accompanying rituals of violence and repression. In this respect, John Hope Franklin was correct to stress the importance of the terror. What he and many subsequent historians missed, however, was the crucial recognition that the later violence was effective in a way that the Klan's was not. In the mid-1870s violence was channeled to achieve well-defined political

23. "Mississippi in 1875," *Senate Reports*, 44th Cong., 1st Sess., Vol. II, 138, 145; William C. Harris, *The Day of the Carpetbagger: Republican Reconstruction in Mississippi* (Baton Rouge, 1979), 635.

24. Simkins and Woody, *South Carolina During Reconstruction*, 514.

25. Fleming, *Civil War and Reconstruction in Alabama*, 755, 795.

26. Harris, *Day of the Carpetbagger*, 685–87; "Mississippi in 1875," *Senate Reports*, 44th Cong., 1st Sess., Vol. II, 145; Simkins and Woody, *South Carolina During Reconstruction*, 514; Peggy Lamson, *The Glorious Failure: Black Congressman Robert Brown Elliott and the Reconstruction in South Carolina* (New York, 1973), 205, 257.

objectives that had been established by the Democratic party leadership; concurrently, a previously apathetic white constituency was mobilized on the basis of race to translate that violence into votes on election day.

Implicit in Franklin's emphasis on the role of violence in overthrowing Reconstruction, of course, was the notion that Republican rule had been brought to an end by the will and the actions of the former Confederates. This is to say, Reconstruction was defeated as much, if not more, by its enemies as by its own weaknesses and shortcomings. Forces that were located in the South and were external to the Republican party contributed decisively to its demise. It did not collapse simply because the southern Republicans themselves were deficient in some way or because their allies in Congress or in the northern states betrayed them.

This was an important observation, and it needed stressing. Nevertheless, despite Franklin's emphasis on the southern opposition in bringing about the overthrow of Reconstruction, the trend in historical scholarship after the appearance of *Reconstruction: After the Civil War* has been, surprisingly, in a quite different direction. During the late 1960s and on into the early 1980s, historians directed their attention elsewhere. There were perhaps three distinct features to this development. The first was a focus on the northern Republicans who were responsible for federal policy toward the postwar South. Historians tried to discover what their intentions were and how they conceived the government's task in protecting the freedmen and reorganizing the region's politics and economy. Initially, most assessments approved of the approach taken by Congress, but by the late 1960s and early 1970s, this tone had changed and a viewpoint had emerged that was quite critical. The congressmen who formulated reconstruction policy began to be seen as politicians who lacked the vision and capacity to rise above the existing constitutional and political restrictions that inhibited radical change. In addition, the Grant administration came under fire for its lack of vigor and commitment in enforcing the rather limited proposals that were advanced. This interpretative stance was described as postrevisionist because its effect was to counter the approach taken during the 1950s and 1960s by the revisionists, who had treated the congressional Republicans with sympathy and had rehabilitated them from the disparaging assessments of the Dunning school. The postrevisionists regarded the Republicans as

conservatives whose provisions for the postwar South were quite inadequate to the demands of the situation. They were portrayed as politicians who lacked boldness and commitment and who therefore deserved much, if not most, of the blame for the deficiencies of
Reconstruction.[27]

The second focus of recent scholarship was on those politicians
who formed the new Republican party in the South and whose mission
was to reconstruct the region and keep it out of the hands of the former Confederates. Historians who embarked on this investigation discovered that the fledgling party quickly became immersed in complex
and destructive factional disputes, which the opposition then used to
divide and split the party. The Republicans' legislative shortcomings,
incompetence, corruption, and even their racism also were emphasized. Studies both of Reconstruction in individual states and of aspects of Republican rule across the entire region produced a perspective in which the southern Republicans were seen as their own worst
enemies, men who relieved the Democratic opposition of the need to
initiate much of a countermovement on its own behalf. In effect, the
historians concluded that the Republican party died of self-inflicted
wounds.[28]

The third and final focus was on the role of blacks in Reconstruction. This line of development actually drew considerably on another
innovative aspect of Franklin's approach—his path-breaking emphasis on the black political leadership during the era. Blacks who previously had been virtually anonymous now became subjects of intense
examination. Soon, both their quality and their influence became

27. See, for example, Michael Les Benedict, A Compromise of Principle: Congressional
Republicans and Reconstruction, 1863–1869 (New York, 1974); Michael Les Benedict, "Preserving the Constitution: The Conservative Basis of Radical Reconstruction," Journal of American History, LXI (1974), 65–90; Michael Perman, Reunion Without Compromise: The South
and Reconstruction, 1865–1868 (New York, 1973); C. Vann Woodward, American Counterpoint: Slavery and Racism in the North-South Dialogue (Boston, 1971), chap. 2; William Gillette, Retreat from Reconstruction, 1869–1879 (Baton Rouge, 1979); Terry L. Seip, The South
Returns to Congress: Men, Economic Measures, and Intersectional Relationships, 1868–1879
(Baton Rouge, 1983); James C. Mohr, ed., Radical Republicans in the North (Baltimore, 1976);
and Richard H. Abbott, The Republican Party and the South, 1855–1877: The First Southern
Strategy (Chapel Hill, 1986).
28. Among the titles on this topic are Otto H. Olsen, ed., Reconstruction and Redemption
in the South: An Assessment (Baton Rouge, 1980); Harris, Day of the Carpetbagger; Carl Mon-
eyhon, Republicanism in Reconstruction Texas (Austin, 1980); Elizabeth Studley Nathans, Losing the Peace: Georgia Republicans and Reconstruction, 1865–1871 (Baton Rouge, 1968);
Sarah Woolfolk Wiggins, The Scalawag in Alabama Politics, 1865–1881 (University, Ala., 1977);
Ted Tunnell, Crucible of Reconstruction: War, Radicalism, and Race in Louisiana, 1862–1877
(Baton Rouge, 1984); and Perman, Road to Redemption.

known through biographies of such leaders as Robert Brown Elliott, Robert Smalls, and Martin Delaney, all from South Carolina; Josiah Walls of Florida; James Rapier of Alabama; and P. B. S. Pinchback of Louisiana. In addition, the role of blacks in the politics of several states was scrutinized. Finally, the experience of emancipation and the conditions of life for the freed slaves were the focus of many studies, dealing in particular with race relations and the systems of land tenure and labor that involved and were affected by blacks.[29]

All of this scholarly activity focused on groups and individuals who were engaged in promoting and supporting Reconstruction. As a result, attention was drawn away from the role played by the southern resistance. Indeed, there seemed to be so many indications that the proponents and agents of Reconstruction were flawed and deficient that it appeared unnecessary to look for external causes to explain the failure of the experiment. This impression was strengthened by a major reinterpretation of one of the acknowledged instances of a highly successful and decisive southern initiative during Reconstruction—the southerners' Machiavellian maneuver to cajole Rutherford B. Hayes into handing over control of the South in exchange for the help of southern Democrats in his effort to obtain the presidency during the contested election of 1876–1877. The view that the South's role in this bargain was critical was so widely accepted by the early 1960s that Franklin simply reiterated it without comment in *Reconstruction: After the Civil War*.[30]

The central role of southern Democrats in this crisis was formulated initially by C. Vann Woodward in his influential *Reunion and Reaction* (1951). In this study, Woodward claimed that a group of southern Democrats, quite aware of Hayes's political predicament and

29. The literature on this aspect of Reconstruction is too vast to cite more than a few significant works, namely, Thomas Holt, *Black over White: Negro Political Leadership in South Carolina During Reconstruction* (Urbana, Ill., 1977); Howard N. Rabinowitz, ed., *Southern Black Leaders of the Reconstruction Era* (Urbana, Ill., 1982); Loren Schweninger, *James T. Rapier and Reconstruction* (Chicago, 1978); Leon F. Litwack, *Been in the Storm So Long: The Aftermath of Slavery* (New York, 1979); Eric Foner, *Nothing but Freedom: Emancipation and Its Legacy* (Baton Rouge, 1983); Janet Sharp Hermann, *The Pursuit of a Dream* (New York, 1981); Louis S. Gerteis, *From Contraband to Freedman: Federal Policy Toward Southern Blacks, 1861–1865* (Westport, Conn., 1973); Rodney Davis, *Good and Faithful Labor: From Slavery to Sharecropping in the Natchez District* (Westport, Conn., 1982); Robert C. Morris, *Reading, 'Riting, and Reconstruction: The Education of Freedmen in the South, 1861–1870* (Chicago, 1981); and Howard N. Rabinowitz, *Race Relations in the Urban South, 1865–1890* (New York, 1978).

30. Franklin, *Reconstruction*, 211–17. See also C. Vann Woodward, *Reunion and Reaction: The Compromise of 1877 and the End of Reconstruction* (Boston, 1951).

of his need for Democratic support in securing a favorable outcome to the electoral count, bargained with him and secured terms that were remarkably beneficial to them and their region. In return for withholding their support from the national Democrats' filibuster against the results of the Electoral Commission's recount, as well as for helping Hayes to organize the House of Representatives under a Republican, James A. Garfield, the southerners pressured Hayes into agreeing to withdraw the remaining federal troops from the South, thereby undermining the precarious, newly elected Republican state governments in South Carolina, Louisiana, and Florida. In addition, Woodward claimed, the wily and insistent southerners had forced Hayes to concede a cabinet post to the South and to promise his support for enactment of a subsidy for the Texas and Pacific railroad that would finance a transcontinental route across the South to match the northern road completed in 1869.[31]

Research appearing between 1973 and 1980 by Allan Peskin, George Rable, Michael Les Benedict, William Gillette, and Keith Polakoff questioned this entire formulation—not only the economic bargain described by Woodward, but even the influence of the South altogether.[32] Although these scholars wrote about various aspects of the crisis and the negotiation, their findings can be summarized by the following five propositions. First, the deal over the House speakership and the Texas and Pacific bill was never fulfilled. Second, the election of Hayes resulted from the inaction of the northern Democrats, not the action of their southern counterparts. Third, the southerners really wanted home rule and had no economic agenda that they were agreed upon and determined to achieve, although some individuals may have thought and acted as if they did. Fourth, the election of Hayes and the resolution of the crisis had been accomplished before negotiations with the candidate actually began. Fifth, Hayes had intended all along—and his predecessor, Grant, had come to the same conclusion

31. Woodward, Reunion and Reaction, 1–21, 122–203.
32. Allan Peskin, "Was There a Compromise of 1877?" Journal of American History, XL (1973), 63–75; Gillette, Retreat from Reconstruction, chaps. 13, 14; Keith I. Polakoff, The Politics of Inertia: The Election of 1876 and the End of Reconstruction (Baton Rouge, 1973); George C. Rable, "Southern Interests and the Election of 1876: A Reappraisal," Civil War History, XXVI (1980), 347–61; Michael Les Benedict, "Southern Democrats and the Crisis of 1876–1877: A Reconsideration of Reunion and Reaction," Journal of Southern History, XLVI (1980), 489–524. See also Vincent P. DeSantis, "Rutherford B. Hayes and the Removal of the Troops at the End of Reconstruction," in Region, Race, and Reconstruction: Essays in Honor of C. Vann Woodward, ed. J. Morgan Kousser and James M. McPherson, (New York, 1982), 417–50.

just before the election—to end the attempt to sustain the remaining Republican governments in the South. Thus, little, if anything, that the southerners did or said influenced Hayes to adopt a line of policy that he felt he could not avoid and that he probably wanted to pursue anyway. Moreover, the railroad subsidy that supposedly showed how assertive and effective the southern Democrats were did not in fact amount to much, either as a critical ingredient in the final bargain or as an actual benefit to the South.

This dismissal of the southern Democrats' most audacious scheme to curtail Reconstruction was the ultimate contribution in a historiographical development that had downplayed or overlooked the role of the southern resistance. Historians seemed to be suggesting, in effect, that the Reconstruction initiative had been so circumscribed and feeble that it had collapsed virtually of its own accord.

Clearly, that was not the case. Although Reconstruction was indeed flawed and vulnerable, it did pose a discernible threat to existing southern institutions and values, and toppling it necessitated considerable maneuvering and ultimately the adoption of extreme measures that mobilized the deepest passions and most elemental resources available to its opponents. Reconstruction did not simply collapse; it was overthrown, even eliminated, by the action of its adversaries. The vigorous and successful attempt of the landowners to regain control of their emancipated labor force—a procedure to which historians have paid considerable attention in recent years—paralleled a similarly determined and triumphant effort to reclaim political ascendancy.[33]

It all amounted to a continuation of the South's campaign for autonomy, a campaign begun in defense of slavery before the war and continued after it in order to uphold the practice of white supremacy. Exactly how this campaign was carried out and who was to rule at home once home rule was attained are topics that demand serious consideration. W. E. B. Du Bois indicated the outlines of such an analysis, and John Hope Franklin stressed the importance of "Counter Reconstruction" in the history of the postwar South. Historians now need to complement the recent focus on Reconstruction by examining the phe-

---

33. See Perman, *Road to Redemption;* Rable, *But There Was No Peace;* Steven Hahn, *The Roots of Southern Populism: Yeoman Farmers and the Transformation of the Georgia Up-Country* (New York, 1983); Foner, *Nothing but Freedom;* Davis, *Good and Faithful Labor;* Michael Wayne, *The Reshaping of Plantation Society: The Natchez District, 1860–1880* (Baton Rouge, 1983); and Roger L. Ransom and Richard Sutch, *One Kind of Freedom: The Economic Consequences of Emancipation* (New York, 1977).

nomenon of Redemption so as to discover its essential characteristics and objectives, as well as to elucidate the power struggle that took place within it. After all, the shape and course of southern history for at least the succeeding fifty years were determined by this successful movement of resistance to Reconstruction.

7

Educational Reconstruction

ᕁ ROBERT C. MORRIS

Freedmen's education was already the subject of heated debate when scholars first began interpreting Reconstruction history. Indeed, well before the withdrawal of federal troops from the South, opinion had divided along sectional lines over the nature and effects of this northern effort to provide schooling for the former slaves. Some saw a necessary, reforming crusade waged by idealistic Yankee teachers; others reacted against what they considered dangerously naive interference in southern affairs.

Educators and social activists later adapted these contrasting viewpoints to their own purposes. W. E. B. Du Bois, the most articulate proponent of academic and professional training for blacks, lauded the postwar school program as the finest thing in American history. The "crusade of the New England schoolma'am," Du Bois observed in 1901, "seemed to our age far more quixotic than the quest of St. Louis seemed to his. Behind the mists of ruin and rapine waved the calico dresses of women who dared, and after the hoarse mouthings of the field guns rang the rhythm of the alphabet." In direct contrast, the South's leading white advocate of public education for both races excoriated these same missionary teachers as ignorant fanatics who "proceeded to make all possible mischief." According to J. L. M. Curry's widely publicized address before the Montgomery Conference on Race Problems, Reconstruction education was unsettling and demoralizing, and it pandered to a wild frenzy for schooling as a quick method of reversing social and political conditions. Alleging that during the "saturnalia of misgovernment" outsiders sought to impose "negro domination" on the South and secure the states permanently for partisan ends, this influential representative of the Peabody and Slater funds blamed Yankee educators for introducing an impractical curriculum in an attempt "to bring the race *per saltum* to the same plane with their former masters, and realize the theory of social and political equality."[1]

As differing sectional views on southern black education converged during the early twentieth century, the negative assessment exemplified in Curry's address prevailed. Formalized by the Dunning school of historians, this thesis reiterated charges made throughout Reconstruction that many Yankee educators were cultural carpetbaggers who taught dangerous social, political, and religious doctrines, soon turning emerging white support into intense, sometimes violent, opposition. Although divided in their appraisals of the average teacher's character and motives, those Dunningites who analyzed the Freedmen's Bureau program in any depth largely agreed that it failed to inaugurate the kind of education best adapted to a race just removed from slavery. "No attention was paid to the actual condition of the negroes and their station in life," Walter L. Fleming generalized in a passage citing Curry, Booker T. Washington, and William Hooper Councill. "False ideas about manual labor were put into their heads, and the training given them had no practical bearing on the needs of life." Turning to more immediate concerns about public education, these studies tended to emphasize the relative lack of pressure for racially "mixed" schools while focusing on allegedly incompetent and corrupt state superintendents. Overall, Dunningite authors judged bureau and public efforts a failure.[2]

Despite challenges from Du Bois, A. A. Taylor, Horace Mann Bond, and other critics of Reconstruction orthodoxy, the traditional interpretation continued to exert a substantial influence through the

---

1. W. E. B. Du Bois, "Freedmen's Bureau," *Atlantic Monthly*, LXXXVII (March, 1901), 358, 361; Southern Society for the Promotion of the Study of Race Conditions and Problems in the South, *Race Problems of the South: Report of the Proceedings of the First Annual Conference . . . at Montgomery, Alabama, May 8, 9, 10, A.D. 1900* (Richmond, Va., 1900), 108–109.

2. Walter L. Fleming, *Civil War and Reconstruction in Alabama* (Cleveland, 1905), 467–68, 624–35; Fleming, *The Sequel of Appomattox: A Chronicle of the Reunion of the States* (New Haven, 1919), 214–15; Joseph G. de Roulhac Hamilton, *Reconstruction in North Carolina* (New York, 1914, 316–20; James W. Garner, *Reconstruction in Mississippi* (New York, 1901), 359–63. Garner and C. Mildred Thompson produced the most balanced of these studies. Thompson even questioned the common contention that white Georgians generally favored educating blacks. C. Mildred Thompson, *Reconstruction in Georgia: Economic, Social, Political, 1865–1872* (New York, 1915), 122–27.

1950s. Even Francis B. Simkins and Robert H. Woody's mildly revisionist *South Carolina During Reconstruction* concluded that freedmen's educators taught a spirit of political and social insubordination and, by emphasizing literary instruction, elevated the race into an unreal world, leaving it "less adequately equipped for the problem of living than did the industrial training given the plantation slave."[3] Subsequent treatments by Henry L. Swint and George R. Bentley lent added weight to criticism accusing northern teachers of advocating inflammatory "ideas of 'social equality,' of remaking the South in the image of New England, and of converting the freedmen into Republican voters." More than thirty years after its publication in 1941, Swint's impressionistic little volume *The Northern Teacher in the South, 1862–1870* represented the only comprehensive treatment of freedmen's education. Although the author considered his study an introductory statement, its depiction of doctrinaire abolitionists and egalitarians carrying out a program that was anathema to southern whites largely defined the terms of the continuing debate well into the 1970s. The first to take advantage of Freedmen's Bureau school records, Swint insisted the southerner did not fear all education of blacks, merely black education in the hands of naive and disruptive Yankee teachers. Simply stated, "The South was universally opposed to the education of the Negro by radical abolitionists from the North."[4]

Direct refutations of this traditional viewpoint developed slowly. Although rejecting Swint's highly selective portrait of meddlesome cultural carpetbaggers, few revisionist historians seriously questioned his generalization that these educators were "abolitionist in sentiment and equalitarian in practice." Such a stance was entirely consistent with the revisionist assessment of the bureau and the various aid societies as being sincerely devoted to improving the freedmen's social, economic, and legal situations. In fact, when John Hope Franklin published *Re-*

---

3. W. E. B. Du Bois, *Black Reconstruction in America: An Essay Toward a History of the Part Which Black Folk Played in the Attempt to Reconstruct Democracy in America, 1860–1880* (New York, 1935); Alrutheus Ambush Taylor, *The Negro in the Reconstruction of Virginia* (Washington, D.C., 1926), 138–73, and *The Negro in Tennessee, 1865–1880* (Washington, D.C., 1941), 168–204; Horace Mann Bond, *Negro Education in Alabama: A Study in Cotton and Steel* (Washington, D.C., 1939); Francis B. Simkins and Robert H. Woody, *South Carolina During Reconstruction* (Chapel Hill, 1932), 424–34.

4. George R. Bentley, *A History of the Freedmen's Bureau* (Philadelphia, 1955), 169–84; Henry L. Swint, *The Northern Teacher in the South, 1862–1870* (Nashville, 1941), v, 35–76, 142.

construction: *After the Civil War,* he signaled a return to Du Bois's earlier position that education represented the greatest success of the Freedmen's Bureau. Countering a persistent emphasis on the program's excesses, Franklin and other revisionists pointed to its accomplishments. With bureau support, northern aid societies by 1870 maintained approximately 4,300 schools and colleges serving a quarter of a million students. Bureau educational officials spent more than $5,000,000 in helping to establish the first schools for southern blacks. As Kenneth Stampp pointed out in his 1965 synthesis, this was "a pitifully inadequate sum but as much as Congress would grant." On a more permanent basis, Reconstruction laid the foundations for black higher education and state-supported public school systems in the South.[5]

Although studies as far back as John and LaWanda Cox's "General O. O. Howard and the 'Misrepresented Bureau'" (1953) presaged a move away from contrasting one-dimensional views of educational reconstruction, it was not until the 1970s that "postrevisionist" historians began to challenge established interpretations by examining the extent to which radical ideals actually influenced northern reform efforts. Reflecting the early concerns of the civil rights movement, Franklin's *Reconstruction* had devoted more attention to segregation and integration in southern schools than to the Yankee schoolmarm. As optimism gave way to a feeling that neither the first nor the second Reconstruction had gone far enough in effecting change, however, postrevisionist scholars "indicted northern teachers for seeking to stabilize the plantation order and inculcate 'middle-class' northern values like thrift, self-discipline, temperance, and respect for authority."[6]

In his historiographical article "Reconstruction Revisited" (1982), Eric Foner linked the emerging criticism of the school program to the social-control theory of education advanced in previous studies of

5. John Hope Franklin, *Reconstruction: After the Civil War* (Chicago, 1961), 38, 52, 107–109, 140–41, 191; Kenneth M. Stampp, *The Era of Reconstruction, 1865–1877* (New York, 1965), 134. James McPherson termed Swint's *Northern Teacher* "a relatively fair-minded study that nevertheless portrays the Yankee teachers as disruptive and naive egalitarians who needlessly alienated Southern whites." James M. McPherson, *Ordeal by Fire: The Civil War and Reconstruction* (New York, 1982), 691.

6. John H. Cox and LaWanda Cox, "General O. O. Howard and the 'Misrepresented Bureau,'" *Journal of Southern History,* XIX (1953), 427–56; Eric Foner, "Reconstruction Revisited," *Reviews in American History,* X (December, 1982), pp. 86, 97 n. 15. See also Eric Foner, *Reconstruction: America's Unfinished Revolution, 1863–1877* (New York, 1988). For an important study concentrating on segregated public education, see William Preston Vaughn, *Schools for All: The Blacks and Public Education in the South, 1865–1877* (Lexington, Ky., 1974).

northern educational reform. By this interpretation, black education was part of an effort to "create a disciplined and docile labor force." Even more influential than the forces cited by Foner in stimulating this reexamination of traditional interpretations were questions raised in the 1960s by works such as "Antislavery Ambivalence: Immediatism, Expediency, and Race" by William and Jane Pease; C. Vann Woodward's "Seeds of Failure in Radical Race Policy"; and William Mc-Feely's *Yankee Stepfather: General O. O. Howard and the Freedmen.* These studies forced revisionists to take a harder look at the racial attitudes and policies of those engaged in the freedmen's aid effort. The result was a shift in emphasis from Swint's uncompromising radical abolitionists to a broader characterization of educators, ranging from sincere egalitarians to paternalists and, in a few cases, outright racists.[7]

Three major reassessments of freedmen's education appeared in the 1970s and early 1980s—Robert C. Morris' *Reading, 'Riting, and Reconstruction,* Ronald E. Butchart's *Northern Schools, Southern Blacks,* and Jacqueline Jones's *Soldiers of Light and Love.*[8]

Seeing herself as complementing and expanding on James Mc-Pherson's sympathetic examination of abolitionist reformers, Jones concentrated on 368 northern teachers who served in Georgia for varying lengths of time between 1865 and 1873. *Soldiers of Light and Love* combined revisionism's twentieth-century civil rights perspective with a focus on women's history, portraying Yankee schoolmarms as women who "turned their backs on racial prejudice and cast off the cloak of female domesticity." Although Jones recognized some of the limits of a reform program that stressed personal improvement as the key to institutional change, her group portrait of idealistic schoolmarms battling both racism and conventional Victorian ideas about women underestimated the conservative aspects of freedmen's educa-

7. Foner, "Reconstruction Revisited," 97 n. 15; Michael B. Katz, *The Irony of Early School Reform: Educational Innovation in Mid-Nineteenth Century Massachusetts* (Cambridge, Mass., 1968); Stanley K. Schultz, *The Culture Factory: Boston Public Schools, 1789–1860* (New York, 1973); Samuel Bowles and Herbert Gintis, *Schooling in Capitalist America: Educational Reform and the Contradictions of Economic Life* (New York, 1976); William H. Pease and Jane H. Pease, "Antislavery Ambivalence: Immediatism, Expediency, and Race," *American Quarterly,* XVII (1965), 682–95; C. Vann Woodward, "Seeds of Failure in Radical Race Policy," *American Philosophical Society Proceedings,* CX (1966), 1–9; William S. McFeely, *Yankee Stepfather: General O. O. Howard and the Freedmen* (New Haven, 1968).

8. Robert C. Morris, *Reading, 'Riting, and Reconstruction: The Education of Freedmen in the South, 1861–1870* (Chicago, 1981); Ronald E. Butchart, *Northern Schools, Southern Blacks, and Reconstruction: Freedmen's Education, 1862–1875* (Westport, Conn., 1980); Jacqueline Jones, *Soldiers of Light and Love: Northern Teachers and Georgia Blacks, 1865–1873* (Chapel Hill, 1980). All three works were based on doctoral dissertations completed in 1976.

tion. By restricting herself almost exclusively to the Yankee school-marm in Georgia, moreover, Jones failed to capture the breadth and diversity of this multifaceted effort. The American Missionary Association teachers, however important, represented only one component of a movement built on three distinct, sometimes conflicting, reform traditions—an evangelical wing dominated by the AMA but including smaller denominational societies; a Garrisonian secular coalition; and an independent black faction rooted in antebellum attempts to develop autonomous cultural institutions.[9]

Although he intended *Northern Schools, Southern Blacks* as a comprehensive study of freedmen's education, Butchart in many respects took a still narrower focus than Jones by centering his chronicle on the ideological struggle between "egalitarian" secular aid societies on one side and "conservative" ecclesiastical and (western) secular groups on the other. Siding with the egalitarian societies, Butchart criticized denominational organizations and the Freedmen's Bureau for providing the former slaves with a placebo—education—when they really needed land, protection, a stake in society, and "meaningful power." Educational work, he argued, might be accepted as the bureau's greatest success "if accommodating the black to oppression, providing him with an institution that sought to discipline him for an emerging industrial servitude, and creating a black petty bourgeoisie of powerless professionals imbued with deference to dominant class values" were the only standards by which to judge the agency. "But if one assumes black freedom rather than white prerogatives as the measure of success, the educational venture, too, was an abysmal failure." Viewed in Butchart's illusory presentist perspective, bureau and denominational leaders lacked commitment to "black power and pride," developing instead an educational and religious ideology of social control that subverted the freedmen's racial and class interests. Ultimately, Butchart saw this education as a form of "cultural imperialism" incapable of stimulating mobility, equality, or liberty.[10]

Butchart's critical approach not only left too little room for the educational program's sincere efforts to prepare freedmen for a new socioeconomic order in the South, but its contrast of conservative

9. Jones, *Soldiers of Light and Love*, 4–13.
10. Butchart, *Northern Schools, Southern Blacks*, 51, 74, 113, 182, 203–207.

evangelicals and egalitarian seculars also was vastly oversimplified. As demonstrated in Morris' *Reading, 'Riting, and Reconstruction* and such subsequent works as Joe M. Richardson's *Christian Reconstruction* and Foner's *Reconstruction: America's Unfinished Revolution*, freedmen's education was a complex blend of reformist and conservative impulses.[11]

Characterizing freedmen's education is complicated both by the size and the diffuseness of the operation. Between 1861 and 1870, the final year under the Freedmen's Bureau, more than fifty organizations participated in some way. By the end of the 1870 academic year, government estimates placed the number of teachers in day and night schools at 3,300. Incomplete statistics for high schools, normal schools, and colleges added another 261, and an unspecified number of teachers in 61 industrial schools brought the final total, in all but sabbath schools, to approximately 3,600. These men and women often took on responsibilities outside of the classroom, acting as missionaries, social workers, dispensers of charity, labor superintendents, legal advisers, and even politicians. As one schoolmarm from upstate New York aptly described her activities, "I preach & teach & civilize & reconstruct generally." [12]

Administration of the educational program was a decentralized affair even after the advent of the bureau and the coalescence of many of the freedmen's aid societies under either the evangelical AMA or the secular American Freedmen's Union Commission (AFUC). The list of those who actually determined the direction of the enterprise extended from bureau commissioner Oliver Otis Howard to the teacher in the field. Within Howard's agency alone, policy making involved an education division run by the general superintendent of schools, John Watson Alvord; assistant commissioners and superintendents in the

11. Morris, *Reading, 'Riting, and Reconstruction;* Joe M. Richardson, *Christian Reconstruction: The American Missionary Association and Southern Blacks, 1861–1890* (Athens, Ga., 1986), 37–53, 123–40, 163–209; Foner, *Reconstruction: America's Unfinished Revolution,* 96–102, 144–48, 284–85, 354, 359, 366–67, 428, 541, 589, 592, 602.

12. See John Watson Alvord, *Third Semi-Annual Report on Schools for Freedmen, January 1, 1867* (Washington, D.C., 1868), 2–3; Alvord, *Fourth Semi-Annual Report on Schools for Freedmen, July 1, 1867* (Washington, D.C., 1868), 2–3; Alvord, *Sixth Semi-Annual Report on Schools for Freedmen, July 1, 1868* (Washington, D.C., 1868), 4–7; Alvord, *Eighth Semi-Annual Report on Schools for Freedmen, July 1, 1869* (Washington, D.C., 1869), 4–10, 64; Alvord, *Tenth Semi-Annual Report on Schools for Freedmen, July 1, 1870* (Washington, D.C., 1870), 4–7, 52–54; [Caroline F. Putnam] to [?], September 27 [1868], in Emily Howland Papers, Cornell University Library, Ithaca, N.Y.

various states; a general school inspector; and a host of local agents. These officials supervised the overall educational effort, while the benevolent societies staffed and managed the schools through their own hierarchy.

As inspector of schools and finances and later as general superintendent, Alvord embodied the moderate-reformist tone of freedmen's education. A veteran abolitionist, Alvord long since had adopted Charles Grandison Finney's passionate evangelical approach, which appealed to slaveholders more in a spirit of love than of hate. Alvord and the equally conciliatory Howard applied this moderate strategy to cultural reconstruction. In selecting assistant school superintendents for the education division, religion and experience with freedmen's affairs were more important than ideological and political criteria. Neither an active abolitionist nor a doctrinaire radical Republican, General Howard was understandably concerned about the precarious position of the bureau under President Andrew Johnson. The "Christian soldier" from Maine personally intervened to prevent the appointment of the militant abolitionist James Redpath in South Carolina, explaining that this controversial disciple of John Brown was "the very worst man to put in." [13]

Such intervention was rarely necessary, however; Howard's assistant commissioners usually avoided extremes in making their appointments. Although there were several former abolitionists among the thirty to forty school superintendents between 1865 and 1870, very few appointees favored draconian reconstruction measures. Most, in fact, were quite solicitous of the feelings of the native white population. G. L. Eberhart, the superintendent in Georgia, expressed a common sentiment in 1866: "We must be governed in this work by great prudence and, so far as we possibly can without any compromise of

13. Asa A. Stone to Theodore Dwight Weld, November 1, 1832, in Gilbert H. Barnes and Dwight L. Dumond, eds., *Letters of Theodore Dwight Weld, Angelina Grimké Weld, and Sarah Grimké, 1822–1844* (2 vols.; New York, 1934), I, 88; John Watson Alvord to Weld, August 9, 1836, *ibid.*, I, 326–27; Alvord to Weld, August 29, 1838, *ibid.*, II, 696; American Tract Society, Boston, *Forty-Fifth Annual Report* (Boston, 1859), 3–11; American Tract Society, New York, *Thirty-Fifth Annual Report* (New York, 1860), 37, 64–69, 351–355; American Tract Society, Boston, *Forty-Ninth Annual Report* (Boston, 1863), 32–33, 97–98; John Watson Alvord, *Fifth Semi-Annual Report on Schools for Freedmen, January 1, 1868* (Washington, D.C., 1868), 5; *American Missionary*, IX (November, 1865); New York *Times*, April 16, 1865; *Nation*, XXI (December, 1865), 799; Benjamin Quarles, *The Negro in the Civil War* (Boston, 1953), 328; James Redpath to Oliver O. Howard, September 5, 1865, Howard to Rufus Saxton, September 15, 1865, both in Oliver Otis Howard Papers, Bowdoin College Library, Brunswick, Maine.

principle, or conflict with truth, be controlled by policy and expediency." Since men were largely the product of their circumstances and education, Eberhart contended, "we can not therefore expect to excite any thing but ill feelings and disrespect among the white people here, if we run too far beyond what they deem the limits of prudence and propriety." [14]

The same trend toward moderation affected the leadership of freedmen's aid organizations. "Iconoclasm has had its day," James Miller McKim declared when resigning as corresponding secretary of the Pennsylvania Anti-Slavery Society in 1862. It was time to change tactics, time to substitute the "hod and trowel" for the "battering ram." Destruction must be followed by reconstruction, Lyman Abbott explained six months before Lee's surrender. Northerners had to occupy the South not only with bayonets and bullets, but also with ideas and institutions. Restoring the safety of the Republic necessitated establishing two essentials of democracy lacking in the Confederate states—schools and churches freely available to all classes and races. [15]

After the militant abolitionism of the 1850s, architects of freedmen's aid were, in effect, returning to an earlier antislavery emphasis on black "intellectual, moral, and religious improvement." Antislavery reformers had been concerned with practical education since the eighteenth century, declaring preparation for freedom to be a prime objective and later establishing a number of schools for free blacks in the East and Midwest. Reviving their antebellum faith in the force of free institutions, cultural reconstructionists considered education and religion essential engines of social change in the postemancipation period. "John Adams's axiom that civil society must be built up on the four corner-stones of the church, the school-house, the militia, and the town-meeting, receives new illustration, of the most distinct kind, as we work out the great problem of to-day," a Garrisonian freedmen's teacher observed in 1865. "Whichever panacea is presented to us in the great work of the admission of the four million negroes into our

14. G. L. Eberhart to Samuel Hunt, May 23, June 4, 1866, in American Missionary Association Archives, Amistad Research Center, Tulane University, New Orleans (hereinafter cited as AMA Archives).

15. J. Miller McKim to Oliver Johnson, January 22, 1862, in National Anti-Slavery Standard, May 3, 1862; Lyman Abbott, "Southern Evangelization," New Englander, XXIII (October, 1864), 699–708. See also Liberator, May 9, 1862, and William Cohen, "James Miller McKim, Pennsylvania Abolitionist" (Ph.D. dissertation, New York University, 1968).

civil society, and the establishment of their social rights, fails to pass test till . . . all four of the essential rights of religion, education, self-defence, and self-government are provided for." [16]

Changing tactics coincided with changes in leadership. Wendell Phillips, Frederick Douglass, and like-minded abolitionists questioned the whole freedmen's-aid concept, contending blacks needed justice more than pity, liberty more than old clothes, rights more than training to enjoy them. Other abolitionist leaders—of the stature of William Lloyd Garrison, Lewis and Arthur Tappan, Samuel May, John Andrew, and Salmon P. Chase—did serve as aid-society officers, but their influence on day-to-day management of freedmen's education was less pronounced than that of Abbott, a vocal critic of what he considered the "impracticable methods and the uncharitable spirit" of abolitionists. As chief executive officer of the AFUC and editor of its monthly journal, this moderate antislavery veteran not only advised teachers on such matters as racial etiquette, but also personally influenced the commission's ultimate decision to abandon its stated commitment to integrated education. [17]

The bulk of historical writing in this area naturally has concentrated on the typical Yankee schoolmarm—a middle-class white woman in her late twenties or early thirties, unmarried, Protestant, and in many cases living in New England at the time of her appointment. [18] Reinforced by burgeoning interests in women's studies and the

16. [William Channing Gannett and Edward Everett Hale], "The Education of the Freedmen," *North American Review,* CI (1865), 528.

17. Frederick Douglass to J. Miller McKim, May 2, 1865, in James Miller McKim Papers, Cornell University Library, Ithaca, N.Y.; *National Anti-Slavery Standard,* May 6, 1865; *Liberator,* January 13, May 6, 1865. Information on Abbott's role in the formulation of AFUC policy is found throughout the McKim Papers; the American Freedmen's Union Commission Executive Committee Minute Book, January 31, 1866–March 29, 1869, Cornell University Library, Ithaca, N.Y.; and the *American Freedman.* See also Lyman Abbott, *Reminiscences* (Boston, 1915), 98, 265–70; Ira V. Brown, *Lyman Abbott, Christian Evolutionist: A Study in Religious Liberalism* (Cambridge, Mass., 1953), 48. Details on the American Missionary Association leadership can be found in the AMA Archives; Clifton Johnson, "The American Missionary Association, 1846–1861: A Study of Christian Abolitionism" (Ph.D. dissertation, University of North Carolina, 1959); Richard B. Drake, "The American Missionary Association and the Southern Negro, 1861–1888" (Ph.D. dissertation, Emory University, 1957); Augustus Field Beard, *A Crusade of Brotherhood: A History of the American Missionary Association* (Boston, 1909); 18; and Richardson, *Christian Reconstruction.*

18. "Teachers: Their Qualifications and Support," *American Missionary,* X (July, 1866), 152–53; "Our Teachers," *Freedmen's Record,* I (May, 1865), 70–71; "The Situation," *Freedmen's Record,* I (April, 1865), 49–50. These generalizations about the "average" northern teacher are based on lists and tables found in *American Missionary; National Freedman; American Freedman;* Horace James, *Annual Report of the Superintendent of Negro Affairs in North Carolina, 1864* (Boston, [1865]), 41–42; Presbyterian Church, General Assembly's Committee

relatively well-documented role of the AMA, this focus in several monographs distorted the group portrait of an educational force that also included many white men, blacks of both sexes, and teachers from outside New England, especially New York and the Midwest. Over the course of Reconstruction, in fact, the dynamics of the teacher corps changed so much that by 1869, blacks outnumbered whites.[19]

Central to this shift was the initial Freedmen's Bureau premise that social reconstruction would be a temporary, short-term process necessitating cooperation from southerners of both races. As Superintendent Alvord suggested while still the bureau's school inspector, the government had no choice but to enlist southern support in educating the estimated one million blacks now "ready to engage in the study of books." A desire to control schooling in their own region, a sense of moral obligation, and recognition that free labor was more contented when educated elicited assent, if not favor, from some whites. Much of the actual teaching force, however, would have to come from among the South's black population. In addition to being more acceptable in the former slave states than the hated Yankee missionary teachers, freedmen could penetrate interior areas unsafe for white schoolmarms; their schools would be largely self-supporting; black youth would soon see honorable employment open to them; and most important, black participation would demonstrate the emancipated slave's independence from outside assistance. "These self-made efforts may not be perfect," Alvord conceded when describing the all-black Savannah Educational Association. "These schools are not, perhaps, as good as those taught by men and women from the North, . . . but we want this colored population to become self-reliant at once, though it be in an imperfect way."[20]

Except in Louisiana, however, few educators shared Alvord's early enthusiasm. Many school officials—and later, Dunningite historians discussing southern support for freedmen's education—realized that

---

on Freedmen, *Annual Reports, 1867–1870* (Pittsburgh, 1867–1870); and Minutes of the Instruction Committee, Friends Freedmen's Association Records, Friends Historical Library, Swarthmore College, Swarthmore, Pa.

19. See John Watson Alvord's semiannual reports on schools for freedmen, January 1, 1867, through July 1, 1870.

20. John Watson Alvord, *First Semi-Annual Report on Schools and Finances of Freedmen, January 1, 1866* (Washington, D.C., 1868), 12–13; W. T. Richardson, report to Michael Strieby, January 2, 1865, in AMA Archives; *National Freedman,* I (February, 1865), 11–12, (April 1, 1865), 98–99, (July 15, 1865), 197–98; *American Missionary,* IX (November, 1865), 256–58; *Freedmen's Record,* II (May, 1866), 91.

native whites often sought teaching positions because of financial need, politics, or a desire to influence what was being taught.[21] Some northerners considered such appointments better than none, but the wisdom of employing former Rebels was questioned enough to keep the number of native white teachers low.

Black educators, on the other hand, were more involved than most specialized studies suggest. Even when one takes into account the varied definitions of what it meant to be a bureau teacher, the increase from 33 percent of the teaching force in 1867 to 53 percent two years later is still significant. Much of the impetus for this increase came from blacks themselves, locally as well as through the African Methodist Episcopal (AME) church and the reconstituted African Civilization Society, an organization of "pious and educated colored people" who believed the black man himself could best instruct, direct, and elevate his race.[22] Self-improvement proponents, while repeatedly acknowledging white efforts, nevertheless asserted black people's peculiar fitness as ministers and teachers among the freedmen. Educated Negroes, it was argued, were better able to gain the confidence of their charges and less likely than whites to "be bribed by the deceptive flippancy of oily-tongued slaveocrats." Blacks in responsible positions would instill self-respect and racial pride, and by their own example they would demonstrate the race's capacity for advancement and leadership.[23]

During the last three years of bureau operations, the proportion of black teachers varied from highs of 50 to 75 percent in North Carolina and Louisiana to below 35 percent in South Carolina, Alabama, and Georgia. These teachers ran the gamut from college-educated free persons of color to barely literate freedmen. Those with the highest qualifications usually were employed in cities like Charleston, New Orleans, Mobile, and Savannah, leaving the less educated in rural and plantation schools considered impracticable for northern women, who often encountered greater opposition than their native black counter-

21. Fleming, *Civil War and Reconstruction in Alabama*, 624–26; Fleming, *Sequel of Appomattox*, 211–12.
22. *Freedmen's Torchlight* (Brooklyn, N.Y.), December, 1866; H. M. Johnson to John W. Alvord, April 15, 1869, in Bureau of Refugees, Freedmen, and Abandoned Lands Records (hereinafter cited as Bureau Records), Education Division, Letters Received, September, 1866–May, 1869, Record Group 105, National Archives, Washington, D.C.; *Christian Recorder*, February 20, April 2, 1864; *National Freedman*, II (January 15, 1866), 25, (February 15, 1866), 49.
23. Henry M. Turner in *Christian Recorder*, August 5, 1865. Numerous similar articles appeared in this AME church newspaper during the Civil War and early in Reconstruction.

parts. Few black applicants were equal to the accomplished schoolmistresses of the North, bureau officials admitted to critics, but some had been aided because the government "could do no better & because we wished to get them to do *something* and arouse an interest in the school work." [24] Moreover, where the cultural gap between free and freed Negroes was widest, black communities tended toward instructors closer to their own status. [25]

Recommendations that aid societies draw from the steadily increasing pool of southern black applicants achieved mixed results. Francis L. Cardozo, a member of Charleston's light-skinned elite, felt it would be better to have all or nearly all northern teachers in his school. "But the great expense prevents this, and perhaps it is best to encourage the native teachers." [26] Cardozo's sponsor, the AMA, was equally concerned about qualifications—and more so about organizations controlled by inexperienced native blacks. While readily assisting what it judged to be qualified teachers and cooperating with the AME church and the African Civilization Society, the AMA withheld essential support from the Savannah Educational Association, whose leaders "started on the principle of managing things themselves & admitting their white friends only to inferior places & as assistants in carrying out their ideas and wishes." [27] Whereas bureau superintendent Alvord and the New England Freedmen's Aid Society representative William Channing Gannett encouraged the admittedly imperfect efforts of the black association, the Reverend S. W. Magill, a white Georgian who had lived in Connecticut during the war, predicted the Savannah enterprise would fail "unless persons of more head than these col'd people yet have, can be in the ascendant." [28]

American Missionary Association officials resisted outside competition for control of territory or institutions; they let the Savannah

---

24. Alvord, *Third Semi-Annual Report,* 3–4, 32; Miss T. C. Roberts to Colonel John R. Lewis, December 7, 1869, in Bureau Records, Education Division, Georgia, Letters Received, 1869–1870; Lewis to Roberts, December 16, 1869, in Bureau Records, Education Division, Letters Sent, July 27, 1869–February 1, 1870.

25. Morris, *Reading, 'Riting, and Reconstruction,* 85–113; Leon F. Litwack, *Been in the Storm So Long: The Aftermath of Slavery* (New York, 1979), 453–55.

26. Francis L. Cardozo to Samuel Hunt, October 10, 1865, in AMA Archives.

27. S. W. Magill to M. E. Strieby, February 26, 1865, in AMA Archives.

28. *Freedmen's Record,* I (June, 1865), 92; Magill to Strieby, February 26, 1865, in AMA Archives; Edwin A. Cooley to Samuel Hunt, March 20, 1866, in AMA Archives; Richardson, *Christian Reconstruction,* 187–209. For detailed treatments of the Savannah Educational Association's brief history, see Morris, *Reading, 'Riting, and Reconstruction,* 37, 120–124, and Jones, *Soldiers of Light and Love,* 73–76.

group succumb to financial difficulties and later fought attempts to take over the fledgling colleges at Tougaloo and Atlanta. Told that blacks might insist on managing Tougaloo themselves, the AMA threatened to sever all ties with the school. Field Secretary Edward Smith warned that with black trustees in charge, school appropriations would "go principally for the aggrandizement of some Dinah and Sambo until they have floundered through two or three years— perhaps five—experience of incompetency." Faced with an analogous situation in Georgia, Atlanta University's president Edmund Asa Ware advised the AMA to select several more black teachers and specifically proposed appointing the former bureau school inspector John Mercer Langston "or some good colored man to some Professorship." Although Langston never joined the Atlanta faculty, the AMA succeeded in thwarting those members of the legislature who "wanted a '*Black College*' managed by black &c &c." [29]

Within the context of the Freedmen's Bureau program, each society had its own approach to cultural reconstruction. The AMA, although technically nondenominational, was closely identified with the Congregationalists; by 1867, the association had begun establishing Congregational churches near its schools. The denomination, however, never attracted many black members, leaving the principal evangelical organization relatively free of sectarian competition not only with the AME church and the African Civilization Society, but to some extent with southern white churches as well. Under greater pressure for reconciliation with their southern brethren, Episcopalians and Presbyterians went further. Shortly after Appomattox the general convention of the reunified Protestant Episcopal church adopted a policy of supporting southern agents, whereas the Presbyterian Committee on Freedmen dramatically increased its black contingent from both sections as part of a program "to raise up Ministers and Teachers of their own race for this people." These conciliatory policies tended to reduce local resistance, especially when measured against the sectarian approach used by northern Baptists and Methodists. [30]

29. Edward Smith to General C. H. Howard, April 2, 1870, Edmund Asa Ware to Erastus M. Cravath, [October 25, 1870], both in AMA Archives.

30. See Amos G. Beman to S. S. Jocelyn, March 7, 1859, Beman to Lewis Tappan, January 16, 1860, Charles B. Ray to Jocelyn, March 19, 1848, all in AMA Archives; Clara Merritt De Boer, "The Role of Afro-Americans in the Origin and Work of the American Missionary Association, 1839–1877" (Ph.D. dissertation, Rutgers University, 1973), 230–32, 337–53; Johnson, "The American Missionary Association, 1846–1861: A Study of Christian Abolitionism";

The secular AFUC espoused a strictly nondenominational line. "To enter the South in a spirit of denominational propagandism to plant churches already formed and organized, as men shipped houses all framed to California," Lyman Abbott wrote prior to becoming the commission's secretary, "would be, at least at present, to undertake a work of doubtful utility, and more than doubtful success."[31]

In many ways the school program was a continuation of the antebellum age of reform, offering a welcome opportunity for abolitionists, women, foreign and domestic missionaries, civil rights proponents, social reformers, suffragists, and temperance advocates. All of these elements were represented among the thousands of freedmen's educators who served in the southern states. But so, to a lesser extent, were certain negative aspects of the prewar era—nativism, anti-Catholicism, and even racial prejudice and discrimination.[32]

Although the vast majority of Yankee teachers began with racial views that were decidedly liberal by nineteenth-century standards, prejudice from some and legitimate fears about southern white resistance combined to limit true equality in relations with the freedmen. At one extreme, some educators treated freedmen as social and intellectual inferiors, and in a number of cases refused to eat or board with their black co-workers. More often, however, prejudice and policy both were involved in attenuating egalitarian ideals. Once they were in the South, egalitarians like the Reverend S. G. Wright might well accommodate to southern racial mores. According to a colleague in Natchez, Wright's susceptibility to public sentiment precluded his treating black teachers from Oberlin College as he would have done back home. Brother Wright hated slavery, John P. Bardwell explained, but the women justifiably "felt they were proscribed on account of

---

Drake, "American Missionary Association and the Southern Negro"; Richard B. Drake, "Freedmen's Aid Societies and Sectional Compromise," *Journal of Southern History*, XXIX (1963), 175–86; Robert A. Warner, "Amos Gerry Beman, 1812–1874: A Memoir on a Forgotten Leader," *Journal of Negro History*, XXII (1937), 200–21; Litwack, *Been in the Storm So Long*, 450–501; Presbyterian Church, General Assembly's Committee on Freedmen, *Second Annual Report . . .* (Pittsburgh, 1868), 7.

31. Abbott, "Southern Evangelization," 707; Lyman Abbott, "Education and Religion," *American Freedman*, I (September, 1866), 94–96; *American Missionary*, X (October, 1866), 225; Minutes for April 25, May 9, September 12, 1866, in AFUC Executive Committee Minute Book.

32. See, for example, *American Missionary*, XII (January, 1868), 14–16; *ibid.*, XI (December, 1867), 276–78; *Christian Intelligencer* quoted *ibid.*, XII (April, 1868), 85; and Charles C. Arms to Charles W. Buckley, in Bureau Records, Education Division, Alabama, Letters Received, 1865–1867.

their colour, and this naturally awakened in them a spirit of resentment."[33]

Freedmen's-aid officials from the bureau commissioner on down were anxious to counteract allegations that teachers openly practiced social equality, a breach of southern etiquette that General Howard considered one of the chief causes of local resistance. Joseph Warren, Howard's school superintendent in Mississippi, expressed a common position when he reported proudly in 1866: "I have not known a single case of association with the people on the ground of social equality. Families have been visited in the proper work of the mission, but beyond this, I think no occasion has been given for even prejudice to find fault." In North Carolina, the AMA educator Samuel S. Ashley maintained a policy of discouraging racial intermingling despite objections from instructors who did not wish to be identified with any such discriminatory arrangement. To do otherwise, Ashley insisted, would create an intolerable situation for white teachers: "We are charged with endeavoring to bring about a condition of social equality between the blacks and the whites. We are charged with teaching the blacks that they have a right to demand from the whites social equality. Now, if they can point to mission families or teachers homes where there is complete social equality between colored and white, they have proved, to their own satisfaction at least, their assertion."[34]

To a greater or lesser degree, such sectional accommodation pervaded every element of the educational program. Native resistance, violence, and schoolhouse burnings were too frequent to be ignored, compelling compromise from radicals and moderates alike. James Redpath himself found it necessary to bend before the winds of expediency while superintendent of public instruction for Charleston. Redpath has been described as "an energetic reformer—always seething with ardor, in some cause or other, scornful of compromise." Yet it

33. W. T. Richardson to Mrs. E. A. Lane, April 29, 1865, J. C. Haskell to Edward P. Smith, October 28, 1867, both in AMA Archives; H. A. Miller to William Colby, December 28, 1869, Bureau Records, Education Division, Arkansas, Letters Received, 1868–1870; John G. Fee, *Autobiography of John G. Fee* (Chicago, 1891), 180–81; H. C. Percy to Edward P. Smith, October 6, 1868, Fannie Gleason to Smith, November 6, 1868, Thomas Henson to Smith, October 6, 1868, D. White to Gen. ———, December 8, 1868, Phebe E. Henson to Smith, May 1, 1869, S. S. Ashley to Samuel Hunt, January 22, 1866, Martha L. Kellogg to George Whipple, December 17, 1866, J. P. Bardwell to Samuel Hunt, June 22, 1866, all in AMA Archives.

34. [John Watson] Alvord to O. O. Howard, July 1, 1866, in Bureau Records, Education Division, Letters Sent, January 1, 1866–October 10, 1867; John Watson Alvord, *Second Semi-Annual Report on Schools and Finances of Freedmen, July 1, 1866* (Washington, D.C., 1868), 7; S. S. Ashley to Samuel Hunt, January 22, 1866, in AMA Archives.

was he who developed the half-measure of allowing blacks and whites to attend the same schools but dividing them into separate classrooms. Getting both races into one building, the antislavery veteran reasoned, was an important "step toward destroying the prejudice against the colored people." [35]

Attempts to promote mixed schools met with little success either in bureau institutions or in the emerging state systems. Commissioner Howard believed the two races could learn together as well as apart but was quite willing to tolerate separate schools on the pragmatic assumption that southerners would not accept any other arrangement. When, early on, the AFUC did stipulate that no school should be established that recognized distinctions based on caste or color, doubts immediately arose as to the likelihood of implementing the policy. In answering a questionnaire sent out by General Secretary Lyman Abbott, most respondents said it was impossible to establish mixed schools in their respective states. "You cannot gather the whites and blacks together in the same school," declared Clinton Fisk, then the bureau's assistant commissioner for Tennessee and Kentucky. "Both rebel against it." From Virginia, R. M. Manly predicted the AFUC "would lose rather than gain by any proposition to mingle whites and blacks in the same school." It would engender charges of social equality against freedmen's teachers, Georgia superintendent G. L. Eberhart specified, and possibly destroy their usefulness entirely. Abbott later admitted that the responses to his questionnaire were among the first influences to change his opinion about the "desirability of the coeducation of the races." At the state constitutional conventions, meanwhile, freedmen's educators were divided on the same issue. Only Louisiana and South Carolina explicitly permitted mixed schools, and in the latter case the black delegates J. J. Wright and Francis Cardozo (the education committee chairman) made it clear that they expected separate institutions to predominate except in sparsely populated areas where the cost of a dual system would be prohibitive. During Reconstruction, Louisiana alone seriously tried integrated education.[36]

---

35. *Freedmen's Record,* I (April, 1865), 61–64.

36. Oliver O. Howard to John M. Schofield, November 5, 1868, in Bureau Records, Bureau Headquarters at Washington, Letters Sent, Vol. V, p. 161; *Proceedings of the Constitutional Convention of South Carolina* (2 vols. in 1; Charleston, 1868), 691–93, 706, 724, 901; *Freedmen's Record,* II (March, 1866), 38, (April, 1866), 67–68, III (December, 1867), 190; *American Freedman,* I (March, 1866), 38, (April, 1866), 5, 6, 43, (May, 1866), 30, (August, 1866), 70–76, 79. Statistics on the number of white students are found in Superintendent Alvord's semiannual reports.

Commissioner Howard set the conciliatory tone of the educational program in an address delivered to the freedmen of Lynchburg, Virginia, soon after Appomattox. Appealing for patience and gradual change, Howard instructed listeners to make and observe labor contracts and to live down predictions that they were unfit for freedom by learning fidelity, industry, and obedience. Education that included such moral lessons, he admonished, would allow freedmen to overcome racial prejudice and put themselves in a position to demand the rights that others would have difficulty guaranteeing on their behalf.[37]

Gaining southern support was a prime concern of the educational program, affecting the most basic formulations of its goals. With time, textbook exercises on John Brown and arithmetic problems involving freedmen capturing or killing Rebel soldiers gave way to more accommodating lessons. Along with the three R's, northern educators taught freedmen their new duties, inculcating "obedience to law and respect for the rights and property of others, and reverence for those in authority; enforcing honesty, industry, and economy, guarding them against fostering animosities and prejudices, and against all unjust and indecorous assumptions." The Reverend Samuel Ashley voiced a common sentiment when explaining the advantages of an AMA school to influential white residents of Lumberton, North Carolina. He and his co-workers, Ashley explained, had "no other desire or purpose than to promote the peace and prosperity of the South" by removing the "causes of dissensions & strife."[38]

Addressing national concerns about the results of emancipation, school officials emphasized the dangers inherent in denying freedmen an education. "Without it," Superintendent Alvord warned in 1866, "they will . . . quickly sink into the depravities of ignorance and vice; free to be what they please, and in the presence only of bad example, they will be carried away with every species of evil." Robert G. Fitzgerald, a black teacher from Delaware, agreed. The product of a black school in Wilmington, of Philadelphia's Institute for Colored Youth, and of Lincoln University, Fitzgerald feared the freedmen he had observed in the South would become a "dangerous element" if not educated. From his days as a teacher at Amelia Court House, Virginia, through his tenure in the public schools of North Carolina, this Union

37. Oliver O. Howard quoted in *The American Freedmen's Union Commission* (N.p., n.d.), 3.
38. Samuel S. Ashley to N. A. McLean, February 7, 1866, in AMA Archives.

veteran promoted education as necessary for the future welfare of both races, making blacks good citizens and preventing southern "prisons & poor houses from being full." [39]

Preparation for responsible citizenship became an integral part of the curriculum as educators constantly cautioned emancipated slaves against abusing their newly acquired freedom. The purpose and tone of these practical lessons are suggested by the chapter headings in a typical book of advice written especially for southern blacks: "How You Became Free," "Duties and Responsibilities," "Be a True Christian," "Be Industrious," "Be Economical," "Be Truthful and Honest," "Be Temperate," "Guard the Family Relation," "Provide for Your Family," "Educate Yourself," "Educate Your Children," "Punctuality," "To Educate Your Children You Must Provide Schools," "Support the Gospel," "Take Care of Your Sick Poor," "Respect One Another," "Be Respectful to All," and "Be Good Citizens." Implicit in this and other instructions was the premise that blacks must *earn* the esteem of whites. "Be always respectful and polite toward . . . those who have been in the habit of considering you an inferior race," Lydia Maria Child advised in a reader simultaneously teaching racial pride and responsibility. "It is one of the best ways to prove that you are not inferior." [40]

The Baptist missionary-teacher Isaac W. Brinckerhoff, responding to objections regarding his discussions of slavery, secession, and the southern "rebellion" in his textbook *Advice to Freedmen*, actually published a revised edition deleting almost everything that conceivably could alienate the former Confederates. The few remaining references to slavery treated it as a national rather that a sectional manifestation, and the wartime chapter urging freedmen to "Be Soldiers" was dropped in favor of a discussion of their "Duties and Responsibilities." [41] The editor of a Southern Baptist periodical compared the two editions in an 1868 article entitled "Conciliation."

> The first edition . . . speaks of the southern people as engaged in "rebellion"—in a war wicked and cruel on their part. This may or may not have

39. Robert G. Fitzgerald to I. N. Rendall, August 28, 1866, and Robert G. Fitzgerald Diary, January 25, 1870, both in Robert G. Fitzgerald Papers (microfilm), Schomburg Center for Research in Black Culture, New York, N.Y.
40. Isaac W. Brinckerhoff, *Advice to Freedmen* (New York, 1864); *ibid.* (2d ed.; New York, 186–[?]); Lydia Maria Child, ed., *The Freedmen's Book* (Boston, 1865), 270.
41. Brinckerhoff, *Advice to Freedmen* (2d ed.).

been well enough at the time, for the issue then was a *living* one, and the closing pages of the tract were employed in urging the colored men of the nation to engage heartily and earnestly in the work of "crushing the South." But since the cessation of armed hostilities, a revised edition of the "Advice" has been published, from which the phraseology implying the wrong of secession disappears, and we read instead simply that "our country was visited by the scourge of civil war."

Hoping to shame other northern writers into following Brinckerhoff's example, the editor concluded by asking, "Now was it misbecoming or detrimental action on the part of the American Tract Society and the author to make these changes for the sake of harmony?" [42]

Whether enunciated by northern whites or blacks, the basic precepts of cultural reconstruction were essentially the same. The stated purpose of the African Civilization Society newspaper-textbook, the *Freedmen's Torchlight,* could just as easily apply to most other evangelical aid organizations: "It is devoted to the temporal and spiritual interests of the Freedmen; and adapted to their present need of instruction in regard to simple truths and principles relating to their life, liberty, and pursuit of happiness. It will carry to and teach them the simplest elementary principles of the English language; of moral science and political ethics; and guide them in their mental, moral, social and political duties." Like their white counterparts, Afro-American educators taught students "to have a very clear idea of the personal responsibilities attending their new relation to society, and fully to understand that the state of FREEDOM is the state of SELF-RELIANCE." [43]

White and black educators called on freedmen to contribute to their own elevation, albeit with considerable assistance from their friends. Over the objections of those who believed rights should take precedence, reformers developed a gradualist strategy based on the assumption that racial improvement was the surest means of achieving equality. "It cannot be done by expostulation or complaint," spokesmen for the New England Freedmen's Aid Society insisted, "still less by self assertion and pushing on the part of those who feel aggrieved; but mainly, if not solely by their persevering effort to elevate them-

42. *Christian Index and South-Western Baptist* (Atlanta), August 6, 1868, p. 122. Mistakenly concluding that Lydia Maria Child's *The Freedmen's Book* was the only text specifically for freedmen used in Georgia, Jacqueline Jones did not analyze these revealing works or discuss Brinckerhoff's educational role in Savannah.
43. *Freedmen's Torchlight* (Brooklyn, N.Y.), December, 1866.

selves morally and intellectually, in all the fields of exertion opened to them . . . to compete for the rewards of talent and industry." [44]

Imbued with a strong Puritan work ethic applicable to both races but especially relevant to freedmen in a period of economic uncertainty, northern educators felt a pressing need to encourage self-help. For many of them, there was but one kind of freedmen's aid entirely free from doubtful results and evil influences—aid in the form of education. In the blunt language of Samuel Chapman Armstrong, at the time a bureau agent and school superintendent in eastern Virginia, it was "far better to build up character, self-respect, and intelligence, which are the conditions of all right living than to fill people with meal, meat, and herring which teach the degrading lesson of dependence." [45]

The curriculum in freedmen's schools represented a patchwork of pedagogic and practical approaches extending from conventional subjects to industrial education. Adapting northern formulas to fit the freed slaves' special situation, educators setting school policies addressed what were thought to be hereditary limitations and the retarding effects of centuries of servitude. The primary objectives centered around elevating the race on a seemingly scientific ladder of civilization, and at the same time specifically aiding southern blacks in gaining an "intelligent understanding" of their rights and duties. In pursuit of these goals, school officials steadily expanded industrial training along with school-related reform societies that encouraged such character-building virtues as temperance, clean language, chastity, marital fidelity, industry, and enterprise. [46]

Concern about the adverse effects of ignorance and immorality inevitably overlapped into the realm of politics. Most aid-society leaders shared the belief of the AFUC's secretary James Miller McKim that "democracy without the schoolmaster is an impossibility" and that "universal suffrage without universal education would be universal anarchy." Prior to passage of the Fourteenth Amendment, those involved with freedmen's affairs warned that if blacks were "left to the

44. *Freedmen's Record,* IV (September, 1868), 140.
45. [Samuel Chapman] Armstrong to "General," July 7, 1866, in Samuel Chapman Armstrong Papers, Hampton University, Hampton, Va.
46. See Alvord, *Fourth Semi-Annual Report,* 3, 73; *American Missionary,* XIII (June, 1869), 123–25; A. J. Montgomery to Edward P. Smith, May 31, 1869, in AMA Archives.

power of intemperance, to the intimidations of their former masters, or to the wiles and control of demagogues," suffrage would be a curse to themselves and the nation.[47] Afterwards, policy makers still stressed that they were interested in politics only as it affected the social and civil welfare of freedmen and other loyal elements in the South. Although bureau and aid-society leaders sometimes allowed more direct partisan involvement, they officially discouraged such participation for most school employees. Convinced that party rivalry intensified opposition to black education, leaders frequently prohibited educators from holding political office and dismissed some who concentrated too heavily on partisan instruction.[48]

As was true to a lesser extent in northern public schools, the distinction between civics instruction and political indoctrination was not always clear. South Carolina state superintendent Reuben Tomlinson came as close as anyone to describing the difference during the summer of 1867: "In the present state of society in the South, any tuition which does not include some information upon the character and condition of our whole country will fail of producing what is most needed, an intelligent and loyal population. But the statement that politics, in a partisan sense, are taught in the schools is without foundation in fact." [49]

It was not unusual for freedmen's teachers to have students read from the Emancipation Proclamation, the Constitution, Reconstruction legislation, and speeches by such radical Republican stalwarts as Samuel Shellabarger and Owen Lovejoy. Outside the classroom, some educators advised freedmen concerning their rights, involved students in the activities of the Union League or similar organizations, campaigned for Republican candidates, and arranged debates on questions such as "Will the election of Grant prove beneficial to the colored

47. J. Miller McKim to Salmon P. Chase, October 15, 1866, in McKim Papers; *American Missionary*, XI (January, 1867), 7–8.
48. See John Mercer Langston to Oliver O. Howard, August 3, 1867, in Bureau Records, Education Division, Letters Received, September, 1866–May, 1869; Caroline F. Putnam to Ralza Morse Manly, September 26, 1869, in Bureau Records, Education Division, Virginia, Letters Received, 1868–1869; *American Missionary*, XII (August, 1868), 183; Alvord, *Eighth Semi-Annual Report*, 17, 50; Robert G. Fitzgerald Diary, February 27, 1868, in Fitzgerald Papers; W. H. Butler to F. A. Fiske, October 23, 1867, Bureau Records, Education Division, North Carolina, Letters Received, 1867; John Scott to Edward P. Smith, April 30, 1868, Alva A. Hurd to Smith, March 2, 1868, both in AMA Archives. For an example of the bureau's tolerating some forms of political involvement, see Henry R. Pease to John W. Alvord, October 22, 1867, quoted in Bentley, *History of the Freedmen's Bureau*, 199, and Alvord to Pease, November 2, 1867, Bureau Records, Education Division, Letters Sent, September, 1867–July, 1868.
49. Alvord, *Fourth Semi-Annual Report*, 23.

people of the country?" and "Whether the Legislature of Georgia had a right to expel its colored members." [50]

Hoping to effect social change through moral suasion, northern educators used the bureau school system as a laboratory for refuting popular theories of racial inferiority.[51] Unrealistic though it seemed to southern critics of the freedmen's school movement, many of the northerners believed blacks should be exposed to the standard academic curriculum at all levels. In the words of Lyman Abbott: "Any scheme of education which proposes to furnish the negro race only with manual and industrial education is a covert contrivance for putting him in serfdom; it tacitly says that the negro is the inferior of the white race, and therefore we will educate him to serve us. The race must have an education which in final outcome shall be complete for the *race as a race,* which shall open opportunities for the highest culture of which any individual of that race is capable." [52] Francis Cardozo established college-preparatory classes in his select school at Charleston shortly after the end of the war, confident that these would prove "the capacity of colored young men to the *Southerners."* Between 1867 and 1870, the bureau allotted over $400,000 to twenty institutions of higher learning. By 1871, eleven colleges and universities and sixty-one normal schools in the South were educating blacks for careers in teaching, the ministry, government service, and the professions.[53]

The establishment of secondary schools and colleges to train black leaders marked a transitional phase in freedmen's education as north-

50. Broadside entitled "High School to Tarboro [N.C.] Commencement Exercises, June 1, 1870," and James H. M. Jackson to Oliver O. Howard, August 28, 1867, both in Bureau Records, Education Division, Letters Received, September, 1866–May, 1869; David Todd to George Whipple, November 1, 1866, and W. D. Harris to Whipple, February 17, 1866, both in AMA Archives; *Freedmen's Record,* III (July, 1867), 122; J. N. Murdoch to R. M. Manly, December 23, 1868, Bureau Records, Education Division, Virginia, Letters Received, 1868–1869; *American Missionary,* XIII (July, 1869), 147; *Freedmen's Record,* III (July, 1867), 122.

51. John W. Alvord to Oliver O. Howard, July 1, 1867, Bureau Records, Education Division, Letters Sent, January 1, 1866–October, 1867. For detailed information on racial theories, see also William S. Jenkins, *Pro-Slavery Thought in the Old South* (Chapel Hill, 1935), 242–84; *De Bow's Review,* After the War Ser., II (1866), 313; J. Stuart Hanckel, *Report on the Colored People and Freedmen of South Carolina* (Charleston, 1866); Thomas Carlyle, "Occasional Discourse on the Negro Question," *Fraser's Magazine* (London), XL (December, 1849), 670–79; Josiah Nott, *Types of Mankind; or, Ethnological Researches Based upon the Ancient Monuments, Paintings, Sculptures, and Crania of Races, and upon Their Natural, Geographical, Philological, and Biblical History* (Philadelphia, 1854); Alvord, *Third Semi-Annual Report,* 22; Alvord, *Fifth Semi-Annual Report;* and Alvord, *Tenth Semi-Annual Report,* 6–7.

52. Lyman Abbott, quoted in Beard, *Crusade for Brotherhood,* 265–66.

53. Francis L. Cardozo to M. E. Strieby, September 12, 1866, Reuben Tomlinson to Maj. O. D. Kinsman, March 15, 1866, Cardozo to Strieby, June 13, 1866, all in AMA Archives; *American Missionary,* X (May, 1866), 110, XIV (January, 1870), 7.

ern support for the school crusade began to decline in the 1860s. By 1867, most societies dependent on private contributions felt the effects of a waning commitment to racial reform. Disbanding in 1869, the AFUC looked to state officials to assume responsibility for the work that the aid societies had begun. Termination of the bureau in 1870, and then the Panic of 1873, further strained the resources of the remaining societies. Throughout most of the decade, all of them had to retrench or to suspend educational activities altogether. At the end of Reconstruction, only four societies maintained major educational programs for southern blacks—the AMA, the Freedmen's Aid Society of the Methodist Episcopal church, the American Baptist Home Mission Society, and the Presbyterian Committee on Freedmen.[54]

Financial difficulty was accompanied in the 1870s by heightened disillusionment with the freedmen and Reconstruction. "If I had known what I know today," Massachusetts abolitionist Charles Stearns confessed after six years as a plantation owner and freedmen's educator in Georgia, "I should not have been likely to have engaged in this almost Quixotic enterprise." Disappointed that the school program had not accomplished more, some teachers admitted they had "underestimated the benumbing effects of centuries of slavery." By the middle of the decade, veteran reformers like James Redpath were openly critical of southern blacks. Following a trip to Mississippi, the former school superintendent fumed that uneducated freedmen were "not fit to rule" in the state. "We ought never have given the negro a vote," Redpath wrote to the *Independent* in 1876, "or we ought to have forced him to learn to read, and build a school for him in every township. . . . The negro governments in Mississippi bore the same relation to orderly Republican administration, that negro minstrelsy burlesques bear to the divine symphonies of Beethoven."[55]

Soon after the end of Reconstruction, a number of past leaders from the freedmen's aid movement were calling for an end to the em-

54. *American Freedman*, II (April, 1867), 195; Philip C. Garrett to George Dixon, October 19, 1867, in Friends Freedmen's Association Records; *Freedmen's Record*, IV (July, 1868), 106–108, (November, 1868), 169; *American Freedman*, III (April, 1869), 1–2; Julius H. Parmelee, "Freedmen's Aid Societies, 1861–1871," in *Negro Education: A Study of the Private and Higher Schools for Colored People in the United States*, ed. Thomas Jesse Jones (2 vols.; Washington, D.C., 1917), I, 274–275, 286, 296–98.
55. Charles Stearns, *The Black Man of the South, and the Rebels* (Boston, 1872), 28, 153. The Redpath article is quoted in *American Missionary*, XX (September, 1876), 204–206. See also *American Missionary*, XIV (October, 1870), 234–35, XVIII (April, 1874), 85.

phasis on civil rights legislation. In a representative statement, President William Patton of Howard University advised his audience that

> neither special legislation, nor military protection, nor favor extended by those in power, nor the peculiar regard and effort of philanthropists, will, of themselves avail to procure the abolition of caste-feeling, and the elevation of the colored people to an entire equality with whites. The effects of ages of slavery are not to be removed in a day, by a mere legislative vote. An amendment to the Constitution alters no fact of ignorance, of poverty, of moral debasement. . . . Prejudices will vanish gradually in the presence of increasing evidence of noble manhood. Developed intellectual power, the higher education, success in industrial pursuits, and acquirement of wealth and culture and character will cause them to disappear.[56]

With Reconstruction giving way to Redemption, those still active in freedmen's affairs revived their emphasis on education as the most acceptable engine for racial reform. After nearly a decade of decline, the surviving missionary societies began an unprecedented period of growth, spending more on black schools in 1885 or 1890 than they had in 1870. Largely leaving mass education to southern public school systems, these societies sharpened the old focus on black self-help, practical training, the refutation of prejudice through education, and the gradual improvement of racial conditions. Most officials, feeling the need to strike a balance between the ideals and exigencies of educational reconstruction, abandoned the rhetoric of abolitionism and adopted a more conservative position on civil rights and racial equality. Less than twenty years in the making, the process owed as much to politics and a willingness to compromise as it did to disillusionment with the excesses of the postwar period.

The best recent scholarship has recognized these compromises without denying the substantial achievements of an effort that laid the foundations of black education in the South. As Eric Foner summed up the resulting synthesis in *Reconstruction: America's Unfinished Revolution,* the bureau's program was a "typical nineteenth-century amalgam of benevolent uplift and social control."[57] Inevitably, special

---

56. *American Missionary,* XXII (January, 1878), 16–17.

57. Foner, *Reconstruction: America's Unfinished Revolution,* 146. See also Lawrence A. Cremin, *American Education: The National Experience, 1783–1876* (New York, 1980), 516–21. For a balanced history of the black secondary school first superintended by Thomas and Francis Cardozo see Edmund L. Drago, *Initiative, Paternalism, and Race Relations: Charleston's Avery Institute* (Athens, Ga., 1990). Covering the period 1865 through 1969, Drago places the

pleading and presentism have influenced interpretations of this crucial area. For instance, in attempting to highlight the "movement by ex-slaves to develop an educational system appropriate to defend and extend their emancipation," James D. Anderson seriously underestimated the significance of the bureau program. "The values of self-help and self-determination underlay the ex-slaves' educational movement," Anderson concluded in 1988. "To be sure, they accepted support from northern missionary societies, the Freedmen's Bureau, and some southern whites, but their own action—class self-activity informed by an ethic of mutuality—was the primary force that brought schools to the children of freed men and women."[58]

Reconstruction's most durable myth, the stereotypical Yankee schoolmarm, has for decades served as a conveniently ambiguous symbol in an ongoing racial and sectional debate. Over the years, those on either side of this debate have shaped the image for particular ends—to make the case for academic or industrial education, to criticize northern involvement in southern affairs, to trace the development of segregated schools, and generally to compare the civil rights crusades of the nineteenth and twentieth centuries. After nearly half a century largely limited to assessing the northern white teacher and the appropriateness of freedmen's education, however, historians have finally begun to recognize the complexity and contradictions in a subject most thought had been exhausted long ago.

institution in the context of class and color within Charleston's black community while also treating external racism and paternalism.

58. In a chapter filled with straw men and selective interpretations, Anderson categorically challenged attributing the freedmen's school movement to "Yankee benevolence or federal largesse." More convincing was his reiteration of the position that Afro-Americans throughout the South "contributed significantly to the origin and development of universal schooling." James D. Anderson, *The Education of Blacks in the South, 1860–1935* (Chapel Hill, 1988), 1–32.

8

Black Economic Reconstruction in the South

୬ LOREN SCHWENINGER

The appearance in 1961 of John Hope Franklin's *Reconstruction: After the Civil War* marked both an end and a beginning. Gracefully synthesizing a growing revisionist literature, Franklin laid bare the myths that for many years had dominated the study of the postwar era. With "notable balance and judicious temper," one reviewer said, he revealed the complex and subtle changes that occurred during a period of rapid transition. In doing so, he demonstrated the inadequacy of the old stereotypes of the greedy carpetbagger, the villainous scalawag, and the lazy, ignorant Negro. Indeed, with regard to blacks, Franklin contended there was a "new dignity, a new pride, a new self-respect" in their economic and social relations following the end of slavery. Although he said relatively little about black economic reconstruction per se, *Reconstruction* was instrumental in opening the field to specialists who could ask new questions and employ new techniques.

In the generation that followed, historians produced a substantial literature about the Reconstruction era. Influenced by the civil rights movement of the 1960s and a growing awareness of the importance of racial matters in American life, scholars examined the political, social, cultural, and economic changes that occurred as a result of the Civil War with an intensity matched perhaps only in recent studies of slavery. Some thought that a better understanding of Reconstruction might lead to brighter prospects during what Franklin and others have termed the "Second Reconstruction" of the modern era. As a result, a number of historians paid particular attention to the economic plight of southern blacks.

Although the writings on this subject are varied, scholars in the field generally fall into one of three categories: those who focus primarily on the political dimensions of black economic problems, those who stress the role of competitive markets, and those who emphasize racial exploitation. The best writers, of course, analyze the political, social, and economic trends in a broader context, seeking to understand the interplay of each with the others. Even these writers, however, tend to accentuate politics, the free market, or black oppression. This essay seeks to assess the strengths and weaknesses of this literature and to offer a new, perhaps more illuminating model for analyzing black economic reconstruction in the South.[1]

During the 1960s and 1970s, revisionist scholars, responding to the racial stereotypes in the works of William A. Dunning and his students at the turn of the century, published a large number of books and articles on the politics of Reconstruction. Although concerned primarily with Congress, the Republican party, and the presidency, these scholars also asked questions about how government agencies and private institutions responded to the economic needs of the former slaves. They discovered that during the war years, neither the president nor northern political leaders nor Union army officers had formulated a clear, coherent policy with regard to assisting freedmen. Fearing that Negroes would never be afforded equal opportunities in the South, Lincoln and other Republicans had seriously considered the possibility of colonizing freed people in West Africa, the Caribbean, or South America. Even after Congress passed a law creating a direct tax on all real estate in the United States, including abandoned plantations, it was not clear how the law might affect former slaves. Would land confiscated for nonpayment of this tax be sold and distributed to freed-

---

1. John Hope Franklin, *Reconstruction: After the Civil War* (Chicago, 1961), 189. Excluding the sources cited below, other books appearing since the early 1960s dealing with the subject include: Robert Francis Engs, *Freedom's First Generation: Black Hampton, Virginia, 1861–1890* (Philadelphia, 1979); Peter Kolchin, *First Freedom: The Responses of Alabama's Blacks to Emancipation and Reconstruction* (Westport, Conn., 1972); Edward Magdol, *The Right to the Land: Essays on the Freedmen's Community* (Westport, Conn., 1977); Daniel A. Novak, *The Wheel of Servitude: Black Forced Labor After Slavery* (Lexington, Ky., 1978); Howard Rabinowitz, *Race Relations in the Urban South, 1865–1890* (New York, 1978); Joel Williamson, *After Slavery: The Negro in South Carolina During Reconstruction, 1861–1877* (Chapel Hill, 1965).

men? Indeed, did Congress have the authority to institute such a tax and then confiscate an individual's property?[2]

At the same time, revisionists explained, Union army officers had initiated their own remedies concerning freedmen and abandoned lands. In the West, Generals Benjamin Butler and Nathaniel Banks instructed former slaveholders to pay wages to their former slaves until more satisfactory agreements could be worked out. Army chaplain John Eaton organized a land redistribution scheme in 1862 at Davis Bend, Mississippi (on two plantations owned by Joseph Davis, Jefferson Davis' older brother), only to encounter opposition from Treasury Department officials, who claimed jurisdiction over the disposition of the land. Eaton's counterparts in the East were General Rufus Saxon, military governor of the South Carolina and Georgia Sea Islands, and General David Hunter, an abolitionist appointed as a member of the tax commission that was charged with the sale and distribution of "plantations heretofore occupied by rebels." By the time Sherman arrived in Savannah in December, 1864, Saxon and Hunter already had supervised the sale of more than 50,000 acres of land to black families. Even as these sales were taking place, several members of the tax commission, as well as some northern politicians, argued that such auctions might be considered illegal at war's end. Shortly after his arrival, Sherman issued an order (later famous as Field Order No. 15) declaring that the territory from Charleston, South Carolina, to the St. Johns River in Florida, and stretching thirty miles inland, be set aside for freed slaves, with each family to receive forty acres of tillable ground and, if available, a surplus army mule (the probable origin of "forty acres and a mule"). Sherman stipulated, however, that Congress would have to make a final decision on this plan. In short, as Willie Lee Rose and others have pointed out, federal policy toward black economic reconstruction was uncertain, contradictory, and ambiguous.[3]

After the war, according to the revisionists, it was much the same

2. Roy P. Basler, ed., *The Collected Works of Abraham Lincoln,* (9 vols.; New Brunswick, N.J., 1953), IV, 561; Benjamin Quarles, *Lincoln and the Negro* (New York, 1962), 108; LaWanda Cox, *Lincoln and Black Freedom: A Study in Presidential Leadership* (Columbia, S.C., 1981), 29; James M. McPherson, *Ordeal by Fire: The Civil War and Reconstruction* (New York, 1982), 158, 271; Claude F. Oubre, *Forty Acres and a Mule: The Freedmen's Bureau and Black Land Ownership* (Baton Rouge, 1978), 8.

3. Peyton McCrary, *Abraham Lincoln and Reconstruction: The Louisiana Experiment* (Princeton, N.J., 1978), 117–19; Janet Sharp Hermann, *The Pursuit of a Dream* (New York, 1981), 5, 44–49; Willie Lee Rose, *Rehearsal for Reconstruction: The Port Royal Experiment*

story. The national government, the state and local authorities, and the various philanthropic organizations were unable to provide more than temporary assistance to the nearly four million recently freed blacks. In many areas freedmen suffered grievously from want of clothing, food, medical supplies, and adequate housing. In a series of books and articles, Joel Williamson, Claude Oubre, Joe Gray Taylor, Carl R. Osthaus, Carol Bleser, William McFeely, Joe Richardson, and Howard Ashley White, among others, have recounted a dreary tale of lost opportunities and failed programs. They showed how radical proposals to distribute land to blacks never materialized; how the Bureau of Refugees, Freedmen, and Abandoned Lands, a federal agency designed to assist blacks, failed to help freedmen gain an economic stake; how the Freedmen's Trust and Savings Bank, although successful in attracting depositors—especially former slaves in their twenties—went into receivership in 1874, destroying the faith of some blacks in banking institutions for a generation; how the 1866 Southern Homestead Act, which set aside forty-four million acres of public lands in Alabama, Arkansas, Florida, Louisiana, and Mississippi, primarily for former slaves, failed to attract more than a few thousand homesteaders; and how the South Carolina Land Commission (the only state institution organized to deal with the problem of putting blacks on their own land) was a study in political wrangling, duplicity, corruption, and fraud. In addition, a number of writers have demonstrated that President Andrew Johnson stood firmly against these various programs and sympathized with former Confederates.[4]

(New York, 1964), 152; Oubre, *Forty Acres and a Mule*, 9; Laura Towne, *Letters and Diary of Laura M. Towne: Written from the Sea Islands of South Carolina, 1862–1884*, ed. Rupert Holland (1912; rpr. New York, 1969), 34; J. M. Fairfield to William Brisbane, February 15, 1864, in Records of South Carolina Direct Tax Commission, Records of Internal Revenue, Record Group 58, National Archives. The origin of "forty acres and a mule" remains obscure and may never be known with certainty, but the slogan most likely evolved in the Sea Islands of South Carolina following Sherman's order. The idea of providing freed slaves with land had its inception among abolitionists prior to the Civil War. See James McPherson, *The Struggle for Equality: Abolitionists and the Negro in the Civil War and Reconstruction* (Princeton, N.J., 1964), 246–68.

4. See Oubre, *Forty Acres and a Mule*; Joe Gray Taylor, *Louisiana Reconstructed, 1863–1877* (Baton Rouge, 1974); Carl R. Osthaus, *Freedmen, Philanthropy, and Fraud: A History of the Freedman's Savings Bank* (Urbana, Ill., 1976); Carol K. Bleser, *The Promised Land: The History of the South Carolina Land Commission, 1869–1890* (Columbia, S.C., 1969); William S. McFeely, *Yankee Stepfather: General O. O. Howard and the Freedmen* (New Haven, 1968); Joe M. Richardson, *Christian Reconstruction: The American Missionary Association and Southern Blacks, 1861–1890* (Athens, Ga., 1986); Howard Ashley White, *The Freedmen's Bureau in Louisiana* (Baton Rouge, 1970); Eric L. McKitrick, *Andrew Johnson and Reconstruction* (Chicago, 1960); John H. Cox and LaWanda Cox, *Politics, Principle, and Prejudice, 1865–1866: Dilemma of Reconstruction America* (New York, 1963).

The revisionist historians were asking political questions about economic problems, and so their findings, although often engaging, gracefully put forth, and interesting, also were often predictable. In fact, writing during the era of the Great Society programs, some of them started out with the assumption that it was government's responsibility to assist disadvantaged people. From a historical perspective, what group was more disadvantaged than slaves emerging into freedom? Thus, revisionists were concerned mostly about how government responded to the needs of freedmen. More important, since it was generally accepted that official responses did little to solve blacks' economic problems, how and why did Reconstruction fail so abysmally in this regard? If Congress had acted differently, if President Johnson's opposition had been less strident, if former plantation owners had not been allowed to regain control of their land, if sympathetic whites had been put in charge of various programs, and if at the moment of defeat the conquered South had been forced to grant sweeping economic concessions, William McFeely argued, not only would the Freedmen's Bureau have had a chance for success, but the specter of "perpetual debt" and virtual bondage also would have been eliminated.[5] Almost invariably, similarly persuaded scholars either implicitly or explicitly expressed their frustrations at the failure of the government or private philanthropy to fulfill the economic promise of Reconstruction. Perhaps in the future, during a Second Reconstruction, a more equitable and economically just society would emerge in the South. "If" history, of course, has its limitations and is cast in large measure around contemporary problems.

Using new statistical tools and asking different questions, a group of economic historians turned their attention during the 1970s to the postbellum South. The revisionists had asked why various agencies had failed to assist the former slaves; the new economic historians asked, What were the economic consequences of emancipation? The earlier scholars had agreed on the main features of the nation's postwar economic development: expansion in the North, retardation in the South, failed federal and state programs. In the writings of the later authors, two distinct and contradictory interpretations emerged.

The first interpretation, which has been called the "competitive

5. William S. McFeely, "Unfinished Business: The Freedmen's Bureau and Federal Action in Race Relations," in *Key Issues in the Afro-American Experience*, ed. Nathan I. Huggins *et al.* (2 vols.; New York, 1971), II, 15, 22, 23.

model," was advanced by Robert Higgs, Joseph R. Reid, Jr., and Stephen J. DeCanio. They asserted that despite the efforts of whites to control freedmen through intimidation, violence, and "restrictive cartels," blacks made significant economic progress following the Civil War. Their per capita income rose at an annual rate of about 2.7 percent; their housing, diet, living standards, and material wealth rose significantly; their ownership of real property increased. Even those who labored as sharecroppers and tenant farmers experienced improvements in areas directly related to material progress: education, literacy, acquisition of skills, and managerial knowledge. Because competitive forces were at work in the South, Higgs explained in his 1977 study *Competition and Coercion,* whites were not always able to control black agricultural workers, whether as wage laborers, sharecroppers, or share tenant farmers. "Competition also prevented the general emergence of racial discrimination in wage payments or farm rental agreements," Higgs noted, and as a result, "economic progress did occur during the first 15 years after the war." The development of the tenancy system actually meant both higher incomes and greater independence for blacks than they might have achieved under other systems. In addition, "land ownership conferred even greater benefits; and some found opportunities in nonagricultural employments." Despite white coercion, asserted those who employed the competitive model, blacks made significant economic advances during the Reconstruction era.[6]

The same year that Higgs published his findings, Roger L. Ransom and Richard Sutch, in *One Kind of Freedom: The Economic Consequences of Emancipation,* advanced a more complex interpretation of blacks in the postwar South. On the one hand, they tended to agree with some of the conclusions put forth by the competitive-model scholars. Focusing on five states in the lower South, they estimated that

---

6. Robert Higgs, *The Transformation of the American Economy, 1865–1914: An Essay in Interpretation* (New York, 1971); Robert Higgs, "Did Southern Farmers Discriminate?" *Agricultural History,* XLVI (April, 1972), 325–28; Robert Higgs, *Competition and Coercion: Blacks in the American Economy, 1865–1914* (Cambridge, Mass., 1977), 61, 134; Joseph D. Reid, "Sharecropping as an Understandable Market Response: The Post-Bellum South," *Journal of Economic History,* XXXIII (1973), 106–30; Joseph D. Reid, "Sharecropping and Agricultural Uncertainty," *Economic Development and Cultural Change,* XXIV (1976), 549–76; Stephen J. DeCanio, "Agricultural Production, Supply, and Institutions in the Post–Civil War South," *Journal of Economic History,* XXXII (1972), 396–98; Stephen J. DeCanio, "Productivity and Income Distribution in the Post-Bellum South," *Journal of Economic History,* XXXIV (1974), 422–46; Stephen J. DeCanio, *Agriculture in the Postbellum South: The Economics of Production and Supply* (Cambridge, Mass., 1974). See Harold D. Woodman, "Sequel to Slavery: The New History Views the Postbellum South," *Journal of Southern History,* XLIII (1977), 525.

black per capita agricultural income increased by 46 percent between 1857 and 1879, with most of this increase coming during the early years of freedom. With a decline of 35 percent in white per capita income during the same period, by 1879 blacks had reached more than half the level of white southerners. This was the greatest proportionate redistribution of income in American history. In addition, there were some small improvements in housing, diet, and landownership. In the end, however, these gains had to be measured against the fact that the freedmen's economic, political, and social freedom was "under constant attack by the dominant white society determined to preserve racial inequalities." "The economic institutions established in the postemancipation era effectively operated to keep the black population a landless agricultural labor force, operating tenant farms with a backward and unprogressive technology." What little income was earned above the bare subsistence level was often "exploited by monopolistic credit merchants." [7]

Whereas Ransom and Sutch were cautious about discussing the exploitative and oppressive nature of black economic reconstruction, suggesting that in some areas there were advances, however limited, several other economic historians offered a more sweeping indictment of the postwar South. The Marxist-oriented scholars Jonathan M. Wiener and Jay R. Mandle, as well as the labor historian William Cohen, contended that with freedom came a new type of slavery. They argued that the continued hold of the planter elite on the land, the creation of the sharecropping system, the institutionalization of the crop lien system, and the agreements among white landowners not to compete with one another for black workers gave white planters a virtual monopoly over the economy of the South. "Planters throughout the South in the years immediately following the war organized to limit competition among themselves," Wiener explained. "At a typical meeting in the fall of 1867, planters in Sumter County, Alabama, unanimously resolved that 'concert of action' was 'indispensable' in hiring labor." Each of them promised to offer exactly the same terms of employment to freed slaves and vowed not to "employ any laborer discharged for violation of contracts." The conspiracies among white

---

7. Roger L. Ransom and Richard Sutch, *One Kind of Freedom: The Economic Consequences of Emancipation* (New York, 1977), 198; Roger L. Ransom and Richard Sutch, "Growth and Welfare in the American South of the Nineteenth Century," *Explorations in Economic History*, XVI (1979), 225.

landholders, along with the pernicious effects of racism, kept freedmen in a condition of perpetual debt and quasi-slavery. Too much of the "recent debate" had treated southern economic and political developments separately, Wiener averred. In fact, the South's poverty and the political oppression of Negroes were inextricably intertwined. White southerners chose to follow the "Prussian Road," rejecting "true democracy" while instituting a savage "labor-repressive system of agricultural production."[8]

Almost as soon as they appeared, these various interpretations came under vigorous attack. In a probing analysis titled "Sequel to Slavery: The New History Views the Postbellum South," Harold Woodman dismissed as too narrow Higgs's argument concerning market forces and the lack of economic discrimination. To define the market strictly in terms of the final economic transactions—the purchase price of labor power, land, and other commodities—Woodman wrote, was to create an artificial distinction between the economic milieu and the social and political context in which such transactions took place. "Because they concentrate on market place behavior and do not consider the political economy of the market itself, Higgs, Reid, and DeCanio failed to consider the fundamental features of the postbellum southern economy," Woodman said. "They ignore social classes and class relations; and violence and intimidation, although recognized, are really irrelevant because they have no discernible effect on income, wage rates, and land-tenure arrangements." But he found the "virtual slavery" argument equally unconvincing. Admitting that there were various forms of labor coercion—"a vicious system of labor repression"—he nevertheless argued that southern tenant farmers and sharecroppers were not "bound" to the land. "They could—and, in fact, did—move more often and more regularly than did their Northern counterparts." Had the various local laws and other coercive methods been fully enforced, it would have been easily discernible, but in fact there was a good deal of movement by blacks. As a result, various forms of tenant farming emerged—thirds and fourths, halves, standing rent, and cash rent—in response not only to the market but also as

8. Jonathan Wiener, *Social Origins of the New South: Alabama, 1860–1885* (Baton Rouge, 1978), 72–73; Jonathan Wiener, "Class Structure and Economic Development in the American South, 1865–1955," *American Historical Review,* LXXXIV (1979), 973–74; Jay R. Mandle, *The Roots of Black Poverty: The Southern Plantation Economy After the Civil War* (Durham, N.C., 1978), 23–27; William Cohen, "Negro Involuntary Servitude in the South, 1865–1940: A Preliminary Analysis," *Journal of Southern History,* XLII (1976), 31–60.

part of the emergence of "new classes and new class relationships." Woodman pointed out the difference between share tenants and share-croppers, the latter having no right to dispose of his "share" since he possessed only a laborer's lien against the landlord equal to the value of his share of the crop, whereas the share tenant, after paying the landlord, could dispose of the crop as he wished. What was emerging in the South after emancipation, Woodman contended, was "a kind of unfettered capitalism," peculiarly southern in that the "evolving bourgeois society" was arising on the "ruins of a premodern slave society."[9]

Drawing on the works of revisionists, cliometricians, and others, as well as the records of the Freedmen's Bureau, the economic historian Gerald David Jaynes recently published the most comprehensive and detailed account of black economic reconstruction. By concentrating on only two decades, expanding the breadth of his inquiry to include such topics as "Work-Leisure and the Meaning of Freedom," "Industrial Relations and the Turnover of Labor," "The Labor-Managed Economy," and "Negro Agrarianism," and by emphasizing "real-world economic phenomena"—for example, violence, intimidation, and convict labor—Jaynes separated himself from economic historians who rely on economic and statistical models. Yet in his analysis of the "inseparable interactions" between racism and economics he portrayed as bleak a picture of the postwar black economic adjustment as that of the most ardent racial-exploitation scholars. "The competition of convict labor, the legal crushing of a free market for mobile wage labor, the landlord-merchant lien, and control of the productive and redistributive process to the exclusion of laborers, who had all the obligations of entrepreneurs but few of the benefits, all confined the southern laborer within a system that bred exploitation."[10]

This ever-increasing literature has greatly expanded understanding of the political and economic forces at work during the Civil War and Reconstruction, producing a clear picture of the unique problems for-

---

9. Woodman, "Sequel to Slavery," 534–35, 552, 554; Harold D. Woodman, "Comment" on Jonathan Wiener's "Class Structure and Economic Development in the American South, 1865–1955," in *American Historical Review*, LXXXIV (1979), 997–1001. See also Gavin Wright, "Comment on Papers of Reid, Ransom and Sutch, and Higgs," *Journal of Economic History*, XXXIII (1973), 170.

10. Gerald David Jaynes, *Branches Without Roots: Genesis of the Black Working Class in the American South, 1862–1882* (New York, 1986), 314.

mer slaves confronted as they made the transition to freedom. There is little doubt that the nation failed to deal adequately with those problems. Yet despite the vitality of the scholarship and the heated debates among economic historians, a comprehensive picture of black economic reconstruction in the South still is lacking. One problem is that some scholars anchor their analyses in theoretical abstractions and, as Woodman notes, either ignore changes over time or treat a particular historical situation as if it had been static. Other historians offer broad generalizations from investigations of specific locations. In both cases, the writers fail to heed the admonition of Ira Berlin that the black experience can be comprehended "only through a careful delineation of temporal and spatial differences," that is, of changes over time in different subregions of the South. Perhaps what is most distressing is the fact that although there is some truth in each of the various interpretations—relatively weak discrimination in some areas allowed market forces to work without hindrance, while in other areas the hegemony of the planter aristocracy remained much as it had during the antebellum era—until the "temporal and spatial differences" are more fully understood, the larger picture must remain incomplete.[11]

One way to gain a better understanding of black economic reconstruction is through a systematic analysis of black property ownership in various parts of the South during what historians refer to as the "middle period," the years just before, during, and just after the Civil War. By focusing on economic politics, the market place, and racial discrimination, scholars—with rare exceptions—have virtually ignored this subject. This neglect is surprising, since any understanding of economic reconstruction, it would seem, should begin with an examination of black wealth. By analyzing Negro property ownership after the war, comparing it with prewar holdings, viewing the South's towns and cities as well as its agricultural regions, and looking at both the upper and lower South, one can shift the focus from the propertyless to the propertied, from white oppression to black aspiration. Most freedmen, of course, remained desperately poor in the years following the Emancipation Proclamation. Yet, as revealed in the musty volumes of the United States population censuses—the only source connecting

11. Ira Berlin, "Time, Space, and the Evolution of Afro-American Society in British Mainland North America," *American Historical Review*, LXXXV (1980), 78.

racial identity with property estimates (real and personal) in 1860 and 1870 for the South as a whole—by 1870, tens of thousands of blacks already had begun the long journey toward self-sufficiency.

The ownership of property among slaves prior to the Civil War has only recently become a subject for historical inquiry. In his detailed investigation of low-country blacks in the Carolinas and Georgia, the historian Philip Morgan has shown that significant numbers of slaves became property owners during the antebellum era. Despite the impressionistic nature of some of the evidence—the testimony of postwar investigators, the recollections of former slaves, contemporary laws designed to curtail "pretended ownership"—blacks in bondage did obtain various types of personal property, including cattle, horses, pigs, fodder, staple crops, wagons, extra clothing, money, watches, and other items. Those who worked in the task system—that is, who were assigned a task at the beginning of the day and once the assignment was completed had the remainder of their time to work for themselves—had the best opportunities in this regard. By the eve of the Civil War, slave property owners could be found not only along the Sea Island coast of South Carolina and Georgia, but all across the lower South, in most towns and cities, and on plantations and farms in the upper South. "I know it is hard for some to realize or imagine how it was possible for slaves to own property," wrote Virgil Hillyer, an investigator in Georgia for the Southern Claims Commission, created by Congress to identify and provide restitution to northern loyalists who had lost personal property to Union soldiers during the Civil War. Yet, Hillyer continued, there "are colored persons in Savannah worth their thousands; some in our market who can buy 30 or 300 head of cattle at a time, and did so before and during the war." After many months of investigation, Hillyer believed that property ownership among slaves was widespread "all through the Southern states." Such comments, coming as they did from a northern-born Unionist who was sympathetic toward freedmen, might have been viewed with suspicion, but subsequent investigators, including southern-born former Confederates, confirmed Hillyer's findings.[12]

---

12. Philip D. Morgan, "The Ownership of Property by Slaves in the Mid-Nineteenth-Century Low Country," *Journal of Southern History,* XLIX (1983), 399–420; Lawrence T. McDonnell, "Money Knows No Master: Market Relations and the American Slave Community," in *Developing Dixie: Modernization in a Traditional Society,* ed. Winfred B. Moore, Jr., *et*

More precision can be brought to analyzing prewar property-holding among free blacks, since United States census takers in 1850 and 1860 asked every head of household in the nation to estimate the value of his or her real estate; in 1860 personal property was estimated as well. On the eve of the Civil War, nearly one of five (9,581 of 52,383) free black family heads owned realty, compared with two of five whites; nearly one of three (16,044) owned real or personal property worth at least $100, compared with three of five whites. In the Gulf States and South Carolina, small groups of skilled artisans and a few Negro plantation owners (mostly mulattoes directly related to the master class) had achieved an economic status not far below—and in some instances well above—the average for whites. In the upper South, especially in Virginia and Maryland, larger numbers of black farmers and farm workers, mostly a generation or so removed from bondage, had acquired land. For many of them, the long road from slavery to freedom had consumed most of their energy and resources, and even those who achieved landed status controlled relatively small amounts of property—the average in Virginia stood at only $648. Even so, when the first shots were fired on Fort Sumter, every southern state had a significant cohort of property-owning blacks, both slave and free.

Following emancipation, former slaves confronted many obstacles in their efforts to become economically self-sufficient: the legacy of bondage, lack of assistance from federal and state authorities, the hold of whites on the land (especially in the lower South), the emergence of the Ku Klux Klan and other terrorist groups, and a host of economic problems—floods, crop failures, lack of credit, scarcity of money, wartime destruction, and increased competition in towns and cities from various immigrant groups. Yet the freed slaves viewed their new status as one of opportunity. Most blacks rejected working on the plantation in gangs, as they had labored in the past. They preferred to move out on their own. Since few could afford to purchase land or even rent farm acreage, they engaged in various kinds of sharecropping. Despite

al. (Westport, Conn., 1988), 31–44; Virgil Hillyer to J. B. Howell, March 22, 1873, Hillyer to Asa Aldis, February 21, 1874, both in Records of the Southern Claims Commission, Records of the Treasury Department, Record Group 56, National Archives; Report to the Commissioners of Claims, July 18, 1876, in William Paine Papers, Georgia Historical Society; William Paine to Charles Benjamin, June 24, 1876, in Records of the Southern Claims Commission.

its limitations, sharecropping offered them the potential of a higher income, capital to engage in farming, the possibility of greater rewards for hard work, and a significant amount of independence from white control.

Only a few former slaves made the transition from sharecropping to landownership, but almost universally, the freedmen expressed their desire to own land. "What's de use of being free," one elderly black asked the journalist Whitelaw Reid in 1865, "if you don't own land enough to be buried in?" One white observer in postwar South Carolina asserted that former slaves had "a passion" to obtain land: they would sacrifice almost anything to obtain a few acres of their own. The Union general Rufus Saxon agreed, saying that freed slaves "have shown that they can appreciate freedom as the highest boon; [that] they will be industrious and provident with the same incitement which stimulates the industry of other men in free societies; that they understand the value of property and are eager for its acquisition, especially of land; that they can conduct their private affairs with sagacity, prudence and success." [13]

Success, of course, was relative and had various meanings for former slaves. Some spoke of "getting ahead" or "accumulating wealth"; others accepted the teachings of black political leaders, northern missionaries, or Freedmen's Bureau officials who entreated them to become frugal, hard-working, and industrious; still others, after a lifetime of bondage, simply wanted to be left alone. By owning a few acres of land, planting vegetables and corn, raising a few head of livestock, hunting and fishing, they could distance themselves not only from the impersonal forces of the market place, but from their former masters as well. This was especially the case in the Sea Islands of South Carolina and Georgia, a region that has claimed the attention of scholars far out of proportion to its importance. There, Eric Foner has suggested, a unique combination of circumstances, including initial government programs, the breakup of the great plantations, black political power, and the collapse of rice production, allowed a majority of

13. *Nation*, I (1865), 354, 393; Whitelaw Reid, *After the War: A Tour of the Southern States, 1865–1866* (1866; rpr. New York, 1965), 564; Edward Ord to Ulysses Grant (telegram), April 19, 1865, in *The Papers of Ulysses S. Grant*, ed. John Simon (14 vols.; Carbondale, Ill., 1985), XIV, 412n; *Senate Executive Documents*, 39th Cong., 1st Sess., No. 27, p. 120; Edwin D. Hoffman, "From Slavery to Self-Reliance: The Record of Achievement of the Freedmen of the Sea Island Region," *Journal of Negro History*, XLI (1956), 19.

blacks to become landowners. Although access to the land made low-country freedmen ("peasants," as Foner calls them) independent and autonomous, they suffered from the same "debilitating disadvantages that afflicted peasant agriculture throughout the world, among them a credit system that made direct access to capital impossible, an inability to invest in fertilizer or machinery, vulnerability to the vagaries of the national and international markets, and the demands for taxation of an oppressive state." In short, black landowners had not risen above the barest subsistence level.[14]

In other regions of the rural South, and in towns and cities, some blacks acquired holdings worth more than a few subsistence acres. Within five years after emancipation, the 1870 census indicates, rural blacks in the western sections of the upper South and some freedmen who migrated to urban areas in the upper and lower South already had made significant advances in accumulating property. Their success depended both on the willingness of whites not to stand in the way of their purchasing land or city property and on favorable economic circumstances. In Kentucky, Tennessee, and Missouri, some former slaves moved with little difficulty from bondage to farm ownership. With the support, and in some sections the protection, of whites, and aided by a strong demand for laborers and farm hands, the number of black rural landholders in these three states increased by 744 percent (from 775 to 6,538) during the 1860s. Some of them were only part-time farmers who also worked as day laborers, harvest hands, woodcutters, and rail-splitters. In Boyle County, Kentucky, for example, Charles Christopher, James Warren, Harrison Bruce, and Jesse Jones, who each farmed several acres, were listed as laborers. In Pike County, Missouri, Thornton Washington, Ned Holloway, and Frederick Ball each owned between $800 and $1,000 worth of farm land, but the first two were listed in the census as hired hands, and the third as a blacksmith. Although the average holdings of these rural realty owners in the western states remained small—between $580 in Kentucky and $709 in Tennessee—the rise in their numbers actually kept pace with the eight-fold increase in the number of free rural black families in the wake of emancipation. By 1870, one of twelve black rural family heads in Mis-

14. Eric Foner, *Nothing but Freedom: Emancipation and Its Legacy* (Baton Rouge, 1983), 108–109; Maris A. Vinovskis, "Have Social Historians Lost the Civil War? Some Preliminary Demographic Speculations," *Journal of American History,* LXXVI (1989), 38–39.

souri, one of fifteen in Kentucky, and one of twenty-two in Tennessee, was a real estate owner.[15]

There was also a sharp increase in the number of urban property owners during the 1860s. In the towns and cities of the upper South, the number of black realty owners rose significantly: in Baltimore, from 169 in 1860 to approximately 435 in 1870; in the District of Columbia, from 497 to 1,019; in Lexington, from 44 to 671; and in Wilmington, North Carolina, from 42 to 408. Representing only 15 percent of the upper South's black population (266,188 of 1,808,655), city dwellers in 1870 comprised 34 percent of the realty owners and controlled 49 percent of the total black wealth ($8,863,500 of $18,197,400). In the District of Columbia in 1870, one out of eight black family heads owned real estate. Its value exceeded $2,305,900, or $2,263 per realty holder. This did not compare favorably with the figures for whites, who made up 68 percent of the city's population but owned 98 percent of the property. Yet the total realty holdings among urban blacks in the upper South had nearly quadrupled (from $2,285,900) in only ten years. In Wilmington, the 42 free blacks listed for 1860 owned $55,600 worth of land; the 408 black realty owners who lived there a decade later controlled holdings valued at $247,900. In Nashville, Tennessee, there were 44 antebellum black landowners, with property worth $119,400; in 1870, 65 black owners controlled $245,300. In St. Louis, 94 black real estate owners controlled $428,600 before the war; afterwards, approximately 128 owners controlled $765,100 worth of property.

Except in Charleston and New Orleans, similar growth occurred in the urban lower South. The rising demand for skilled and unskilled black workers, especially to rebuild buildings destroyed during the war, and the continued importance of small towns as trading and merchandising centers gave some freedmen an opportunity to improve their economic condition. In Selma and Mobile, Alabama; Pensacola, Florida; Savannah, Valdosta, and Augusta, Georgia; Columbia, South Carolina; and other small towns and cities in the region, the number

---

15. United States Manuscript Population Census (hereinafter cited as USMSPC), Boyle County, Kentucky, 1870, p. 220; USMPC, Pike County, Missouri, 1870, pp. 156, 167, 180. In these and subsequent citations of the census returns, the printed page numbers (in the upper right-hand corner) have been used. The left-hand facing page, which is not numbered, is cited as the same page as the right-hand page. This method avoids the confusing pagination by individual census takers.

of propertied blacks rose from 276 in 1860 to 3,366 a decade later, and their total real estate holdings jumped from $415,300 to $2,705,400. In Charleston and New Orleans, rising taxes, competition from whites for skilled jobs, and racial violence—including a major riot in the Crescent City—resulted in a drop in black wealth during the war decade: in Charleston, from $808,300 to $507,100 (or from $2,479 to $2,234 per realty owner); in New Orleans, from $2,521,300 to $2,087,100 (or $4,739 to $2,899 on average). Despite these setbacks, urban blacks in the lower South generally improved their economic position. During a decade that saw real estate values in the South drop by 45 percent, urban blacks in the lower South increased the value of their holdings from $3,744,900 to $5,299,600, an improvement of 42 percent. By 1870, one of nine urban blacks in the region owned an average of $1,229 worth of real estate.[16]

A far greater expansion of black property ownership appears when personal as well as real property is considered (see table). Between 1860 and 1870, the number of blacks who owned at least enough personal possessions—horses, mules, cows, wagons, plows, machinery, tools, furniture, carts, carriages—to bring their total assets above $100 grew by 947 percent, from 16,044 to 168,034. This total represented nearly one out of five black families in the South. Unlike realty owners, who were proportionately more numerous in the upper South and a few scattered areas of the Deep South, these owners of modest amounts of personal property were most numerous in the heart of the lower South—Georgia, Alabama, and Mississippi. Some former bondsmen had preserved the small personal holdings they had acquired in slavery, but most simply found it easier to buy livestock and tools than to purchase a plot of ground. Mississippi and Georgia, the two lower South states with the largest antebellum slave populations (and two of the smallest free-black populations), led all states in the total number of black property owners—Mississippi with 23,665, Georgia with 17,739. The contrast with the antebellum period also appears in the fact that 94 percent of the 1870 property owners were

16. The totals and percentages in this and the preceding paragraph are computed from USMSPC, 1860, 1870. Despite its limitations, including a probable 6.6 percent undercount of blacks in 1870 (though probably substantially less among property owners), the census is the best source for *estimating* black wealth holding in the South. Local and state tax assessment records are scattered and incomplete. For the decline in real estate values in the South after the war, see Lee Soltow, *Men and Wealth in the United States, 1850–1870* (New Haven, 1975), 64. This decline varied in urban and rural areas, and in the upper and lower South. See also Ransom and Sutch, *One Kind of Freedom,* 51, 82.

Black Property Ownership in the South, 1860 and 1870

Black Property Owners in the Lower South

State	Estimated Total Property Holdings		Average Property Holdings Per Owner		No. of Owners	
	1860	1870	1860	1870	1860	1870
Alabama	$ 468,300	$ 5,060,300	$2,072	$330	226	15,317
Arkansas	4,500	2,419,400	1,125	340	4	7,113
Florida	168,400	1,052,100	1,604	317	105	3,315
Georgia	256,200	5,237,000	896	295	286	17,739
Louisiana	8,159,300	7,530,200	3,674	517	2,221	14,569
Mississippi	210,500	8,248,100	3,972	349	53	23,665
South Carolina	1,895,200	4,628,700	1,760	421	1,077	10,997
Texas	53,800	3,049,800	1,681	243	32	12,535
Totals (Lower South)	$11,216,200	$37,225,600	$2,801	$354	4,004	105,250

Black Property Owners in the Upper South

State	Estimated Total Property Holdings		Average Property Holdings Per Owner		No. of Owners	
	1860	1870	1860	1870	1860	1870
Delaware	$ 595,100	$ 1,108,000	$ 562	$ 899	1,059	1,232
Dist. of Columbia	788,500	2,702,300	1,109	1,712	711	1,578
Kentucky	976,200	5,564,500	832	479	1,173	11,629
Maryland	2,581,500	4,389,800	643	701	4,013	6,262
Missouri	637,800	4,416,500	1,787	558	357	7,914
North Carolina	1,073,800	2,759,500	640	329	1,679	8,375
Tennessee	638,300	6,514,400	1,244	385	513	16,904
Virginia	1,745,800	3,847,600	656	433	2,663	8,890
Totals (Upper South)	$9,037,000	$31,302,600	$ 743	$ 499	12,168	62,784
Totals for Entire South	$20,253,200	$68,528,200	$1,252	$ 408	16,172	168,034

Source: Computed from the United States Manuscript Population Census, 1860, 1870. To obtain property owners in 1870 with estates valued at from $100 to $999, a sample of 7,855 propertied blacks (from every twentieth printed page in the manuscript census) was used.

men (compared with 81 percent in 1860), 87 percent lived in rural areas (compared with 66 percent), 84 percent were listed as black rather than mulatto (compared with 53 percent), and 84 percent were illiterate or semiliterate (compared with 45 percent). In view of the fact that southern whites were 3.5 times more likely to own some property and that their holdings dwarfed those of blacks, these gains may seem modest, but in relation to the property blacks owned before the Civil War the change was substantial. By 1870, blacks in the South owned $68,528,200 worth of property—an average estate of only $408, but a rise of 240 percent in a decade, and a significant step away from the destitution of slavery.[17]

The decline in black property ownership in Charleston and New Orleans, coupled with the substantial expansion among those who controlled at least $100 worth of personal property in rural areas of the Deep South, suggests some of the economic changes occurring during the Reconstruction era among blacks who had been free before the war. The few historians who have compared the pre- and postwar condition of blacks, including Thomas Holt and David Rankin, have concentrated almost solely on the property acquisitions of black political leaders. This emphasis has tended to obscure the complex and dynamic economic transformations that were taking place among free persons of color. In the lower South free blacks, like their white neighbors, suffered from wartime destruction, the loss of slave property, and a multitude of economic problems. During the 1860s, the mean value of real estate held by black "planters" in South Carolina, Louisiana, and a few other Gulf states dropped from about $10,000 to less than $2,000, a decline nearly double the general depreciation in land values. Even those free blacks who survived the war with their estates intact—primarily urban dwellers who had invested heavily in real estate instead of in slaves—found it difficult to adjust to the rapid changes occurring in the wake of emancipation. Within a decade, most of them had passed from the scene through either death or mismanagement of their holdings.[18]

17. Computed from USMSPC, 1860, 1870. The total wealth in the South in 1870 was approximately $5.5 billion. Calculated from "Valuation of Property—1870, 1860, 1850," in U.S. Department of the Interior, Census Office, A Compendium of the Ninth Census (Washington, D.C., 1872), 639. See also Soltow, Men and Wealth in the United States, 65.
18. Computed from USMSPC, 1860, 1870; Thomas Holt, Black over White: Negro Political Leadership in South Carolina During Reconstruction (Urbana, Ill., 1977); David Rankin, "The Origins of Black Leadership in New Orleans During Reconstruction," Journal of Southern

Prewar free blacks in the upper states fared somewhat better than those in the lower South during the postwar period. Nearly one out of four free blacks who owned land in 1850 or 1860 could be found as property owners in 1870, at least as roughly gauged by the "persistence rate" in the United States population censuses. In rural areas of western states—Kentucky, Tennessee, and Missouri—where white antiproprietorship attitudes were less pronounced and the black population more widely dispersed, and in towns and cities, where there were new economic opportunities for service employment and establishing small businesses, some antebellum free blacks substantially improved their economic position during Reconstruction. Some became the most prosperous blacks in their communities—for example, Kentucky farmer Dennis Lane; Tennessee landholder Rubin Caldwell; Baltimore barber Augustus Roberts; District of Columbia restaurateur Richard Francis and hotel owner James Wormley; Alexandria, Virginia, butcher William Gray; Shelbyville, Kentucky, merchant Thomas Ballard; and St. Louis steward James Young. Others, like the Baltimore shoemaker George Adams, advanced from owning small amounts of personal property to real estate ownership. Still others entered the property-holding group for the first time.[19]

Even with these shifts, the vast majority of postwar black property owners were former slaves. Among the 43,268 black landowners in the South in 1870, only about 2,300 had been property owners in

---

History, XL (1974), 417–40. Several studies of the antebellum era point to this decline in certain locales. See Larry Koger, *Black Slaveowners: Free Black Slave Masters in South Carolina* (Jefferson, N.C., 1985), 120–24, 193–95; Michael Johnson and James Roark, *Black Masters: A Free Family of Color in the Old South* (New York, 1984), 314–20; and Gary B. Mills, *The Forgotten People: Cane River's Creoles of Color* (Baton Rouge, 1977), 237. See also George Rawick, ed., *The American Slave: A Composite Autobiography* (19 vols.; Westport, Conn., 1972–), Vol. V, Pt. 4, p. 158; Petition for Relief of Antoine Meullion, December, 1889, in Meullion Family Papers, Louisiana State University Library, Baton Rouge; Adolphe Garrigues to Charles Benjamin, January 28, 1876, in Records of the Southern Claims Commission, Records of the Treasury Department, Record Group 56, National Archives; Records of the Parish Probate Court, Iberville Parish, La., Deeds, Book 9, July 5, 1868, pp. 221–23; Records of the Parish Probate Court, Pointe Coupée Parish, La., Successions, No. 203, July 11, 1865; Records of the Parish Probate Court, Natchitoches Parish, La., Conveyances, Vol. 69, December 20, 1873, pp. 601–604, 637–39; Records of the Parish Probate Court, New Orleans, La., Successions, No. 38677, May 27, 1876, in New Orleans Public Library; and Loren Schweninger, "Antebellum Free Persons of Color in Postbellum Louisiana," *Louisiana History,* XXX (1989), 345–64.

19. Computed from USMSPC, Mason County, Kentucky, 1860, p. 279; 1870, p. 518; *ibid.,* Greene County, Tennessee, 1860, p. 368; 1870, p. 364; *ibid.,* District of Columbia, 1st Ward, 1860, p. 217; 1870, p. 231; Records of the Probate Court, District of Columbia, Estates, No. 1700, October 31, 1884; USMSPC, Alexandria, Virginia, 1860, p. 841, (5th Ward), 1870, p. 134; *ibid.,* Shelby County, Kentucky (Shelbyville), 1870, p. 415; *ibid.,* St. Louis, Missouri (9th Ward), 1870, p. 519; *ibid.,* Baltimore County, Maryland (Baltimore, 6th Ward), 1860, p. 541, (5th Ward), 1870, p. 159.

1850 or 1860; among the 168,034 blacks who owned at least $100 worth of real or personal property in 1870, fewer than 4,000 had been in the same class before the war. Only estimates can be made of the number of propertyless free blacks who entered the property-owning group for the first time after the war, but even if their numbers were twice as great as the number of prewar owners, by 1870 at least 84 percent of the black landowners and fully 94 percent of all black property owners had recently emerged from slavery.[20]

Statistical evidence, of course, may be viewed from many perspectives, and it tends to minimize the human dimensions of historical change. Yet by turning attention away from political failures, market systems, and labor repression, and by focusing on the statistics of the "temporal and spatial differences" in the upper and lower South, before, during, and after the war, one can better understand the aspirations and achievements of freedmen in their first half-generation of freedom. One also can understand more fully the complex and dynamic dimensions of black economic reconstruction in the South. It is remarkable that despite regional variations, such significant numbers of freedmen became property owners during this brief period. Some acquired homes and small farms, symbols of their movement away from the past. It was a slow, tedious process, often requiring many years. Such was the case for the illiterate North Carolina black Isaac Forbes, who saved his extra earnings for more than a decade before purchasing his first farm. On December 14, 1872, at the age of fifty, Forbes put his mark on an "Indenture" between himself and Francis T. and Hanna G. Hawks:

20. Computed from USMSPC, 1850, 1860, 1870. The difficulties of tracing individuals from one census to the next are obvious. People died, women married and took new names, some free blacks changed their names (this was rare), and others left the South. There was also, as noted previously, a probable undercount of blacks in the 1870 returns. The procedure used to gain an *estimate* of propertied prewar blacks who appeared in 1870 as property owners was the following: Three data lists of black property owners (for 1850, 1860, and 1870) were compiled from the original returns. These lists were alphabetized and then "sorted" according to state. The resulting "directories" were then checked and cross-checked individual by individual. For the great majority, the match-ups were obvious. For those whose names were spelled differently or whose ages did not match exactly, the comparisons were more difficult. But in all except a few cases the combination of all the variables—family name, given name, location, age, gender, color, occupation, state of birth, literacy, and (except for those with wealth between $100 and $999 in 1870) the names of those living in the same household—served as a virtual fingerprint for identification. The sampled wealth holders were considered to represent 5 percent (the sample size) of the "repeats" in 1870. For a discussion of this methodology, as well as an in-depth analysis of the strengths and weaknesses of the census as a primary source, see Loren Schweninger, *Black Property Owners in the South, 1790–1915* (Urbana, Ill., 1990), 371–79.

Witnesseth That said Hawks & wife for & in consideration of Five thousand dollars to them in hand paid by the said Forbes, have granted bargained & sold and by these presents do grant bargain & sell unto the said Isaac Forbes, his heirs & assignees, a body of land lying on Brices Creek in Craven County, bounded by the Creek on the west, by Boleyns swamp on the south, by the lands of Henry R. Bryan on the North, and by the lands of G Moye & others on the east, being the entire body of lands owned by the late Judge Gaston on the north side of Boleyns Swamp, containing twelve hundred acres more or less, To have & to hold the said lands with all privileges and appurtenances thereunto belonging to him the said Isaac his heirs, and assignees forever.

How Forbes acquired such a large amount of money is not known, but his sense of accomplishment and triumph must have been substantial, and it undoubtedly was shared by other former slaves who struggled to move beyond the suffering and degradation of perpetual bondage.[21]

These were small beginnings, but despite a severe depression during the 1870s, former slaves continued their quest for property ownership. Prior to the Civil War, three fifths of the white farmers and planters in the South had owned their land. By 1880, some whites, lacking capital and forced into debt by increased taxation, lost their holdings. Others migrated from marginal lands in the up-country and became renters and laborers in more fertile areas. At the same time, many freedmen, by hard work, thrift, and good luck, purchased land. By 1880, the number of rural black landowners in the South had risen substantially. Living primarily in the upper South and a few peripheral regions of the lower South, these rural blacks owned less than half the average acreage of whites; furthermore, black-owned real estate was worth less per acre than white-owned real estate. Nevertheless, as James McPherson points out, for a people emerging from bondage "to have done this well by 1880 was a significant achievement, all the more remarkable because it occurred while many white farmers were losing their land." A decade later, one of five black farmers in the South owned his own farm; in the upper South it was one out of three; in Virginia, where 43 percent of black farmers owned their farms, there

---

21. Records of the County Probate Court, Craven County, N.C., Deeds, Vol. 76, December 14, 1872, pp. 478–79; Eric Anderson, *Race and Politics in North Carolina, 1872–1901: The Black Second* (Baton Rouge, 1981), 22.

were twice as many black farm owners as there had been black rural landholders in the entire South on the eve of the Civil War. Similarly, in urban areas such as Baltimore, District of Columbia, Richmond, Lexington, Nashville, Atlanta, Montgomery, and Little Rock, blacks had substantially enhanced their economic standing, acquiring homes, small businesses, and urban real estate.[22]

Black economic reconstruction in the South, then, was a period of economic adjustment and change. Like John Hope Franklin's synthesis of the period, it was both an end and a beginning. Although conditions varied in different regions, in rural and urban areas, and in areas of former free-black concentration as against areas where the masses of blacks had lived in slavery, most blacks left slavery with new hope and new energy. Cast into freedom with few resources, they often found it difficult to forge ahead, especially in rural areas of the lower South where whites were determined to maintain their control over their former slaves. But even in this hostile environment, former bondsmen discovered that freedom offered new opportunities. In areas where there was less resistance to black advancement, the small improvements during Reconstruction served as harbingers of greater economic progress. It is little wonder that shortly after the end of Reconstruction, in the wake of an emigration movement to Kansas, some black leaders, including the famous former slave Frederick Douglass, cautioned their brethren not to be overcome by "emigration fever." He and others could not help but be impressed by the distance most former slaves had traveled in acquiring land and other property. After all, it had been only two decades since blacks themselves had been considered a "species of property."

22. McPherson, *Ordeal by Fire*, 579–80; Soltow, *Men and Wealth*, 33; Richard R. Wright, "The Colored Man and the Small Farm," *Southern Workman*, XXIX (1900), 483; W. H. Brown, *The Education and Economic Development of the Negro in Virginia* (Charlottesville, Va., 1923), 89; Samuel T. Bitting, *Rural Land Ownership Among the Negroes of Virginia, with Special Reference to Albemarle County* (Charlottesville, Va., 1915), 104–105; U.S. Department of the Interior, *Report on Farms and Homes: Proprietorship and Indebtedness in the United States at the Eleventh Census, 1890* (Washington, D.C., 1896), 167–72.

9

The Constitution and Reconstruction

❧ HERMAN BELZ

During the Constitutional Bicentennial, in a widely noted speech cautioning against making "a blind pilgrimage to the shrine of the original document," Supreme Court Justice Thurgood Marshall posed the issue that is central to the study of the Constitution and Reconstruction. Accepting as historical authority Chief Justice Roger Taney's assertion in the Dred Scott case that Negroes had no rights under the Constitution, Justice Marshall stated that "while the Union survived the Civil War, the Constitution did not." "In its place," he said, "arose a new, more promising basis for justice and equality"— the Fourteenth Amendment. In essence, the Fourteenth Amendment was a new Constitution. It was made by men who "refused to acquiesce in outdated notions of 'liberty,' 'justice,' and 'equality'" contained in the original Constitution. The framers of the Reconstruction amendments conceived of "new constitutional principles" guaranteeing "respect for the individual freedoms and human rights . . . we hold as fundamental today." Marshall argued, in effect, that historical knowledge about the constitutional significance of Reconstruction would enable Americans to understand the nature of constitutional government in our own time and liberate us from the error and injustice of the nation's founding.[1]

Justice Marshall's historical reflections attracted attention because

The author wishes to thank the Earhart Foundation for its support of the research on which this essay was based.

1. Thurgood Marshall, "Reflections on the Bicentennial of the United States Constitution," *Harvard Law Review,* CI (1987), 2–4.

they were not, of course, merely historical. The Constitution to which he referred, whether it be regarded as the framers' document or a new instrument produced in the upheaval of civil war, is the same one that governs our political order today. Since historical analysis continues to be one of the basic approaches to interpreting the Constitution, historical knowledge about the document may be pertinent to resolving constitutional controversies and public-policy disputes.[2] The relevance of constitutional history usually has been discussed in relation to the problem of ascertaining the original intent of the framers. This problem presents itself with even greater clarity and urgency in relation to the Reconstruction amendments, which provide the basis for national civil rights policy. Thus there has been a constant impetus for studies of the constitutional impact of the Civil War by a long line of jurists, lawyers, and constitutional scholars. Analysis of this body of writing may afford a deeper understanding of the constitutional significance of Reconstruction.

The importance of the Constitution and Reconstruction as a subject of historical study needs little demonstration. The object of postwar policy was to bring the former Confederate states back into the system of republican state governments provided by the Constitution. This process required asking whether the states of the defeated Confederacy were still states in the sense of the Constitution and, if so, what status they occupied and powers they possessed. To answer these questions, it was necessary to consult constitutional principle, theory, law, and history, and there were corollary issues to untangle concerning the status and rights of the freed people and former rebels. Reconstruction, in the sense that is most pertinent to us today, consisted in the civil rights settlement embodied in the Thirteenth, Fourteenth, and Fifteenth amendments, which together nationalized civil liberty in the United States. Reconstruction was a constitutional problem in the further sense that alternative courses of action were encouraged and reinforced by the separation of powers between the president and Congress, which eventually helped to precipitate the only presidential impeachment in American history. The final phase of Reconstruction concerned the conduct of government and politics in the former rebel-

2. Walter F. Murphy, James E. Fleming, and William F. Harris II, *American Constitutional Interpretation* (Mineola, N.Y., 1986), 292.

lious states after their return to Congress. Here, too, a significant constitutional question was raised, namely, whether free republican institutions existed in the Reconstruction South or whether southern politics was so thoroughly based on force and violence as to undermine the assumption of peaceful resolution of conflict on which constitutionalism depends.

As a first step toward addressing these issues, a brief consideration of the basic approaches to the Constitution that have shaped historical writing in this field will be useful. Naturally, what lawyers, jurists, and historians have said about Reconstruction and the Constitution has depended in part on their conception of the Constitution and its relationship to political life.

In many accounts the Constitution is regarded as an instrument of power that, although apparently having a fixed and objective form, is in its essential features protean, plastic, and capable of assuming any meaning that those in control of the government decide it should have in order to justify expedient political action. According to this point of view, which one may refer to as the *instrumental* approach, the Constitution does not really limit or control government, but rather functions as a form of rationalization required by the people's quasi-religious attachment to the constitutional text as a symbol of governmental legitimacy. Thus, the Constitution may be said to function in the proper manner when it is rhetorically deployed and manipulated to achieve political ends. A second approach to the Constitution emphasizes its *intrinsic,* rather than its instrumental, value. In this view the Constitution is the forms, procedures, and principles expressed or implied in the documentary text for the conduct of government in accordance with the nature, character, and purposes of the people as constituent power. Without denying that the Constitution was created to accomplish political ends and that it is a useful instrument of power, the argument of intrinsic constitutionalism holds that in order to have force and effect, the document must be regarded as having inherent value. The Constitution must be seen as something good in itself, worthy of being followed for its own sake or for the wisdom, justice, and sound principles it embodies, quite apart from the outcome of specific controversies.[3]

3. For further discussion of the distinction between instrumental and intrinsic constitutionalism, see Martin Spencer, "Rhetorics and Politics," *Social Research,* XXXVII (1970), 597–623, and Shirley Letwin, "Law Without Law," *Policy Review,* XXVI (1983), 7–16.

Informed by both the instrumental and intrinsic perspectives, writing on the Constitution and Reconstruction has been concerned with two general issues: the effect of the Constitution on the events of Reconstruction, and the impact of Reconstruction on the Constitution. Although it is impossible to maintain a fixed distinction between these two analytical concerns, historians and other academic scholars have tended to be more interested in the former question, whereas lawyers and jurists, reflecting the practitioner's greater interest in the pragmatic value of history, have dwelt more on the latter issue.

The earliest historical statements that command attention here appeared in Supreme Court opinions interpreting the Reconstruction amendments and the civil rights laws enacted to enforce them. In a series of decisions from the *Slaughter House Cases* through the *Civil Rights Cases,* the Court stated that protection of Negro freedom was the "one pervading purpose" of the Reconstruction amendments.[4] This purpose did not require revolution or fundamental alteration in the constitutional system. Although temporarily deprived of their rights as governmental entities, the former rebellious states were not out of the Union as a result of secession and civil war.[5] The amendments guaranteed personal liberty and civil and political rights for freed blacks and other citizens of the United States. Yet these measures did not essentially alter the division of sovereignty and federal equilibrium that the Constitution provided for between the national government and the states.

The impact of Reconstruction on the Constitution, according to Supreme Court decisions of the postwar period, can be described in a series of general propositions. The Fourteenth Amendment, the principal enumeration of civil rights requirements and other conditions on which the southern states could be readmitted to Congress, prohibited state action denying civil rights. It did not ban private discrimination. Although state failure to protect civil rights might be considered a form of state action, congressional legislation based on this assumption was required to stipulate that the private discrimination in question was racially motivated. The Thirteenth Amendment was a guarantee of personal liberty against both state and private action depriving persons of liberty, and Congress could define and legislate

4. *Slaughter House Cases,* 16 Wallace 36 (1873).
5. *Texas* v. *White,* 7 Wallace 700 (1869).

against "badges and incidents" of slavery. (The refusal to admit blacks to a privately owned theater, however, was not a badge of slavery according to the Supreme Court's decision in cases in which this claim was raised.) The rights of United States citizenship were relatively few in number compared with the rights derived from state citizenship, which continued to provide the substance of civil liberty in the American republic. Accordingly, the Fourteenth Amendment did not significantly alter the structure of the federal-state relationship with respect to ordinary civil rights. Finally, blacks were not a separate class, and state laws that were explicitly racially exclusionary, such as laws barring Negroes from jury service, were unconstitutional.

From the perspective of the late twentieth century, the Supreme Court's assertion of Negro freedom as the principal meaning of the Reconstruction amendments may seem disingenuous, if not patently insincere, since the Court's decisions did not prevent wholesale denial of blacks' civil rights. Considered in historical context, however, the Court's holdings on civil rights protected the liberty of the freed people while maintaining the essential principles of the constitutional order. The Court helped prevent the total exclusion and denial of rights for blacks, the alternative desired by the more racist elements in southern society. And the justices rejected the conservative argument that the national government lacked effective power in civil rights matters and must defer to the states.[6]

During the segregation era, roughly from the 1890s to World War II, the Supreme Court's interpretation of the Fourteenth Amendment formed a central theme in the development of constitutional law. In the line of cases delineating substantive due process, the Court protected the civil rights of United States citizens and persons against state interference, in accordance with the broad intent of the authors of the Reconstruction amendments. The rights that received protection, however, were those of economic entrepreneurs and corporations. A new historical interpretation of the purpose of the Fourteenth Amendment—the "conspiracy theory" advanced by Charles A. Beard and other progressive historians—served to explain this development. Ac-

---

6. Michael Les Benedict, "Preserving Federalism: Reconstruction and the Waite Court," *Supreme Court Review* (1978), 39–79; Robert C. Palmer, "The Parameters of Constitutional Reconstruction: *Slaughter-House, Cruikshank,* and the Fourteenth Amendment," *University of Illinois Law Review* (1984), 739–70.

cording to the conspiracy theory, the framers of the Fourteenth Amendment included "persons" along with citizens in the due process clause with a view toward protecting corporations against state regulation. Meanwhile, black Americans, the intended beneficiaries of the Fourteenth Amendment under the earlier Negro-freedom theory, were disfranchised and denied civil rights as federal officials acquiesced in the imposition of legal segregation in the southern states.

Virtually throughout the segregation era, historical scholarship on the Constitution and Reconstruction was sympathetic to the South and critical of postwar Republican policy. The best scientific historians of the age, including those of the progressive school, described Reconstruction as a tragic time of political error, opportunism, and corruption, precipitated especially by the partisan and irresponsible decision to reorganize southern state governments on the basis of black suffrage. The name of William Archibald Dunning, more than that of any other scholar, is associated with the tragic view of Reconstruction. Dunning's analysis of the postwar period focused on the Constitution and set a scholarly standard for many years to come.

In Dunning's view, the purpose of Reconstruction was to give freedmen and white Unionists power to organize governments and control the former Confederate states indefinitely. This was the political expression of a general effort "to stand the social pyramid on its apex" and impose on southern whites "permanent subjection to another race." Concerned especially with the impact of political events on the Constitution, Dunning treated congressional reconstruction measures as a virtual overthrow of the fundamental law. "Only in a very narrow sense," he wrote, "was it true that the Union had been preserved." The territorial integrity of the nation had been maintained, but the outcome of Reconstruction revealed that "a new Union had been created." [7]

A student of political thought, Dunning was attentive to theoretical considerations, and into his narrative he wove analyses of theories of reconstruction and the status of the former Confederate states. Regarding the guarantee clause of the Constitution (Article IV, Section 4) as the principal basis of congressional policy, he showed how Republicans had redefined republican government in order to include blacks

7. William A. Dunning, *Essays on the Civil War and Reconstruction*, (1897; rpr. New York, 1965), 250; William A. Dunning, *Reconstruction, Political and Economic, 1865–1877* (New York, 1907), 1, 5.

as voters, positing a new national power to regulate the suffrage, in deliberate disregard of history and constitutional law. As a progressive intellectual, Dunning admired the energy and capacity for discipline evident both in Republican party rule and in the "just and efficient" rule of military commanders in the occupied South. Nevertheless, the outcome of Reconstruction—"a huge social and political revolution under the forms of law"—placed it outside the constitutional tradition. "The process of reconstruction," Dunning concluded, "presented many situations which could be explained as readily by assuming a revolution to have occurred as by strained interpretation of the constitution."[8]

John W. Burgess, Dunning's Columbia University colleague, offered a more complex analysis of the Constitution and Reconstruction, combining approval of the end—national protection of black civil rights—with disapproval of the means by which it was approached. Strongly Unionist in sympathy, Burgess held that the Constitution permitted—and Congress should have provided—territorial civil government for the former rebellious states until white southerners could be entrusted with local self-government. Meanwhile, a constitutional amendment should have been adopted nationalizing civil liberty. Burgess appreciated the threat to the freedmen's liberty posed by the Black Codes, and he thought Congress morally and legally justified in rejecting President Johnson's reconstruction policy. Yet he severely criticized congressional Republicans, motivated by partisanship and passion, for the colossal error of creating a new electorate of the freed slaves. Expressing the almost universal judgment of his day, Burgess wrote: "It was a great wrong to civilization to put the white race of the South under the domination of the Negro race."[9]

In Burgess' view, Congress used its power not only unwisely, but also unconstitutionally in enacting military reconstruction. "There was hardly a line in the entire bill," he said of the Reconstruction Act of 1867, "that would stand the test of the Constitution."[10] Congress further contradicted the organic law in requiring the southern states, as a condition of readmission to the national legislature, to accept

---

8. Dunning, *Essays*, 132–34, 174–75, 250, 135.
9. John W. Burgess, *Reconstruction and the Constitution* (New York, 1902), viii, 134–35, 53–54, 111, 133.
10. *Ibid.*, 113. Burgess pointed out that Congress wrongly resorted to martial law where the circumstances did not warrant it, deprived the president of the power to act as commander-in-chief of the army, and denied civil liberties guaranteed by the Bill of Rights.

terms and provisions that were not yet part of the Constitution. As a political realist, Burgess held that the Johnson governments should have accepted the Fourteenth Amendment, its constitutional irregularity notwithstanding.[11] As a constitutionalist, however, he concluded that imposing on the southern states things not obligatory on the states already in the Union "was tantamount to the creation of a new sort of union with another kind of constitution by an Act of Congress."[12] More so than Dunning, Burgess saw Republican attachment to constitutional ideas as a shaping influence on events. He lamented, for example, Republican lawmakers' regard for the "phantom of the 'indestructible State,'" their willingness to be "haunted by that spectre of an abstract, unorganized 'State' . . . which is nothing more than a Platonic idea."[13]

If they did not stand the test of time, the interpretations of Dunning and Burgess nonetheless served the purposes of historians and the educated public in the early twentieth century. Integrating detailed constitutional analysis into political narrative, their works were not soon superseded. Part of the reason was that historians in these years were turning away from constitutional history, preferring instead to study the social and economic forces that to the progressive mind formed the basis of government, politics, and law.[14] Those persuaded by the basic political argument of the Dunning-Burgess interpretation were therefore little inclined to reexamine its constitutional dimension. Progressive historians also expressed impatience with the constitutionalist assumption—apparent in the work of Burgess and Dunning—that the Constitution possessed intrinsic and not merely instrumental value. Commenting on theories of reconstruction, Walter Lynwood Fleming wrote in 1919: "Unfortunately, American political life, with its controversies over colonial government, its conflicting interpretations of written constitutions, and its legally trained statesmen, had by the middle of the nineteenth century produced a habit of political thought which demanded the settlement of most governmental matters upon a theoretical basis." A decade later, Howard K.

---

11. *Ibid.*, 80–81, 110. Burgess wrote: "Logically and Constitutionally the whole thing was irregular. But it was as it was, and all understood that the way to cut the knot was for the legislatures of the reconstructed 'states' to adopt the proposed Fourteenth Amendment."

12. *Ibid.*, 116. At another point (p. 81), Burgess described the conditions required of the South as "the exaction of . . . an unlawful promise, imposing . . . a degrading discrimination."

13. *Ibid.*, 85.

14. *Cf.* James G. Randall, "The Interrelation of Social and Constitutional History," *American Historical Review,* XXXV (1929), 1–13.

Beale summed up the progressive complaint against intrinsic constitutionalism. Analyzing the critical election of 1866, Beale observed that lawyers and politicians "made lengthy speeches on constitutionality, for this gave them an air of erudition, and satisfied the legalistic conscience of their constituents." Beale added, however, that "constitutional discussions of the rights of the negro, the status of Southern states, the legal position of ex-rebels, and the power of Congress and president determined nothing. They were pure shams." Constitutional arguments were "mere justifications of practical ends." [15]

Yet not all constitutional argument was bombast and rationalization. In spite of themselves, progressives like Beale betrayed a residual belief that valid constitutional principles did exist, possessing intrinsic value and worthy of being defended for their own sake. "Out of a maze of constitutional argument that was mere embroidery for more practical desires," Beale asserted, "there stands out one fundamental constitutional issue that in importance outranks the whole reconstruction question." This was the radical attempt "to remodel the very form of our government into a parliamentary system" and to make "Congress paramount not only to the president, but to the Constitution." Fortunately, Andrew Johnson tenaciously resisted the radicals, defending the separation of powers, the concept of limited government, and politics based on reason and compromise rather than hatred and distrust. In short, Andrew Johnson was seeking "to preserve the principle of constitutional government." [16]

As forces of social and economic change began to penetrate the South in the 1930s, the received view of Reconstruction as a tragic era came under criticism. A few scholars presented a more favorable view of the postwar period as a time of constructive social and economic reform when the South began to catch up with the rest of the country in matters such as public education and industrial development. If the early revisionists judged political and social results differently from the orthodox view, however, they were little disposed toward a different constitutional perspective.

W. E. B. Du Bois, for example, one of the first and most forceful

15. Walter Lynwood Fleming, *The Sequel of Appomattox: A Chronicle of the Reunion of the States* (1919; rpr. Toronto, 1970), 54; Howard K. Beale, *The Critical Year: A Study of Andrew Johnson and Reconstruction* (1930; rpr. New York, 1958), 147, 150.

16. Beale, *Critical Year*, 211, 214; Robert Selph Henry, *The Story of Reconstruction* (1938; rpr. Gloucester, Mass., 1963), 184.

of the revisionist writers, regarded constitutional discussion of reconstruction legislation as "of the same metaphysical stripe characterizing all fetich-worship [sic] of the Constitution." At some level, however, Du Bois, like Beale, was forced to acknowledge the objective reality of the Constitution. As the South unconstitutionally made the Constitution a proslavery document, he reasoned, so the North unconstitutionally prevented the destruction of the Union. After the Civil War "revolutionary measures rebuilt what revolution had disrupted, and formed a new United States on a broader basis than the old Constitution and different from its original conception." Du Bois approved this result, for it was "idiotic" for a people "to follow a written rule of government 90 years old" that definitely had been broken. Thaddeus Stevens and the radicals, understanding that "rule-following, legal precedence, and political consistency are not more important than right, justice, and plain common sense," broke through "the cobwebs of such political subtlety" and imposed military rule on the South until democracy was established. Du Bois thus saw revolutionary constitutionalism sweeping away the Constitution of the framers.[17]

Although mainly interested in social and economic history, Du Bois as an early revisionist was perhaps uncharacteristic in treating the constitutional dimension of Reconstruction. Revisionists who in the 1940s and 1950s elaborated a new view of the postwar period generally ignored the constitutional issues that had concerned earlier writers. John Hope Franklin's *Reconstruction: After the Civil War* illustrates the point. Describing the constitutions in the reconstructed states as satisfactory instruments of state government, Franklin dealt only briefly with the national Constitution. Ignoring the significance that theories of reconstruction had for contemporaries, he referred to the former Confederate states, without qualification, as "out of the Union, awaiting readmission at the pleasure and mercy of the North." Insofar as Reconstruction warranted consideration as a constitutional conflict, it amounted to a contest between Andrew Johnson's adherence to the southern dogma of states' rights, and Charles Sumner's belief that "anything for human rights is constitutional." Franklin noted the conflict between the executive and legislative branches that

17. W. E. Burghardt Du Bois, *Black Reconstruction in America, 1860–1880* (1935; rpr. Cleveland, 1962), 336.

culminated in impeachment, but he viewed it as merely a political struggle rather than a confrontation arising out of the structure of the government and involving essential constitutional principles.[18]

Surveying two decades of Reconstruction historiography, Bernard A. Weisberger in 1959 identified inadequate understanding of the constitutional aspect of postwar events as one of the reasons why the revisionist interpretation had failed to win general acceptance. Weisberger asserted that Reconstruction had been treated as an almost isolated episode in federal-state relations. Recalling Du Bois, he attributed this narrow outlook partly to the "national fetish of Constitution-worship." Implying that historians of Reconstruction thought otherwise, Weisberger declared that "constitutional history is not valid as a study of inviolable principles." Therefore, "to talk of Reconstruction's 'constitutionality,' he advised, "is not very useful except as a theoretical exercise." Instead, historians should ask "how the Constitution itself was reconstructed." Weisberger thus identified himself with the instrumental approach to the Constitution. Yet, with a degree of puzzlement, he also noted in the Reconstruction era evidence of intrinsic constitutionalism, that is, a conviction that certain constitutional principles *were* valid and inviolable. President Johnson and other conservatives, for example, believed the victorious North, out of respect for the Constitution, would promptly restore the southern states to their place in the federal system. "This is a high order of abstraction!" Weisberger exclaimed. "Yet it was fundamentally American." The radical Republicans too, he observed, "showed a surprising concern for maintaining the forms of the federal system, whatever the realities, and for the appearances of constitutionalism." In Weisberger's view constitutional forms and constitutionalism were perhaps not full-fledged realities. Yet how else to explain why the radicals did not simply resort to military force and rule the South indefinitely as conquered territory?[19]

A second stage of revisionist writing about Reconstruction began in the 1960s, the era of the civil rights movement. Perhaps persuaded by contemporary events that principled political action was genuinely

---

18. John Hope Franklin, *Reconstruction: After the Civil War* (Chicago, 1961), 3, 27, 69–79, 118.
19. Bernard A. Weisberger, "The Dark and Bloody Ground of Reconstruction Historiography," *Journal of Southern History,* XXV (1959), 427–47.

possible, historians more readily acknowledged the existence in the Civil War decade of intrinsic constitutionalism. Consider, for example, Kenneth Stampp's synthesis of the revisionist interpretation of Reconstruction. Stampp described how the radicals and President Johnson engaged in a political dialogue for two years after the end of the war. Although conceding that some of the talk was shrill and irresponsible, Stampp said that much of it was an intensely serious discussion of fundamental problems, such as "the proper relationship of the legislative and executive branches [and] the legitimate areas of federal and state responsibility." Certainly the place of blacks in American society was the central problem, but Stampp believed that "vaguely defined constitutional issues," including "the abstract question of whether the southern states had or had not ever been out of the federal Union," also were relevant to the political conversation over Reconstruction.[20]

To speculate on why history is rewritten would take this essay far beyond its intended scope. In relation to the Constitution and Reconstruction, however, it appears that political and legal efforts to end segregation and secure black civil rights—efforts that in part involved historical arguments about the original intent of the Civil War amendments—helped stimulate further revisionist historical writing.

The constitutional revolution of 1937, which swept away substantive due process and the economic interpretation of the Fourteenth Amendment, had the long-range effect of introducing into constitutional law a distinction between property rights and human or civil rights. Approving federal and state economic legislation, the courts in effect served notice that they would no longer protect property rights against government regulation. A parallel development, also beginning in the 1930s, was judicial support of Negro civil rights claims in a few cases involving criminal procedure, voting rights, and segregation in higher education. These judicial trends were not unrelated, for rejection of the economic interpretation of the Fourteenth Amendment implied a revival of the Negro-freedom theory of the nature and purpose of the Reconstruction amendments. The Court's race-relations decisions signaled a new phase in judicial construction and historical interpretation of national civil rights policy based on the Reconstruction amendments.

20. Kenneth M. Stampp, *The Era of Reconstruction, 1865–1877* (New York, 1965), 86.

As civil rights issues began to emerge in constitutional law, two reform-minded legal scholars, Howard Jay Graham and Jacobus ten Broek, carried on pioneering researches that laid the basis for a new view of the Constitution and Reconstruction. Actively seeking to promote racial equality, Graham and ten Broek traced the origin of the Thirteenth and Fourteenth amendments to the antebellum abolitionist movement. They held generally that the framers of the amendments wrote the natural-rights principles of the Declaration of Independence into the Constitution in order to establish civil and political equality for blacks as citizens of the United States. Graham and ten Broek further contended that the Reconstruction amendments revolutionized the federal system by giving the national government plenary power to legislate directly to protect black civil rights against state and private discrimination. The lawyers John P. Frank and Robert F. Munro advanced a similar original-intent argument concerning the liberal, humanitarian nature of the equal protection clause of the Fourteenth Amendment, a clause Frank and Munro believed was intended to prohibit segregation in public accommodations.[21]

The new, egalitarian view of the Constitution and Reconstruction, based on "law-office history" as its proponents candidly acknowledged, was reinforced by the use of history in civil rights litigation aimed at overthrowing the Jim Crow system. *Brown v. Board of Education,* the school desegregation case, was the principal focus of the attempt to provide a historical jurisprudence to support civil rights. The Supreme Court itself encouraged historical revisionism when it requested the parties to the school desegregation case to submit arguments concerning the intent of the framers of the Fourteenth Amendment on the question of segregated public education.[22] In striking down segregation, the Court ultimately based its decision on contemporary cultural-psychological reasoning, rather than on original in-

21. Howard Jay Graham, "The 'Conspiracy Theory' of the Fourteenth Amendment" (Pt. 1), *Yale Law Journal,* XLVII (1938), 371–403; "The 'Conspiracy Theory' of the Fourteenth Amendment" (Pt. 2), *Yale Law Journal,* XLVIII (1938), 171–94; Howard Jay Graham, "The Early Antislavery Backgrounds of the Fourteenth Amendment," *Wisconsin Law Review* (1950), 479–507, 610–61; Jacobus ten Broek, *The Antislavery Origins of the Fourteenth Amendment* (Berkeley, 1951; rev. ed. published under title *Equal Under Law* [New York, 1965]); John P. Frank and Robert F. Munro, "The Original Understanding of 'Equal Protection of the Laws,' " *Columbia Law Review,* L (1950), 131–69.

22. Howard Jay Graham, *Everyman's Constitution: Historical Essays on the Fourteenth Amendment, the "Conspiracy Theory," and American Constitutionalism* (Madison, Wisc., 1968), 21, 268, 337; Richard Kluger, *Simple Justice: The History of "Brown v. Board of Education" and Black America's Struggle for Equality* (New York, 1976), 617–56.

tent. Nevertheless, the historical research stimulated by the case became part of the literature of Reconstruction. A number of constitutional lawyers and historians, some of whom were involved in the school desegregation case, wrote accounts emphasizing the far-reaching egalitarian purposes of the Thirteenth and Fourteenth amendments and their impact on the federal system. Moreover, civil-rights-inspired accounts described the framers of the Reconstruction amendments as humanitarian idealists dedicated to the principle of equal rights. By the mid-1960s, a substantial body of legal-historical writing existed that formed the basis for a constitutional interpretation of Reconstruction and provided historical continuity between the framers' original intent and present-day use of the amendments in the civil rights struggle.[23]

Political histories of Reconstruction written in the 1960s offered a positive assessment of Republican constitutional motives, at the same time calling attention to issues that had been largely ignored since the days of Dunning and Burgess. Less presentist than the legal-historical activists, the revisionist historians in their concern for the impact of the Constitution on Reconstruction reflected the outlook of intrinsic constitutionalism more than instrumentalism. In his study of Andrew Johnson, for example, Eric L. McKitrick did much to restore the seriousness of constitutional theory as an aspect of political action. McKitrick analyzed theories of reconstruction and the status of the seceded states as an expression of constitutional principle and conviction that both accommodated and restricted political passions and policy choices. Without ingrained constitutional scruples to mark the boundaries of dispute, he suggested, it might have taken much longer to achieve a postwar settlement.[24]

LaWanda Cox and John H. Cox described Republicans as principled supporters of equal rights, rather than as expedient politicians seeking to ruin or revolutionize the constitutional order. In the Coxes'

---

23. Howard Jay Graham, "The Fourteenth Amendment and School Segregation," *Buffalo Law Review*, III (1953), 1–24; Howard Jay Graham, "Our 'Declaratory' Fourteenth Amendment," *Stanford Law Review*, VII (1954), 3–39; Alexander M. Bickel, "The Original Understanding and the Segregation Decision," *Harvard Law Review*, LXIX (1955), 1–65; Alfred H. Kelly, "The Fourteenth Amendment Reconsidered: The Segregation Decision," *Michigan Law Review*, LIV (1956), 1049–1086; Laurent B. Frantz, "Congressional Power to Enforce the Fourteenth Amendment Against Private Acts," *Yale Law Journal*, LXXIII (1964), 1352–84. C. Vann Woodward, a consultant to the NAACP in the Brown case, also wrote *The Strange Career of Jim Crow* (New York, 1955), showing segregation to be a late-nineteenth-century development and thus not part of the original civil rights settlement of the Reconstruction period.

24. Eric L. McKitrick, *Andrew Johnson and Reconstruction* (Chicago, 1960), 93–119.

view, Andrew Johnson was constitutionally inconsistent in opposing any modification of states' rights even for the sake of protecting black civil rights, and he was primarily responsible for the Reconstruction controversy. Indeed, according to the Coxes, the nationalization of civil rights, asserted as a moral and constitutional principle, was the central fact of Reconstruction. Writing from an English point of view, W. R. Brock explored tensions within Republican constitutionalism and claimed that in asserting national power over the states and congressional authority over the executive, Republicans verged on a constitutional revolution. The revolution was incomplete, however, because despite a tendency to believe in the unlimited power of the majority to do right, Republicans were unwilling to give up the idea of constitutional checks on the popular will. Evaluating the effects of the Constitution on Reconstruction, Brock observed critically that it magnified unwise actions and encouraged deadlock between opposed interests. Yet it remained the one symbol of nationality on which Americans could unite.[25]

More specialized studies by constitutional historians extended the revisionist analysis of the Constitution and Reconstruction as an intellectual foundation for civil rights advances. Cognizant of the contemporary relevance of his subject, Harold M. Hyman did much to constitutionalize revisionism.[26] Hyman disposed of the lingering notion that Republicans were constitutional radicals or revolutionists by presenting Reconstruction as a positive expression of American constitutionalism. Drawing on a wide array of popular as well as professional legal writings, Hyman introduced the idea of "constitutional adequacy" as an organizing principle of Civil War and Reconstruction politics. He told how northerners, having come within a hair's breadth of losing their Union and Constitution in the secession crisis, discovered in the actions of Abraham Lincoln that they had a real government and a real constitution that provided all necessary power. Far from repudiating

25. John H. Cox and LaWanda Cox, *Politics, Principle, and Prejudice, 1865–1867: Dilemma of Reconstruction America* (New York, 1963), viii–ix, 136–38; W. R. Brock, *An American Crisis: Congress and Reconstruction, 1865–1867* (New York, 1963), 250–73.

26. Hyman wrote in 1966: "Constitutional concepts and political attitudes analogous to those of the Civil War and Reconstruction scene are again current. One can hope that when a century hence historians come to evaluate our time, they will give it as good a report as the young French journalist Georges Clemenceau felt able to send from Washington in 1865: 'The events of the last four years have taught me never to give up hope for this country.' Harold M. Hyman, "Reconstruction and Political-Constitutional Institutions: The Popular Expression," in *New Frontiers of the American Reconstruction*, ed. Hyman (Urbana, Ill., 1966), 39.

the nation's organic law, Unionists based the war effort on "the concept of constitutional adequacy for any ends that political institutions demanded." Americans' insistence on quarreling over constitutionalism, Hyman reasoned, showed renewed reverence for the Constitution. It indicated their "addiction to constitutional bases for political positions."[27] If this characterization superficially recalled Beale's description of constitutional arguments as claptrap, the difference lay in Hyman's belief that constitutional forms and principles had a real impact on events. Constitutional debate was evidence of principled political action and of the intrinsic value of constitutionalism.

To those less certain of the blessings of liberal nationalism, the muscular constitutionalism of Hyman's revisionist account might appear to contradict the idea of limited government.[28] Yet Hyman contended that wartime and postwar policies also reflected the belief that whether at the state or federal level, "coping had to be done constitutionally." He added that "constitutional permissiveness" was "never absolute." In his account of emancipation in particular, Hyman described tensions between constitutional doctrines of national power and the "felt limitations on the allowable functions of government."[29]

A number of studies in the 1960s and 1970s focused on specific constitutional problems of Reconstruction. These included accounts of wartime reconstruction efforts, with emphasis on the constitutional status of the rebellious states; of the civil rights settlement and federal-state relations as defined by the Reconstruction amendments and civil rights laws; of executive-legislative relations and the impeachment of Andrew Johnson; and of the reconstruction acts of 1867 and 1868.[30]

27. *Ibid.*, 38, 285.
28. See Alfred H. Kelly, "Comment on Harold M. Hyman's Paper," in *New Frontiers of the American Reconstruction,* ed. Hyman, 40–58. Kelly viewed Hyman's "adequacy constitutionalism" as the assertion of a new constitution based on the revolutionary doctrine of the popular will, along the lines of the Dunning-Beale point of view.
29. Harold M. Hyman, *A More Perfect Union: The Impact of the Civil War and Reconstruction on the Constitution* (New York, 1973), 414–15.
30. Herman Belz, *Reconstructing the Union: Theory and Policy During the Civil War* (Ithaca, N.Y., 1969); Charles Fairman, *Reconstruction and Reunion, 1864–88* (New York, 1971), Pt. 1; William M. Wiecek, *The Guarantee Clause of the U.S. Constitution* (Ithaca, N.Y., 1972); Michael Les Benedict, *A Compromise of Principle: Congressional Republicans and Reconstruction, 1863–1869* (New York, 1974); Michael Les Benedict, "Preserving the Constitution: The Conservative Basis of Radical Reconstruction," *Journal of American History,* LXI (1974), 65–90; Phillip S. Paludan, *A Covenant with Death: The Constitution, Law, and Equality in the Civil War Era* (Urbana, Ill., 1975); Herman Belz, *A New Birth of Freedom: The Republican Party and Freedmen's Rights, 1861–1866* (Westport, Conn., 1976); Raoul Berger, *Government by Judiciary: The Transformation of the Fourteenth Amendment* (Cambridge, Mass., 1977); Donald G.

The general argument of constitutional revisionism was that Republican Reconstruction aimed at extending the principles of liberty, equality, and consent in the original Constitution to all persons or citizens of the United States, doing so within the framework of a modified but still essentially state-centered federal system. The "grasp-of-war" theory of federal power and the guarantee-of-republican-government clause of the Constitution were identified as sources of authority that could be used to reorganize state governments without the need for a radical restructuring of the Union. Even the most far-reaching national intervention under the Military Reconstruction Act refrained from outright and unilateral coercion, allowing southerners public space within which voluntarily to participate in and consent to state reorganization. Similarly, the Thirteenth Amendment, although authorizing federal intervention against both state and private action, was adopted under a narrow theory of the slavery/freedom dichotomy. When the prohibition of slavery was found to be insufficient protection for the freed people, the Civil Rights Act of 1866 and the Fourteenth Amendment were adopted to provide more effective safeguards for civil rights. These measures confined their effects to state actions, however, and did not reach private discrimination. The states continued to have primary or initial responsibility to regulate civil liberty, albeit under federal constitutional guarantees of equality before the law within local jurisdictions. The federal-state balance was altered, but no revolution in federalism occurred. Finally, the revisionist constitutional interpretation, emphasizing the legitimacy of the civil rights issue, regarded presidential impeachment as a politically and constitutionally justified response to Andrew Johnson's obstruction of congressional legislation.

Establishing the historical basis on which modern civil rights policy rested, constitutional revisionism reopened the question of the failure of Reconstruction. In the Dunning-Burgess interpretation, Reconstruction failed because Republicans reorganized southern governments on the basis of black suffrage, preventing sectional reconciliation and dividing American politics along the color line. In the 1960s,

Nieman, *To Set the Law in Motion: The Freedmen's Bureau and the Legal Rights of Blacks, 1865–1868* (Millwood, N.Y., 1979); Earl Maltz, "Reconstruction Without Revolution: Republican Civil Rights Theory in the Era of the Fourteenth Amendment," *Houston Law Review,* XXIV (1987), 221–79.

as the civil rights movement gave rise to black power politics, the failure of Reconstruction appeared to some scholars to lie in the fact that blacks were denied real equality, notwithstanding the civil rights constitutional amendments and statutes.[31] Without denying that full equality lay in the future, revisionists offered a more positive assessment that emphasized the achievements and partial success of Reconstruction. Harold Hyman, for example, although acknowledging pervasive racism in American society, nevertheless concluded that "in the face of . . . enormous impediments, further complicated by the politics and constitutionalism of federalism, there was considerable advance." Neither the nation nor the states, Hyman said, "ever abandoned the constitutional law or the sense of social responsibility implicit in policies and institutions created during the . . . Reconstruction decade. Even constrained constitutionalism allowed maintenance of the war's great advances." LaWanda Cox, answering the argument that Reconstruction failed because Republicans were unwilling to use maximum force to uphold blacks' civil rights, explained that "the amount of force necessary to realize equal civil and political rights in the South was impossible to sustain in a nation whose democratic tradition and constitutional structure limited the use of power, exalted the rule of law, and embodied the concept of government by the consent of the governed."[32]

In the constitutional revisionist view, the crux of the Reconstruction problem was the tension between Republicans' desire to protect the liberty of the freed blacks and their commitment to preserving the essential principles of the constitutional order. Constitutional limitations restricted the range of options open to reconstruction policy makers. Yet considerable progress was made in securing the results of emancipation by establishing a foundation for national civil rights policy; moreover, the preservation of constitutional limitations was an achievement of great importance. Even if adherence to constitutional principle restrained the humanitarian impulse to secure more complete justice for the freedmen, the nation in the long run benefited from the revival of intrinsic constitutionalism that shaped Reconstruction.

31. Cf. C. Vann Woodward, "Seeds of Failure in Radical Race Policy," in *New Frontiers of the American Reconstruction*, ed. Hyman, 125–47.

32. Hyman, *More Perfect Union*, 416, 544; LaWanda Cox, *Lincoln and Black Freedom: A Study in Presidential Leadership* (Columbia, S.C., 1981), 169.

* * *

The revisionist interpretation of the Constitution and Reconstruction confirmed the principle of equal rights without distinction as to color as the historic basis of the civil rights movement. As that movement took a more radical turn in the late 1960s, asserting the idea of "affirmative action" to overcome the effects of past discrimination, further historical revisionism occurred. Historians reflecting a neo-abolitionist perspective, for example, contended that Reconstruction failed because it neglected to address the problem of economic democracy. Without confiscation and redistribution of property to the freed blacks, they argued, measures for securing civil and political rights were bound to be ineffectual. Republicans thus were seen not only as immobilized by constitutional restrictions, but also as concentrating on the wrong area of public policy. Permitted to retain its economic and social power, the southern planter class was able to overthrow the Reconstruction governments, deprive blacks of their civil and political rights, and rule them as a servile labor force.[33]

The view that Reconstruction could have succeeded had it been more radical with respect to economic redistribution or political and military coercion was expressed in the writings of a number of legal scholars in the post–civil rights period.[34] Concerned to provide a historical justification for affirmative action, neoabolitionist legal writers argued that the Civil War amendments and civil rights laws were the kinds of genuinely radical measures needed to make Reconstruction successful. If blacks did not achieve real equality after the war, the fault lay in a failure of political will rather than a lack of constitutional authority. In fact, contended neoabolitionist legal historians, Reconstruction revolutionized the constitutional system, giving the national

33. Cf. Eric L. McKitrick, "Reconstruction: Ultraconservative Revolution," in *The Comparative Approach to American History*, ed. C. Vann Woodward (New York, 1968), 146–59; Louis S. Gerteis, *From Contraband to Freedman: Federal Policy Toward Southern Blacks, 1861–1865* (Westport, Conn., 1973); C. Peter Ripley, *Slaves and Freedmen in Civil War Louisiana* (Baton Rouge, 1976); William Cohen, "Negro Involuntary Servitude in the South, 1865–1940: A Preliminary Analysis," *Journal of Southern History*, XLII (1976), 31–60; George C. Rable, *But There Was No Peace: The Role of Violence in the Politics of Reconstruction* (Athens, Ga., 1984). For discussion of the relevant writings, see Herman Belz, "The New Orthodoxy in Reconstruction Historiography," *Reviews in American History*, I (1973), 106–13, and Eric Foner, "Reconstruction Revisited," *Reviews in American History*, X (December, 1982), 82–100.

34. Cf. Michael Perman, *Reunion Without Compromise: The South and Reconstruction, 1865–1868* (Cambridge, Mass., 1973), for a political history emphasizing the theme of political coercion.

government all necessary power to fulfill the promise of equality contained in the Civil War amendments.

As noted earlier, the attempt to ground the 1954 school desegregation decision in the original intent of the Fourteenth Amendment was unsuccessful. Partly as a result of criticism of the sociological and psychological bases of *Brown* v. *Board of Education,* and partly because of the need to establish historical continuity between the Reconstruction amendments and modern civil rights policy, the quest for original intent persisted.[35] An original-intent argument justifying Fourteenth Amendment equal protection claims was incorporated in concurring opinions in *Bell* v. *Maryland* (1964), dealing with the sit-in controversy and the right of private property owners to discriminate.[36] In 1968 the Supreme Court adopted a neoabolitionist historical interpretation in deciding an open-housing case on the basis of an original-intent argument concerning the Thirteenth Amendment. The Court declared in *Jones* v. *Alfred H. Mayer Co.* that a right to be protected against private discrimination in the purchase of property under the Civil Rights Act of 1866 was constitutionally justified by the power of Congress under the Thirteenth Amendment to prohibit the "badges and incidents" of slavery.[37] In response to this decision, as well as to the general redirection of civil rights policy signified by affirmative action, neoabolitionist scholars elaborated an interpretation of Reconstruction and the Constitution aimed at justifying the egalitarian vision of contemporary civil rights policy makers.

The general conclusion of neoabolitionist revisionism was that the Reconstruction amendments were intended to give Congress primary, plenary, and ultimate authority to protect the civil rights of United States citizens and other persons.[38] Despite the apparent focus of the Fourteenth Amendment on state action, the neoabolitionists denied

---

35. *Cf.* Charles L. Black, Jr., "The Lawfulness of the Segregation Decision," *Yale Law Journal,* LXIX (1960), 421–30.

36. 378 U.S. 226 (1964). In this sit-in case, Justices Douglas and Goldberg said a right to equal public accommodations was an attribute of United States citizenship and was inherent in the historic purpose and original intent of the framers of the Fourteenth Amendment. *Cf.* Charles A. Miller, *The Supreme Court and the Uses of History* (Cambridge, Mass., 1969), 100–18.

37. 392 U.S. 409 (1968).

38. *Cf.* Arthur Kinoy, "The Constitutional Right of Negro Freedom," *Rutgers Law Review,* XXI (1967), 387–441; Robert L. Kohl, "The Civil Rights Act of 1866, Its Hour Come Round at Last: *Jones* v. *Alfred H. Mayer Co.*," *Virginia Law Review,* LV (1969), 272–300; G. Sidney Buchanan, *The Quest for Freedom: A Legal History of the Thirteenth Amendment* (Houston, 1976); Robert J. Kaczorowski, *The Politics of Judicial Interpretation: The Federal Courts, Department of Justice, and Civil Rights, 1866–1876* (New York, 1985); Robert J. Kaczorowski,

any limitation on national sovereignty in the field of civil rights. If Congress chose, according to Robert Kaczorowski, "it could legislate criminal and civil codes that displaced those of the states." Indeed, it could even destroy the states as separate and autonomous political entities. More important than the identification of specific civil rights was the transfer of sovereignty to the national government in order to implement the egalitarian vision of the authors of the Thirteenth and Fourteenth amendments.[39] Although neoabolitionist scholars deny that Reconstruction abolished federalism and created a unitary government, the denial appears insignificant. For although the states continued to exist, they possessed only the power to protect civil rights— and only as that power was defined and regulated by the national government. Old constitutional forms continued, but in reality a new Constitution came into existence.

Neoabolitionist legal historians further found in Reconstruction an egalitarian vision of "an undefined and indefinitely broad body of natural rights" that expands in accordance with the changing demands of national civil rights policy. According to one scholar, the Reconstruction amendments created a substantive and absolute right of black freedom that was intended to make blacks equal participants in the American political community. The amendments did not confer ordinary civil rights on the freed people, but rather a special body of rights—separate, distinct, and exclusively national in nature—that was enforceable by the federal government through direct and affirmative legislation. In a general sense, this argument supports race-conscious policies intended to eliminate the effects of historic societal discrimination. Neoabolitionist legal historians also seek, in freedmen's legislation enacted after the Civil War, more specific justification for affirmative action.[40]

"To Begin the Nation Anew: Congress, Citizenship, and Civil Rights After the Civil War," *American Historical Review,* XCII (1987), 45–68; Robert J. Kaczorowski, "Revolutionary Constitutionalism in the Era of the Civil War and Reconstruction," *New York University Law Review,* LXI (1986), 863–940.

39. Kaczorowski, *Politics of Judicial Interpretation,* 1–3, 8; Robert J. Cottrol, "The Thirteenth Amendment and the North's Overlooked Egalitarian Heritage" (paper presented to the American Society of Legal History, October, 1987), 18–19 and *passim;* Paul Finkelman, "Prelude to the Fourteenth Amendment: Black Legal Rights in the Antebellum North," *Rutgers Law Journal,* XVII (1986), 415–82.

40. Kaczorowski, *Politics of Judicial Interpretation,* 8; Kinoy, "Constitutional Right of Negro Freedom"; Eric Schnapper, "Affirmative Action and the Legislative History of the Fourteenth Amendment," *Virginia Law Review,* LXXI (1985), 753–98.

The litigation-driven neoabolitionist interpretation finds expression in recent general accounts of Reconstruction. Harold Hyman and William Wiecek emphasize the Thirteenth Amendment as an institutionalization of abolitionist ideas that provided protection in "the full and equal rights of freedom, some of which history had identified and a multitude of which remained for the inscrutable future to reveal." Indeed, the nature and purpose of the Fourteenth Amendment, they reason, can best be understood not by examining the debates on the amendment, but by considering the intentions of the framers of the Thirteenth Amendment. Eric Foner reflects neoabolitionist, affirmative-action ideas in stating that blacks claimed a right to the land as compensation for their unrequited toil as slaves and viewed the accumulated property of the planters as illegitimately acquired. He argues that the freedmen forged from the American and black experience a coherent political response to emancipation, the distinctive feature of which was a black interpretation of the concept of full incorporation as citizens of the republic.[41]

In adopting the Constitution, Publius observed in *The Federalist,* Americans had the opportunity to decide "whether societies of men are really capable or not of establishing good government from reflection and choice, or whether they are forever destined to depend for their political constitutions on accident and force."[42] This question was raised anew at the end of the Civil War as Americans faced the problem of resuming a common political life. Were the Reconstruction amendments principally the result of accident and force, despite the forms that marked their adoption? And did they establish a new Constitution?

Historians of the tragic interpretation of Reconstruction saw the Civil War amendments as a new Constitution imposed by force. They believed the Fourteenth Amendment was invalid and unconstitutional because of the methods used to secure its adoption. Revisionist historians in the civil rights era disagreed, contending that Reconstruction extended and completed the original Constitution by applying the

41. Harold M. Hyman and William M. Wiecek, *Equal Justice Under Law: Constitutional Development, 1835–1875* (New York, 1982), 390; Eric Foner, *Nothing but Freedom: Emancipation and Its Legacy* (Baton Rouge, 1983), 55–56; Foner, "Reconstruction Revisited," 90.
42. James Madison, Alexander Hamilton, and John Jay, *The Federalist,* ed. Edward Mead Earle (New York, 1938), 3.

principles of liberty and equality of the Declaration of Independence to the entire nation. Neoabolitionist writers have revived the thesis of revolutionary constitutionalism, but from a perspective of racial equality opposite that of the white-supremacist Dunning-Burgess school. In the neoabolitionist view, the Reconstruction Constitution, despite formal continuity, differed from the framers' Constitution in two fundamental respects. First, the original Constitution, recognizing and protecting slavery, contained no principle of equality and excluded blacks from membership in the national political community. Second, the idea of liberty embodied in the Constitution was in fact a fundamentally flawed concept of possessive individualism that permitted property in man. The Thirteenth and Fourteenth amendments, containing a more valid conception of liberty and introducing the principle of equality, replaced the framers' outdated ideas and established a new Constitution. In neoabolitionist legal history one thus can see the provenance of Justice Thurgood Marshall's argument rejecting the Constitution of the framers.[43]

Whether the framers' Constitution was destroyed in the Civil War and replaced by a new organic law adopted in Reconstruction is a historical question. It has political and philosophical implications, however, that make it difficult to resolve on strictly empirical historical grounds. It might seem realistic, for example, to argue that whether the nation retained its original Constitution or made a new one is merely a theoretical question. Yet however the framing and ratification of the Fourteenth Amendment be conceptualized—as a valid exercise of the amending power or as a revolutionary congressional act—the fact is that this key measure, the real substance of the Reconstruction Constitution, became an accepted rule of action. As a result of history alone, if nothing else, it acquired legitimacy.[44]

From another standpoint, however, the theoretical question of

43. Justice Marshall developed his historical argument more fully in his dissenting opinion in *University of California Regents* v. *Bakke,* 438 U.S. 265 (1978), at 369–97.

44. An important issue in the discussion of Reconstruction until well into the twentieth century was whether the Fourteenth Amendment was illegitimate and unconstitutional because ratified by the former Confederate states under compulsion of national authority. The matter apparently was laid to rest by the Supreme Court in *Coleman* v. *Miller* (1939), holding that the question was a political one resolved by the action of Congress declaring the amendment ratified, and confirmed by history and usage. In the civil rights era, however, the issue arose once again and provoked scholarly comment. See Walter J. Suthron, Jr., "The Dubious Origins of the Fourteenth Amendment," *Tulane Law Review,* XXVIII (1953), 22–44; Pinckney G. McElwee, "The Fourteenth Amendment to the Constitution of the United States and the Threat That It Poses to Our Democratic Government," *South Carolina Law Quarterly,* XI (1959), 484–519; Joseph L.

whether the Reconstruction amendments extended the principles of the founding or made a revolutionary new beginning is a realistic and historically legitimate one to ask insofar as there is an obligation to understand the amendments as their authors intended them to be understood. Then as now, the question of constitutional theory—in particular the issue of the authority of the founding—formed a real part of the political situation.

The theory of the American Constitution posits a fixed, binding, and permanent supreme law, superior to the government and alterable by the people only in the manner prescribed in the document. The high public status accorded the document as the source and symbol of governmental legitimacy expresses and is a consequence of this theory. The theory is the key to understanding the intrinsic value of the Constitution as the foundation for the rule of law in the United States. If history shows the theory to be false, if during the Civil War and Reconstruction Americans revolutionized their government and made a new constitutional beginning, that would be a precedent of great importance. It would make it easier in future political crises further to abandon the constitutionalism of the founding. Much is at stake, therefore, in the historical controversy over the Constitution and Reconstruction.

Of the three interpretations of Reconstruction examined in this essay, the revisionist view is the most historically accurate. Republicans in the 1860s sought to implement more fully and effectively the principles of liberty, equality, and consent set forth in the Declaration of Independence. Anchored in the founding, the Reconstruction amendments were intended to complete the Constitution and make permanent the expansion of liberty and civil rights resulting from the abolition of slavery.

This purpose was evident in the first Republican abolition proposal introduced into Congress in December, 1863: "A bill to give effect to the Declaration of Independence and also to certain provisions of the Constitution of the United States." [45] Numerous statements in support of the Thirteenth and Fourteenth amendments in the next sev-

---

Call, "The Fourteenth Amendment and Its Skeptical Background," *Baylor Law Review,* XIII (1961), 1–20; Ferdinand F. Fernandez, "The Constitutionality of the Fourteenth Amendment," *Southern California Law Review,* XXXIX (1966), 378–407.

45. H.R. 21, 38th Cong., 1st Sess., introduced by Owen Lovejoy, in Record Group 233 (38A–B1), National Archives.

eral years expressed the same intention. Congressman Godlove Orth of Indiana explained in January, 1865, that the prohibition of slavery would result in a practical application of the principle that life, liberty, and the pursuit of happiness were inalienable rights of all men. According to the Republican congressman John A. Kasson of Iowa, the Thirteenth Amendment would carry into effect the clause of the Constitution entitling citizens of each state to "all Privileges and Immunities of Citizens in the several States." During the debate on the Thirteenth Amendment, Senator Charles Sumner of Massachusetts said: "It is only necessary to carry the Republic back to its baptismal vows, and the declared sentiments of its origins. There is the Declaration of Independence: let its solemn promises be redeemed. There is the Constitution: let it speak, according to the promises of the Declaration." Defending the civil rights section of the Fourteenth Amendment in 1866, Congressman George F. Miller of Pennsylvania argued that it was "so clearly within the spirit of the Declaration of Independence . . . that no member of this House can seriously object to it." [46]

In a philosophical sense, moreover, the authors of the Reconstruction amendments appealed to the same conception of liberty that guided the making of the Constitution. This was not a narrowly self-seeking, strictly economic conception of freedom, as progressive historiography has assumed. Property was a natural right and interest protected by the Constitution, yet it received no special sanction, nor was it elevated to a position of political dominance.[47] Replacing classical virtue as the end or purpose of government, self-interest properly considered—enlightened self-interest—assumed positive moral meaning in a balanced system of republican freedom. Comprising political, religious, social, and economic aspirations, the liberty of the founding began in individuality and ended in common choice, under constitutional forms and procedures agreed upon by the people.[48] The liberty

46. *Congressional Globe*, 38th Cong., 2nd Sess., 142, 153; *ibid.*, 38th Cong., 1st Sess., 1202; *ibid.*, 39th Cong., 1st Sess., 726.

47. Henry Steele Commager, "The Constitution: Was It an Economic Document?" *American Heritage*, X (1958), 58–61; James H. Hutson, "The Constitution: An Economic Document?" in *The Framing and Ratification of the Constitution*, ed. Leonard W. Levy and Dennis J. Mahoney (New York, 1987), 259–70.

48. Glen E. Thurow, "'The Form Most Eligible': Liberty in the Constitutional Convention" (paper presented to the Liberty Fund Conference on Liberty and the Constitution, Philadelphia, November, 1987), 13. See also Richard Vetterli and Gary Bryner, *In Search of the Republic: Public Virtue and the Roots of American Government* (Totowa, N.J., 1987); Thomas L. Pangle, *The Spirit of Modern Republicanism: The Moral Vision of the American Founders and the Philosophy of Locke* (Chicago, 1988).

defended by the Republican party in the Civil War and Reconstruction was similarly grounded in the natural rights of individuals and the principles of equality and consent.

Reflection on the nature of liberty in the American regime requires comment on the place of slavery in the original Constitution. Since slavery was part of the social environment in which the Constitution was adopted, it is possible to argue that the document was intended in principle as well as practical effect to sanction and preserve the South's peculiar institution. Provisions concerning fugitive slaves, the three-fifths ratio for federal representation, and the importation and migration of slaves are seen as expressing the framers' proslavery original intent.[49] This argument has the effect of discrediting the Constitution as "fundamentally imperfect" and unworthy of surviving the Civil War.[50]

More historically sound is the view that although the Constitution recognized the existence of slavery, it did not in principle sanction the institution, but rather placed upon it marks of disapprobation that were the source of antislavery aspiration. This argument was advanced by Frederick Douglass and Abraham Lincoln before the Civil War. Douglass, after philosophical reflection, concluded that slavery lacked authority and was not established under the Constitution. Reasoning that not a word in the document authorized slavery, Douglass elevated constitutional principle above the practice of the government in rejecting the Garrisonian view that the Constitution was a proslavery document. Lincoln, noting that slavery was mentioned in the Constitution only in "covert language," stated that the founders "marked" the institution "as an evil not to be extended, but to be tolerated and protected" only insofar as was necessary to form the Union.[51]

At issue in the controversy over slavery and the Constitution is the

---

49. Denying that the Constitution was essentially open-ended or noncommittal on the question, Paul Finkelman states that "slavery was given both explicit and implicit sanction throughout the Constitution." Paul Finkelman, "Slavery and the Constitutional Convention: Making a Covenant with Death," in *Beyond Confederation: Origins of the Constitution and American National Identity,* ed. Richard Beeman *et al.* (Chapel Hill, 1987), 190–93; William Wiecek, although using somewhat less forceful language describing how the Constitution "acknowledged," "accommodated," and "protected" the institution, concludes that slavery was "ensconced" and "established" in the Constitution. William M. Wiecek, *The Sources of Antislavery Constitutionalism in America, 1760–1848* (Ithaca, N.Y., 1977), 62–74.

50. Finkelman, "Slavery and the Constitutional Convention," 190.

51. Waldo E. Martin, Jr., *The Mind of Frederick Douglass* (Chapel Hill, 1984), 37; Roy P. Basler, ed., *The Collected Works of Abraham Lincoln* (9 vols.; New Brunswick, N.J., 1953), III, 307, 535, IV, 22.

problem of ascertaining the meaning of the Constitution. Ultimately, as Don E. Fehrenbacher has written, "the law inheres most essentially in the text of the document." [52] And the undeniable fact is that the text of the Constitution did not contain the word "slavery." Although neoabolitionist historians discount the significance of this fact, it seems accurate to say that the framers' choice of language conveys the idea of moral disapproval of slavery.[53] The conclusion follows that the founders gave slavery as little political protection as possible in an instrument of government that contained emancipationist potential. James Madison put the matter aptly in stating at the constitutional convention that it would be "wrong to admit in the Constitution the idea that there could be property in man." [54]

The Reconstruction amendments were intended to remove the exceptions to liberty and equality signified by the slavery provisions and complete the Constitution by bringing it into conformity with the Declaration of Independence. Republicans did not regard the Thirteenth Amendment as a declaratory measure that merely expressed the true meaning of the Constitution. They viewed it rather as a change in the organic law, a change consistent with the principles of liberty that were embodied in the Constitution but had been imperfectly realized because of the existence of slavery. The purpose of the amendment was to remove impediments to the exercise of constitutional rights and to

52. Don E. Fehrenbacher, *The Dred Scott Case: Its Significance in American Law and Politics* (New York, 1978), 27. See also Robert C. Palmer, "Liberties as Constitutional Provisions, 1776–1791," in *Liberty and Community: Constitution and Rights in the Early American Republic*, ed. William E. Nelson and Robert C. Palmer (New York, 1987), 142–43.

53. See John Alvis, "The Slavery Provisions of the U.S. Constitution: Means for Emancipation," *Political Science Reviewer*, XVII (1987), 241–65. Alvis writes: "The one thing evidently agreed upon between the delegates from slaveholding states and their opponents at Philadelphia was the propriety of excising any direct mention of slavery from the clauses that would regulate the institution. . . . Consequences attach to the Framers' verbal fastidiousness. Disinfecting the document of any direct acknowledgement of slavery imparts to the concessions regarding the census and the return of fugitive slaves a shame-faced character. . . . Lincoln said that the draftsmen of the Constitution 'left [slavery] with many clear marks of disapprobation upon it.' Conspicuous omission is one such mark of disapprobation. More substantial for antislavery constitutionalism, the avoidance of any explicit acknowledgement of slavery suggests that one cannot look to the supreme law of the land for authorization in owning human beings" (247). See also Fehrenbacher, *Dred Scott Case*, 20–27. Even neoabolitionist scholars acknowledge the significance of the language of the Constitution on this point. Referring to the omission of the word "legally" to describe persons "held to Service of Labor in one state, under the Laws thereof" (Art. IV, sec. 2), Finkelman concedes that "in the most technical linguistic sense" it was true that "the Constitution did not recognize the legality of slavery." Finkelman, "Slavery and the Constitutional Convention," 224.

54. Robert Goldwin, "Why Blacks, Women, and Jews Are Not Mentioned in the Constitution," *Commentary*, LXXXIII (1987), 28–33; Walter Berns, "Comment: Equality as a Constitutional Concept," *Maryland Law Review*, XLIV (1987), 22–27. Madison quotation in Fehrenbacher, *Dred Scott Case*, 21.

complete the American system of liberty. When the Thirteenth Amendment proved inadequate for the task of protecting civil liberty, Republicans proposed the Fourteenth Amendment to secure the civil rights of United States citizens against denial by the states. The framers of the Reconstruction amendments intended neither a revolution in federalism nor a radical transformation in the meaning of liberty and equal rights. Their aim was to extend to the freed people the protection of person and property that delineated the condition of civil liberty under United States citizenship.[55]

The Reconstruction amendments embodied a racially impartial conception of equality before the law. Their purpose was to remove the racial qualification that had impaired the implementation of the principles of equality and consent contained in the Constitution. Reconstruction policy makers conferred on the emancipated slaves citizenship and ordinary civil rights, not a special right of Negro freedom and equality. In a practical sense, of course, any postemancipation measures reasonably related to the end of integrating the freed people into the political order were bound to operate mainly for the benefit of blacks, and hence might be regarded as compensatory or preferential. The question is whether the nature and meaning of the constitutional principles that provide the foundation of civil rights policy are to be defined with reference to this historical circumstance, or to the universal principles of liberty and equality expressed in the language and legislative history of the Reconstruction amendments. Although context and circumstance are necessary considerations in policy making and political action, common sense suggests that changing historical circumstances and relative social conditions can never be the source of the fixed principles and standards on which constitutional government and the rule of law depend. In basing the Reconstruction amendments on the natural-rights principles of the Declaration of Independence, the constitution makers of the 1860s recognized this fact.

Historical study of the Constitution has practical consequences because the document is directly pertinent to the conduct of government. Accounts of constitutional changes during Reconstruction have had a bearing on race relations and civil rights policy, and will prob-

55. Herman Belz, *A New Birth of Freedom: The Republican Party and Freedmen's Rights, 1861–1866* (Westport, Conn., 1976), 113–34; Michael P. Zuckert, "Completing the Constitutional Power Under the Fourteenth Amendment: The Original Understanding of Section Five," *Constitutional Commentary*, III (1986), 123–56.

ably continue to be relevant if the present controversy over affirmative action is to be resolved conclusively. What the historical record shows is that the framers of the Reconstruction amendments neither intended nor effected a revolutionary destruction of the states, as the tragic interpretation held, nor did they posit black freedom and equality as salient features of a new constitution, as the neoabolitionist view argued. The intent of the Reconstruction framers was to protect the civil rights of United States citizens, including most importantly the freed slaves, under the Constitution of the Founding Fathers. This is the principal conclusion to be drawn from historical reflection on the Constitution and Reconstruction.

Afterword
Whither Reconstruction Historiography?

❧ ERIC ANDERSON

"The author of this work feels that there can be no sensible departure from the well-known facts of the Reconstruction program as it was applied to the South," declared E. Merton Coulter, introducing his 1947 study *The South During Reconstruction, 1865–1877.* Working "within the reasonable bounds of established facts" revisionists might make "lasting contributions," of course, but "no amount of revision can write away the grievous mistakes made in this abnormal period of American history." [1]

"What are the well-known facts of Reconstruction?" asked John Hope Franklin in a devastating review of Coulter's volume. "Are they the facts on which the Reconstruction historians of the early part of this century based their conclusions?" Are the facts of Reconstruction, asked Franklin, to be drawn from "melodramatic" accounts, emphasizing "wild-eyed conspirators" and "masses of barbarous freedmen"? "Is it not possible that time has not only served to 'heal' feelings of hurt, but also to provide the serious student with information and perspective with which to reinterpret the period?" [2]

Coulter's confidence was misplaced. Expecting to be revised, most historians are addicted to such phrases as "could well have been"; "other things being equal"; "to a considerable extent"; "whatever the

---

1. E. Merton Coulter, *The South During Reconstruction, 1865–1877* (Baton Rouge, 1947), xi.
2. John Hope Franklin, "Whither Reconstruction Historiography?" *Journal of Negro Education,* XVII (1948), 448.

ERIC ANDERSON

motivating factors"; and "impossible, perhaps, to prove." Except for
a few ideologues, historical scholars put forward new interpretations
tentatively, awaiting the vigorous assault certain to fall upon any generalization that is too sweeping or inadequately supported.

In this collection of essays, the authors follow respectable academic procedure, thoughtfully analyzing discrete parts of the historiography on Reconstruction and skillfully suggesting "new direc-
tions" for future research. Several authors venture into the midst of
heated historical controversies with definite conclusions and firm judgments. As a group, the essays in *The Facts of Reconstruction* demonstrate the importance of John Hope Franklin both as a synthesizer of
earlier research on Reconstruction and as an asker of new questions,
although none of the essayists would assign him an inerrant last word.

No single essay offers a comprehensive new interpretation of Reconstruction, but it is possible to find the general outline of an emerging view in the group of nine essays. If one ignores occasional contradictions and numerous cautious qualifications, this new picture of
Reconstruction highlights the following points:

1. The political *ideas* behind Reconstruction—not merely conflicting economic and social interests—deserve careful study. A famous
book review accused Sir Lewis Namier of removing "mind" from the
study of history, much as Darwin might be said to have taken mind out
of the universe.[3] Gertrude Himmelfarb has complained recently that
the "new social history" distorts the past by downplaying "the ra-
tional ordering and organization of society by means of constitutions,
political institutions, and law."[4] Such criticism could not be applied to
the contributors to this volume.

Though Paul Finkelman has no intention of endorsing a jurisprudence of "original intention," the foundation of his essay is the assumption that historians (if not judges) can best understand the Fourteenth Amendment by studying the purposes of those who put it in the
Constitution. Carefully examining pre–Civil War legislative debates,
court cases, and statutes, he finds the key to understanding Reconstruction in "the struggle for racial equality as carried on in the antebellum North by abolitionists, Free-Soilers, and ultimately Republi-

3. *London Times Literary Supplement,* August 28, 1953, cited in E. H. Carr, *What Is History?* (New York, 1961), 46.
4. Gertrude Himmelfarb, *The New History and the Old* (Cambridge, Mass., 1987), 21.

220

cans." As Republicans rewrote the Constitution after the war, he argues, they employed the ideas and vocabulary of the earlier debates. Finkelman is also able to demonstrate that the formal legal position of blacks was improving in the 1850s, not deteriorating as Abraham Lincoln and a host of modern scholars have asserted.

Herman Belz's essay also illustrates the centrality of political ideas—specifically the Constitution—in the new picture of Reconstruction. Belz differs from Finkelman, however, in questioning the view that the Constitution is "an instrument of power," essentially "protean, plastic," and capable of a range of meanings, each serving a particular policy objective. Instead, he prefers to emphasize the "intrinsic value" of the Constitution. According to Belz, "The Constitution must be seen as something good in itself, worthy of being followed for its own sake or for the wisdom, justice, and sound principles it embodies, quite apart from the outcome of specific controversies."

With this understanding of the fundamental law, Belz rejects the judgment of those scholars who saw the Reconstruction era's Constitutional arguments as "sham" or "mere justification of practical ends" or even foolish "fetish-worship." Like William A. Dunning, he treats the constitutional issues as real issues, but he disagrees with Dunning's claim that Reconstruction represented a revolutionary or reckless attack on the American constitutional tradition. "Republicans in the 1860s sought to implement more fully and effectively the principles of liberty, equality, and consent set forth in the Declaration of Independence" and embodied in the Constitution, asserts Belz. Their intention, he adds, was to confer "on the emancipated slaves citizenship and ordinary civil rights, not a special right of Negro freedom and equality."

If Reconstruction was a conservative reform designed to preserve the founders' ideals in the new environment created by emancipation, perhaps its ending deserves reexamination. Historians sometimes have been content to describe the end of Reconstruction in simplistic or moralizing terms: fainthearted, inconstant reformers lost interest in southern problems, betraying the Negro by succumbing to the pervasive national mood of racism. Here again, as Michael Les Benedict shows, ideas have been slighted. It is true, of course, that the northern public did become "tired out with these annual autumnal outbreaks in

the South," as President Grant put it.[5] But something more than wea-
riness or racism was at work.

According to Benedict, the nation's intellectual elite became alienated from the Republican "southern policy" because that policy was
inconsistent with a coherent and powerful set of "scientific" ideas.
These new ideas, particularly in the realm of political economy, offered
a strong critique of "class legislation" and nonevolutionary social
change. A few stalwart politicians continued to defend prolonged federal intervention in the South, but they already had lost the battle of
ideas among academics and intellectual journalists, most of whom believed that Reconstruction already had accomplished its practical objectives. What remained of the Reconstruction agenda, according to
these thinkers, could not be justified on the basis of expediency or extraordinary urgency.

In short, Reconstruction was a continuation of the Civil War argument about the meaning of self-government. Molded by the peculiar, legalistic language of American constitutionalism, the process of
rebuilding the Union was essentially *political,* both in its origins and
conclusion.

2. It is anachronistic to judge the Republican party by present-day
standards. Although the majority in Lincoln's party was not committed to integration, "social equality," or the repudiation of "scientific"
racism, the party was committed to a clear, coherent vision of political
equality and civic inclusion for Negroes. The achievement of narrowly
defined "civil rights" for blacks and the establishment of the principle
of "separate but equal" in education and other public services were
not contemptible or insignificant successes.

Robert Morris and Roberta Alexander both warn against applying twentieth-century standards to the Freedmen's Bureau, for example. "Bureau agents were not New Dealers committed to a policy
of strong federal intervention," Alexander observes. "If they were not
completely colorblind, they were certainly more enlightened than were
the southern whites in control of the state governments during Presidential Reconstruction."

5. Eric Foner, in *Reconstruction: America's Unfinished Revolution, 1863–1877* (New
York, 1988), 560, points out that Grant's statement has usually been cited out of context, since
the president added that the federal government should not ignore Governor Ames's request for
help in Mississippi.

Alexander also applies the principle of seeking to understand Reconstruction in its own terms to Thomas Holt's Marxist strictures on the black political elite of South Carolina.[6] "Why should anyone expect the black middle-class leadership to have acted differently than politicians do in other communities?" she asks. "To expect black political leaders in nineteenth-century South Carolina to have behaved like radical socialists removes them from the context of time and place." Cautioning against "straw men" and "special pleading," Morris finds a "complex blend of reformist and conservative impulses" in cultural reconstruction. By implication he rejects any interpretation relying on false dichotomies and oversimplification to portray all educational missionaries as self-serving "cultural imperialists."

Perhaps the surest antidote to presentism and unfair judgment is to focus on the goals of Reconstruction. Like Herman Belz, Howard Rabinowitz argues that Reconstruction "was primarily about securing black suffrage and civil rights such as the right to contract, to perform jury service, and the like." The "basic aim" was to promote equality of opportunity—but not integration or "equality of condition." Indeed, Rabinowitz sees an "essential continuity between the Civil Rights Act of 1875 and the *Plessy* v. *Ferguson* Supreme Court decision" and describes the ideal of separate but equal treatment as "one of the few achievements of Reconstruction."

Certainly the rapidly deteriorating status of black Americans in the 1890s and the early twentieth century cannot be blamed primarily on the theoretical inadequacy of the Reconstruction commitments or the inherent flaws in the principle of "separate but equal." Indeed, by 1910 equal funding for racially segregated institutions would have represented immense progress in every southern state. The same can be said for impartial voting regulations, full access to the courts (including jury participation), and basic security from mob violence. As the witticism goes about Christianity, the problem was not so much that the Reconstruction formulas were tried and found wanting as that they were never tried wholeheartedly.

3. The expectations and demands of blacks, whether former slaves or not, were central in the evolution of Reconstruction. Although the

6. Thomas Holt, *Black over White: Negro Political Leadership in South Carolina During Reconstruction* (Urbana, Ill., 1977).

definition of black freedom was constantly threatened, any theory that reduces blacks to the level of hapless victims is unsound.[7] Even when their bargaining power was limited, as in matters of labor and credit, Negroes were able to force some changes in the preferred plans of the former slaveholders. In addition, historians cannot gain a clear understanding of the emancipation era if they ignore black entrepreneurs and landowners.

Although historians have focused on black political power, black demands for autonomy were perhaps strongest in economic and cultural matters. Arguing that it is particularly important to understand the prospering minority among Afro-Americans, Loren Schweninger may have found a way around an important historiographical stalemate. Yes, federal intervention was often halfhearted and ineffective; yes, whites often tried to trump "economic laws" with racial calculations; and yes, competition, as well as coercion, shaped black economic choices. Yet each affirmation is incomplete, requiring qualification in the light of what blacks themselves achieved and attempted.

Schweninger delineates the sharp increase, in the "first half-generation of freedom," in southern black property ownership, including personal property, farm land, and urban real estate. Compared to the deprivation of slavery, the "small improvements during Reconstruction" were an exhilarating change, "harbingers of greater economic progress." Moreover, any study of black economic reconstruction must take into account the impact of hope and opportunity on the freedmen.

In education and community life, blacks also had aspirations—and demands—that white friends and foes sometimes failed to understand, as students of the "black agenda" in education have discovered. Even some forms of segregation represented black choice rather than white commands. According to Howard Rabinowitz, "much of the segregation during and after Reconstruction was initiated or supported by blacks," including separate schools, welfare institutions, and benevolent and fraternal societies. "Any discussion of segregation," he observes, "must go beyond the narrow limits of white-enforced segregation in public accommodations if it is to illuminate the reality of the cultural urges that southern blacks shared with other American ethnic

---

7. As Foner has observed, blacks were "active agents" during Reconstruction, not "simply a problem confronting white society." *Reconstruction: America's Unfinished Revolution,* xxiv.

groups." In addition, Rabinowitz argues that historians must consider the possibility "that the altered attitudes and especially the behavior of some blacks themselves" might have helped provoke white excesses in the 1890s. The sole black congressman in the Fifty-fifth Congress made a similar suggestion in 1899: the "peculiar crisis" Negroes were then enduring, said Representative George H. White, had been brought about by the "tendency on the part of some of us to rise and assert our manhood along all lines." [8]

4. In addition to recognizing the importance of black aspirations, historians must give due credit to the differences among white Americans, resisting the temptation to write as if white racism were unchanging, unremitting, universal. "They were all racists" is a well-nigh useless insight, blurring the vital differences between Salmon P. Chase and Roger Taney, Andrew Johnson and U. S. Grant, Thaddeus Stevens and Charles Francis Adams. Equally misleading is the subtle invocation of the *tu quoque* argument by thoughtful modern southerners, including C. Vann Woodward.[9] Whatever "the seeds of failure" in Republican or northern racial attitudes, there were profound differences of principle at stake in the sectional conflict of the Reconstruction era.

Paul Finkelman's essay masterfully illustrates the vital differences between the slave-owning South and the "Negrophobic" North, as well as the distinctions among northerners. Although northern public opinion was "profoundly racist," tainting even antislavery activists, Finkelman finds significant variations from one region to another. More importantly, he is able to show change over time, with "a growing contradiction . . . between public manifestations of equality—in law and politics—and private racism." Republican leaders, although sometimes opportunistic or inconsistent, were able to move prevailing opinion in an egalitarian direction well before Reconstruction.

In this light, the ultimate defeat of Reconstruction is not plausibly explained by the assertion that North and South were not so different after all. The significant differences between the sections and the parties, in fact, help explain the intensity of southern white opposition to Reconstruction. Michael Perman persuasively argues that southern white resistance, not the deficiencies of Congress or southern Republi-

8. *Congressional Record,* 55th Cong., 3d Sess., 1124.
9. C. Vann Woodward, "Seeds of Failure in Radical Race Policy," in *New Frontiers of the American Reconstruction,* ed. Harold M. Hyman (Urbana, Ill., 1966), 125–47.

cans, overcame Reconstruction. "Although Reconstruction was indeed flawed and vulnerable," he writes, "it did pose a discernible threat to existing southern institutions and values"—and it required the "adoption of extreme measures" to topple it. "Reconstruction did not simply collapse; it was overthrown, even eliminated, by the action of its adversaries."

Perman's argument touches on the most debatable issue in *The Facts of Reconstruction:* What was required for the success of Reconstruction? Was Reconstruction doomed to failure in the absence of land reform or other radical economic changes? Is it possible that the experiment would have succeeded if northerners and their southern allies had been more patient or determined? Would "a little more of the same" have made Reconstruction's achievements permanent?

Perman's focus on the role of violence from 1874 to 1876 offers empirical support for W. E. B. Du Bois's shrewd comment: "It is argued that Negro suffrage was bad because it failed, and at the same time that its failure was a proof of its badness. Negro suffrage failed because it was overthrown by brute force." [10] But one might equally well conclude, from Perman's evidence, that Reconstruction was a hopeless enterprise once southern white opinion became thoroughly aroused and ready to hazard open violence.

5. The claim of Du Bois that Radical Reconstruction in the South was a brief moment of lower-class insurgency crushed by a "counterrevolution of property" is little better than wishful thinking. [11] Indeed, most historians recognize that Republicans generally did not make a class appeal, though some would argue that the attempt should have been made.

It is more plausible to argue that class divisions undermined the southern Republican parties, as Carl Moneyhon's essay suggests. In calling for a detailed regional and class analysis of ordinary southern voters, Moneyhon observes that many studies "have been views from the top down, usually making broad assumptions about the motivations of individual voters—assumptions that then inform conclusions about the cause or causes of Republican failure." Only by the most careful application of state and local research can historians learn

---

10. W. E. Burghardt Du Bois, *Black Reconstruction: An Essay Toward a History of the Part Which Black Folk Played in the Attempt to Reconstruct Democracy in America, 1860–1880* (1935; rpr. New York, 1970), 631.

11. *Ibid.,* 210, 350, 580–636.

more about "the real and potential Republican voters." Moneyhon's study of local Republican officeholders in Arkansas hints at one possible Republican majority: small farmers resentful of "the old political and social elites." He believes that these men "were ready for a radical change" that would topple the "gentlemen." The Republican party simply failed to produce such a program, "and potential constituents quickly drifted away."

If Moneyhon's essay raises tantalizing questions of what might have been possible in local politics, Michael Les Benedict certainly makes clear that soak-the-rich populism and a platform of "class legislation" were not practical alternatives for any organization allied with the national Republican party—or hoping to secure the approbation of its influential wing of "respectable" reformers.

6. The more deeply scholars study the Reconstruction era, the more apparent it becomes that reconstruction was a long-term process, extending in many respects well beyond 1877 and beginning before 1865. At the very least, historians have found the extension of Reconstruction patterns into the 1880s—in the lingering black political power, for example, of North Carolina's Second Congressional District,[12] the Sea Island region of South Carolina, southside Virginia under Mahone, Mississippi's shoestring district, and several urban polities. In a broader sense, a limited renewal of Reconstruction remained a possibility until 1892, as is shown in the debates over the Blair Bill, the Lodge Elections Bill, and repeated Republican invocations of bloody-shirt rhetoric. The continuing importance of Reconstruction is also clear in the state civil rights laws passed in the North during the 1880s.

Several of the contributors to this volume have looked beyond the conventional boundaries of Reconstruction. If historians wish to understand Reconstruction, Paul Finkelman suggests, they must study the 1840s and 1850s. Howard Rabinowitz turns to the 1890s for important parts of his explanation of Reconstruction.

Perhaps Reconstruction's essence was defined in the years 1865 to 1869, especially in the conflict between President Johnson and Congress over what John Hope Franklin called "Confederate Reconstruction." Later choices, from President Grant's decision to suppress the

---

12. Eric Anderson, *Race and Politics in North Carolina, 1872–1901: The Black Second* (Baton Rouge, 1981).

Klan to key Supreme Court judgments in the 1880s and 1890s, were no more than a defense (or cautious clarification) of what was then established. Even many of the opponents of "Grantism" and "bayonet rule" accepted, for a time, the consensus of 1868, that is, black political rights, but no long-term federal intervention in the South or permanent limits on "local self-rule."

As the contributors to *The Facts of Reconstruction* remark time and again, there are many open questions in the study of Reconstruction. Without imitating E. Merton Coulter's proclamation of the "reasonable bounds" for future research, it is safe to assume, however, that the best work will take seriously the constitutional debates of the Reconstruction era, avoid anachronistic standards of judgment, recognize the impact of black expectations and demands, and give appropriate weight to the differences among whites, North and South. In addition, future students of Reconstruction will probably avoid artificially restrictive periodization, choosing instead to examine Reconstruction as a process—and a set of questions—beginning with the outbreak of the Civil War and continuing until the disfranchisement of southern blacks.

The scholars contributing to the emerging picture of Reconstruction are cautious in making direct applications of their work to current political issues, recognizing the limitations of " 'if' history," as Loren Schweninger puts it. Historians, like other citizens, are concerned with the "urgent matters" of their own time, John Hope Franklin commented in 1980, but "we must take care not to permit those matters to influence or shape our view of an earlier period." Historians who "seek confirmation" of their own views of Reconstruction "in the events of our own day," trying "to bolster their case in their own political arena," are likely to write poor history.[13]

There is no party line in the essays that make up this volume. Representing a variety of political perspectives and academic commitments, the authors have sought to follow John Hope Franklin's admonition that Reconstruction should not be used "as a mirror of ourselves." If they have succeeded, this book in honor of a profound scholar and inspiring teacher will provoke renewed discussion about "the facts of Reconstruction."

13. John Hope Franklin, "Mirror for Americans: A Century of Reconstruction History," *American Historical Review,* LXXXV (1980), 1–14.

CONTRIBUTORS

ROBERTA SUE ALEXANDER received her Ph.D. from the University of Chicago, where she was a student of John Hope Franklin. She is an associate professor of history at the University of Dayton and chairperson of the History Department. Her publications include *North Carolina Faces the Freedmen: Race Relations During the Presidential Reconstruction, 1865–1867;* and "Salmon P. Chase," *Encyclopedia of American Business History Biography: Banking and Finance to 1913.*

ERIC ANDERSON received his Ph.D. from the University of Chicago, where he was a student of John Hope Franklin. He is professor of history at Pacific Union College, where he has served as chair of the History Department. His publications include *Race and Politics in North Carolina, 1872–1901: The Black Second;* "James O'Hara of North Carolina: Black Leadership and Local Government," in *Southern Black Leaders of the Reconstruction Era;* and "The Populists and Capitalist America: The Case of Edgecombe County, North Carolina," in *Race, Class, and Politics in Southern History: Essays in Honor of Robert F. Durden.*

HERMAN BELZ received his Ph.D. from the University of Washington. He is professor of history at the University of Maryland, College Park. His publications include *Reconstructing the Union: Theory and Policy During the Civil War; A New Birth of Freedom: The Republican Party and Freedmen's Rights, 1861–1866;* and *Emancipation and Equal Rights: Politics and Constitutionalism in the Civil Rights Era.*

MICHAEL LES BENEDICT received his Ph.D. from Rice University. He is professor of history at Ohio State University. His publications include *A Compromise of Principle: Congressional Republicans and Reconstruction, 1863–1869; Civil Rights and Civil Liberties,* in the American Historical Association's series Bicentennial Essays on the

Constitution; and "The Problem of Constitutionalism and Constitutional Liberty in the Reconstruction South," in *An Uncertain Tradition: Constitutionalism and the History of the South.*

PAUL FINKELMAN received his Ph.D. from the University of Chicago, where he was a student of John Hope Franklin. He is a member of the faculty at Brooklyn Law School. His publications include *An Imperfect Union: Slavery, Federalism, and Comity; Slavery in the Courtroom;* and *The Law of Freedom and Bondage: A Casebook.*

CARL H. MONEYHON received his Ph.D. from the University of Chicago, where he was a student of John Hope Franklin. He is professor of history at the University of Arkansas at Little Rock. His publications include *Republicanism in Reconstruction Texas;* "Public Education and Texas Reconstruction Politics, 1871–1874," in the *Southwestern Historical Quarterly* (1989); and "George T. Ruby and the Politics of Expediency in Texas," in *Southern Black Leaders of the Reconstruction Era.*

ROBERT C. MORRIS received his Ph.D. from the University of Chicago, where he was a student of John Hope Franklin. He is Director of the National Archives, Northeast Region, and has held teaching appointments at the University of Maryland, College Park; Rutgers University; and Teachers College, Columbia University. His publications include *Reading, 'Riting, and Reconstruction: The Education of Freedmen in the South, 1861–1870; Freedmen's Schools and Textbooks: Black Education in the South, 1861–1870;* and "To Elevate This People," a segment in the University of Wisconsin's CPB/Annenberg Series, *Sound Studies in American History.*

ALFRED A. MOSS, JR., received his Ph.D. from the University of Chicago, where he was a student of John Hope Franklin. He is associate professor of history at the University of Maryland, College Park. His publications include *The American Negro Academy: Voice of the Talented Tenth;* "Northern Philanthropy in the South," in the *Encyclopedia of Southern Culture;* and "Alexander Crummell: Black Nationalist and Apostle of Western Civilization," in *Black Leaders of the Nineteenth Century.*

Contributors

MICHAEL PERMAN received his Ph.D. from the University of Chicago, where he was a student of John Hope Franklin. He is professor of history and research professor in the humanities at the University of Illinois at Chicago. His publications include *Reunion Without Compromise: The South and Reconstruction, 1865–1868; The Road to Redemption: Southern Politics, 1869–1879;* and *Emancipation and Reconstruction, 1862–1879.*

HOWARD N. RABINOWITZ received his Ph.D. from the University of Chicago, where he was a student of John Hope Franklin. He is professor of history at the University of New Mexico. His publications include *Race Relations in the Urban South, 1865–1890* and *Southern Black Leaders of the Reconstruction Era.* A forthcoming study will be entitled *The First New South, 1877–1920.*

LOREN SCHWENINGER received his Ph.D. from the University of Chicago, where he was a student of John Hope Franklin. He is professor of history at the University of North Carolina–Greensboro and the author or editor of three books and a number of articles on southern and African-American history. His most recent publication is *Black Property Owners in the South, 1790–1915,* which received the Elliott Rudwick Award.

INDEX